Fichte's Ethics

Michelle Kosch received a BA from Harvard College in 1990 and a PhD from Columbia University in 1999. She was employed as a postdoctoral research fellow at the Søren Kierkegaard Research Center in Copenhagen, and thereafter as an assistant professor in the philosophy department at the University of Michigan, before moving to Cornell in 2006.

Fichte's Ethics

Michelle Kosch

OXFORD
UNIVERSITY PRESS

OXFORD
UNIVERSITY PRESS

Great Clarendon Street, Oxford, OX2 6DP,
United Kingdom

Oxford University Press is a department of the University of Oxford.
It furthers the University's objective of excellence in research, scholarship,
and education by publishing worldwide. Oxford is a registered trade mark of
Oxford University Press in the UK and in certain other countries

Published in the United States of America by Oxford University Press
198 Madison Avenue, New York, NY 10016, United States of America

British Library Cataloguing in Publication Data
Data available

Library of Congress Cataloging in Publication Data
Data available

ISBN 978–0–19–880966–1 (Hbk.)
ISBN 978–0–19–884975–9 (Pbk.)

For Daniel and Leonid

Contents

Acknowledgments   ix
Note on Texts, Translations, and Citations   xi

1. Introduction   1
   1.1. The Idea of Material Independence   1
   1.2. Fichte and Kant   5
   1.3. Scope of the Project and Overview of the Text   7

2. Rational Agency   12
   2.1. Spontaneous Self-Determination   12
   2.2. Reflection   16
   2.3. Necessary Conditions of Reflection   22
       2.3.1. Empirical Cognition   22
       2.3.2. Drive   24
       2.3.3. Energy   29
       2.3.4. Causal Efficacy; Embodiment   30
       2.3.5. Social Interaction; Individuality   31
   2.4. Variability   34
   2.5. 'freedom—for the sake of *freedom*'   36

3. Material Independence   39
   3.1. Textual Evidence   40
       3.1.1. Evidence in the *System of Ethics*   40
       3.1.2. Evidence in Other Texts of the Jena period   47
   3.2. Material Independence in the Doctrine of Duties   52
       3.2.1. Embodiment and Causal Efficacy   54
           3.2.1.1. Physical Preservation   55
           3.2.1.2. Physical Cultivation   67
           3.2.1.3. Property   68
       3.2.2. Good Deliberation and True Beliefs   70
           3.2.2.1. Conscience   71
           3.2.2.2. True Beliefs   73
           3.2.2.3. Knowledge and Control: Property   75
           3.2.2.4. Knowledge and Control: Research and Technology   77
           3.2.2.5. Aesthetic Experience   80
           3.2.2.6. Kant and Fichte on Ends that are Duties   81
       3.2.3. Individuality   85
           3.2.3.1. A Conflict of the Moral Law with Itself?   86
           3.2.3.2. The Place of Rights in the Moral Project   90
           3.2.3.3. Coordination   94

3.2.3.4. Fichte's Theory of the Social Contract 100
3.2.3.5. Ideal and Non-Ideal Communities 108
3.2.3.6. Right as a System of Hypothetical Imperatives 112
3.2.3.7. The Summons and the Problem of Right 115
3.2.3.8. Fichte's Positivism 121
3.2.3.9. Particular Duties 125

4. Formal Independence 128
4.1. Conscientiousness 129
4.1.1. Formal Formal Independence 131
4.1.2. Material Formal Independence 141
4.2. Moral Evil 143
4.3. The Formal Condition and Formal Freedom 149

5. Independence as Constitutive End 152
5.1. Material Independence and Kant's *Doctrine of Right* 153
5.2. From Rational Agency to Material Independence 157
5.2.1. The Argument in *Foundations* §11 158
5.2.2. Limiting Conditions 165
5.2.3. Control as Necessary End and Control as End in Itself 166
5.3. Autonomy and Material Ethical Principles 167
5.4. The Hegemony of Instrumental Reason? 171

6. Conclusion 178

Works Cited 181
Index 189

Acknowledgments

For their generous feedback on components of this project at various stages I am grateful to Elizabeth Anderson, Sarah Buss, Taylor Carman, Stephen Darwall, Michael Demo, Dina Emundts, Patrick Farr, John Martin Fischer, Eckart Förster, Sebastian Gardner, Stefanie Grüne, Paul Guyer, Rolf-Peter Horstmann, Rachana Kamtekar, Paul Katsafanas, Pierre Keller, Wolfgang Mann, Frederick Neuhouser, Nedim Nomer, David Plunkett, Andrews Reath, Katie Smith, Jennifer Uleman, David Velleman, Owen Ware, Noam Weinreich, Andrea Westlund, Reed Winegar, Allen Wood, Christopher Yeomans, Daniel Young, Günter Zöller, many anonymous referees, and audiences and workshop participants at the University of California at Riverside, Syracuse University, Johns Hopkins University, Columbia University, the University of Arizona, the Eastern and Pacific divisions of the APA, the 2012 Boston University Colloquium on Late Modern Philosophy, the 2013 Dartmouth Workshop on Autonomy in Ethics and Political Philosophy, and the Eighth (2012) and Ninth (2015) International Fichte Congresses. For funding for research leaves, office space, library access, and research support of various kinds in the nearly twelve years in which this project has been underway, I am grateful to the University of Michigan, Cornell University, the Humboldt University in Berlin, and the University of Paris VII.

Earlier drafts of much of the material in this book have appeared in papers published in the *International Yearbook of German Idealism* (M. Kosch 2013), *Philosopher's Imprint* (M. Kosch 2014 and M. Kosch 2017), and *Philosophy and Phenomenological Research* (M. Kosch 2015a).

Acknowledgments

Note on Texts, Translations, and Citations

I cite Fichte according to the pagination of the first edition of his collected works, published by his son I.H. Fichte in 1845–6 and reprinted by De Gruyter in 1971 (J.G. Fichte 1971). This pagination is reproduced in the margins of the latest edition by the Bavarian Academy of Sciences (J.G. Fichte 1962–2011) and is also reproduced parenthetically in the modern English translations of Fichte's works. Only where I cite material unpublished in the I.H. Fichte edition do the page numbers refer to the Bavarian Academy edition. (The difference is indicated by the note 'GA' and the two-part volume numbers of the *Gesamtausgabe*.) All translations of Fichte are mine. I cite Kant according to both the Akademie edition and the Cambridge edition of Kant's works. Translations of Kant are taken from the Cambridge editions, often with substantial modification. Throughout the book all in-text page references are to Fichte's works; all other references are confined to footnotes.

1

Introduction

1.1 The Idea of Material Independence

That nature can limit human autonomy, and that technology can overcome some of those limitations, seems to me one of the perfectly evident propositions with which any moral philosophy in which autonomy has a place must reckon. But this is not an idea that has much currency in contemporary moral philosophy; and reactions to some of the material I will present here, from a variety of audiences, have convinced me that not everyone finds that proposition as perfectly evident as I do. In fact many profess to find it simply puzzling.

By 'autonomy' here I mean just the set of psychological dispositions required for planning one's actions rationally and governing one's choices according to principles that one can endorse on rational reflection. I do not mean the power to put one's choices into practice or to have one's life actually go as one has planned; nor do I have in mind specifically Kantian moral autonomy. By 'nature' I mean every non-human force that might constrain human activity in any way.

Of course the idea that autonomy in the narrow psychological sense I have in mind requires independence of some part of the agent's psychological nature (instinctive drives; recalcitrant desires) has a long history. There is likewise a long tradition in moral and political philosophy in which autonomy is seen as requiring freedom from certain sorts of external interpersonal interference, its value as grounding substantive constraints on what other agents can do to, with, and even for an individual. The nature of the connection is not always clearly spelled out, but the assumption that the lack of some degree of interpersonal independence is a threat to an agent's capacity to govern herself—a literal threat—is a common theme, and one that seems to have a basis in the texts (of Kant and Rousseau) in which this tradition has its modern roots.[1]

In the mainstream of this tradition it is customary to distinguish sharply between freedom from interference on the part of other human beings and

---

[1] This is one of the assumptions of Rousseau's argument in *On the Social Contract*; it also figures in Kant's account in the *Groundwork for the Metaphysics of Morals* and in the *Doctrine of Right*.

from interference on the part of non-human agents (animals; pathogens) and the forces of nature more generally. Nature might undermine human happiness or human flourishing, but it cannot limit human autonomy.

But there is a strand of the same tradition, nearly as old, in which no deep moral distinction between human and non-human threats to autonomy in the psychological sense is acknowledged, apart from the obvious fact that the former but not the latter are imputable to morally responsible agents. Marx was an early voice in this tradition, as was Feuerbach and (on some readings) Hegel. In the post-Kantian period its earliest and historically most influential proponent was Johann Gottlieb Fichte.

'Autonomy' is not a word Fichte was especially fond of using. But his is a moral theory built on the idea that autonomy is a constitutive end of rational agency—autonomy both in a psychological sense and in an external/material sense encompassing not only freedom from domination or constraint by other individuals, but more broadly freedom from limitation by any force external to rational agency, including the forces of nature.

Instead of the notion of 'autonomy' Fichte preferred to operate with the notion of 'independence' or 'self-sufficiency' (terms he used interchangeably). Independence, on his theory, has a psychological component (viz. the full and undistorted exercise of rational agency's characteristic activity of practical reflection in deliberation and the formation of intentions and plans). It also has an external, relational component (viz. the set of abilities and opportunities required to manipulate one's environment as one decides, and to give an objective existence in the world whatever freely chosen ends one might embrace).

Independence in this constellation of senses is the substantive end toward which moral action is directed in Fichte's normative ethics. This is an agent-neutral end, in that it is the independence of rational agency generally that is said to be the constitutive end of each rational individual. More precisely: membership in a rationally organized moral community is partially constitutive of the independence of each individual rational agent; and a constraint on the proper organization of such a community is the protection of the individual independence of its members from certain kinds of interference on the part of other members. But within the constraints imposed by such organization, individuals should seek, both on their own and collectively, to promote an aim that goes beyond the establishment and maintenance of relations of mutual noninterference, namely the independence of all rational agents with respect to non-rational nature.

Fichte's defense of the idea that material independence in this sense is a necessary end of rational agency appeals to a set of links between what he argues to be necessary features of self-consciousness on the one hand, and the causal and constitutive conditions of these features on the other. He first argues that self-consciousness is possible only for an embodied intellect that is one of several of its kind; and he then argues from these features (intellectuality, embodiment, individuality) to a set of conditions that are either constituents of these or causal conditions of their maintenance. This set of conditions then forms the basis of his substantive normative ethics. So Fichte's strategy is to link agency itself, through a set of transcendentally necessary features and their conditions of possibility, to a set of concrete aims that, he argues, any agent is rationally required to have.

A modest version of Fichte's basic claim is uncontroversial, insofar as a being disposed to form intentions cannot rationally avoid concern with its independence in the sense at issue. What it aims at in forming intentions is shaping the world in certain ways; and doing that is seldom a function solely of intending, but typically requires control over objects in the environment as well as the cooperation of other agents. An interest in external causal efficacy is part of the package of rational end-setting, one might say without courting much controversy.

Fichte's theory steps out of the realm of the uncontroversial with the claim that the overarching substantive constitutive end of rational beings per se encompasses the maximal material independence of rational beings in general from all external limitations. It is this idea, rather than the modest one, that I will examine and defend in this book.

Much of today's philosophical literature on autonomy is focused on formulating views of what autonomous agency, or morally responsible agency (for this is often the underlying question), minimally requires. This is not Fichte's concern. He assumes that the set of psychological dispositions of which autonomy is composed comes in degrees, develops over childhood, and maintains itself to differing extents within an adult population depending on the personal characteristics and external circumstances of the individuals in it. His concern is not to specify the point on this continuum at which moral responsibility emerges, but instead to articulate the necessary ends shared by individuals anywhere on it.

One such end he takes to be rationality in decision-making, and he argues that this depends directly on environmental factors in a number of ways. This is the significance of the necessary features of physical embodiment and individuality. For rational agents who are embodied individuals, a feedback loop connects the conditions for success in acting on their ends and their capacity to form ends freely and rationally, a loop that runs through interactions with both the natural and the social environment.

Several features of Fichte's theory of rational agency are noteworthy in this connection. One is his emphasis on the social character of human rationality, in particular his view that the disposition to develop second-order evaluative attitudes and so to impose normative demands of any kind upon oneself relies on social-ization, and his view that the standards of rationality in belief and in practical deliberation are set and reinforced by interactions with one's peers. Another is his emphasis on the embodied character of human intellect, in particular his recogni-tion that practical deliberation is effortful and that the capacity to expend the effort it requires depends on somatic as well as environmental factors.[2] A third is his emphasis on the material conditions of possibility of the cognitive attitudes that figure in deliberation. The rationality of beliefs about what it is possible to do, what is an adequate means, whether and where such means are available, and the like, depends (he argues) on an environment that is sufficiently stable and predictable. Stability and predictability are in many areas a function of effective control; and this fact is key to the justification not only of social institutions that minimize interpersonal interference, but also of technologies that minimize interference from non-rational natural forces.

The idea that freedom from such interference is the necessary end of any being whose end is rationality in decision-making has been taken seriously in virtually no discussion of Fichte's ethics to date, despite the fact that nearly everything that is interesting about Fichte's ethical theory depends upon it.[3] But an examination of this least well-understood aspect of Fichte's ethical thought is at the same time an examination of the central substantive contribution his thought has (yet) to make to contemporary moral philosophy. For the idea that nature can place limits on our ability to govern ourselves and that knowledge can push back against those limits, and that anyone who values autonomy is thereby committed to the value of basic research and of the development of autonomy-enhancing technologies, is an idea that is strikingly absent from the mainstream of contem-porary ethics. Questions about the nature and extent of duties of self-improvement and mutual aid and of duties to future generations are productively reconsidered in light of Fichte's framework. The same is true of currently under-theorized areas like the ethics of enhancement and of reproductive choice, among many others. Duties to engage in and support education and basic research in the arts and sciences are an especially good example here. Kantians have little to say

---

[2] In this respect Fichte's view anticipates contemporary research connecting problem-solving performance not only to innate capacity (itself in part a function of childhood environment) but also to current conditions ranging from nutritional status to the presence or absence of external distractions and temptations.

[3] The two exceptions I am aware of are P. Rohs 1991a and 1991b.

about these; and the value theories adopted by many contemporary consequentialists give the wrong account of them: they are valuable not only insofar as they
contribute to happiness or preference satisfaction, but also and primarily because
they expand human capacities, and thereby enable people to formulate, rationally, ever broader and more complex plans of action.

1.2 Fichte and Kant

Fichte was one of the first generation of post-Kantian philosophers, and he saw
himself as articulating and expanding Kant's basic project, in ethics as in other
areas. Most fundamentally, he agreed with Kant that moral virtue (which he
understood to be action in accordance with duty from the motive of duty) is a
constitutive end of rational agency; and he agreed that it is in virtue of that fact
that moral requirements necessarily provide us with reasons for action, reasons
that override those stemming from prudence or other sources, and that are
always to at least some degree motivating. (In fact Fichte was committed to
stronger versions of these last two Kantian claims, insofar as he thought that
moral reasons are the only genuine reasons that we have, and that they are always
adequately motivating insofar as we recognize them.)

But Fichte was convinced that adherence to the spirit of the Kantian approach
sometimes required departures from the letter of Kant's texts. This was true in
ethics as in other areas, and in the *System of Ethics* he in fact made some quite
radical departures from the Kantian letter. Not all of these departures can have
been intentional, since Fichte found himself in the interesting position of
working out his practical philosophy able to refer to the *Groundwork* and the
second *Critique* and some of Kant's essays, but independently of the strictly
parallel works by Kant (the two parts of the *Metaphysics of Morals*), because
these were published too late for him to build upon them. (The first, foundational half of Fichte's *Foundations of Natural Right* (March 1796) appeared
before Kant's *Doctrine of Right* (January 1797); and the *System of Ethics* (March
1798), though published after Kant's *Doctrine of Virtue* (August 1797), was
conceived independently, its main ideas articulated already in the *Lectures on
the Scholar's Vocation* (1794) and most of its details on display already in the
lectures on moral philosophy of summer 1796.) Fichte's works present us, then,
with a practical philosophy that is recognizably Kantian, but that was developed partially independently of Kant's own, and that departs from Kant's in
important ways.

The most fundamental departure from the Kantian letter lies in Fichte's
account of the nature of the highest principle of morality. For Kant, the

fundamental principle of morality requires that we choose only in such a way that the maxim of choice can at the same time be willed as a universal law by and for a realm of rational agents. Kant calls this principle 'formal,' arguing that no material principle can be a principle of autonomy. A material principle would prescribe the production of an end and judge the goodness of acts, rules, or policies on the basis of their tendency to produce or further that end. It will be clear from what I have said so far that Fichte's moral principle is material in this sense: it requires that we pursue the substantive end of rational agency's perfection and material independence from external limitations of all kinds. (I explain why this does not disqualify it as a principle of autonomy in §5.3.)

The normative portion of Fichte's theory is thus consequentialist in form, and it differs from Kant's on a number of counts in virtue of this. One of these is the account of practical reasoning it presupposes. The only principles of practical reasoning Fichte admits are the familiar principles of consistency and means–ends coherence. In fact he argues explicitly that the idea of universal legislation is only a heuristic, and that Kant was wrong to have presented the categorical imperative in its universal law formulation as a constitutive principle of practical reason. Another difference lies in the fact that, while Kant's theory is one on which practical reason in most cases fails to designate a unique action as morally required, on Fichte's theory practical reason will fail to demand a single specific action only in the special case in which several actions are equally conducive to the end of independence.

On Fichte's view, independence is an agent-neutral end of rational agency per se and it gives rise to agent-neutral reasons for action. So in contrast to Kant, who is usually taken to have offered a powerful argument on behalf of agent-centered restrictions (and, on some readings, also agent-centered prerogatives), Fichte rejects these. (More precisely: although the formal condition on the morality of action (which I will describe in Chapter 4) imposes a kind of agent-centered restriction, it is purely procedural and has no systematic substantive upshot.) Fichte's theory leaves ample room for patient-centered constraints tied to political rights, and for associative duties; but all of these are justified by the fact that they are conducive to or (partially or wholly) constitutive of institutions and practices which themselves are conducive to or partially constitutive of the end of independence. To the standard objection that a theory of this form—a maximizing consequentialism that does not admit agent-centered prerogatives—is extremely demanding, Fichte's reply is that this is no objection at all, but simply the truth.

Fichte's treatment of duties that are teleological even on Kant's theory, like the duty of beneficence, is (unsurprisingly, given these other differences) more straightforward than Kant's. Kant's treatment of these duties is, on the usual reading, complicated by his denial that practical reason is the source of substantive ends. Duties of beneficence are justified by the assumption that human beings invariably aim at their own happiness, coupled with the universal law formulation of the categorical imperative in its contradiction-in-willing application. One consequence of this strategy is that for Kant these duties are indexed directly to individual preferences and indirectly to social conditions. Kant's account thus shares with other accounts of mutual aid based on (broadly) preference-satisfaction conceptions of welfare a susceptibility to objections pushed forcefully by, among others, Amartya Sen against welfarist consequentialism. Fichte's account of duties of mutual aid is not only more straightforward (in that duties of mutual aid and self-improvement are derived directly from the end of independence); it also escapes these criticisms in just the way that Sen takes his capabilities approach to escape them.

I will return to these contrasts, and others, in more detail below. Here let me simply note that my chief motivation for drawing them out is to orient the reader on familiar terrain. I am well aware that there are readings of Kant that bring him closer to Fichte in virtually every domain I will mention. (If those readings are correct, I say, so much the better for Kant.) Readers who do not share my interpretation of Kant on these topics or who find the comparisons to Kant distracting for other reasons are invited simply to ignore them, since nothing in my interpretation of Fichte hinges on the depth of any of the contrasts I draw between Fichte and Kant. That said, these contrasts do seem to me to have some intrinsic interest in addition to their usefulness for orienting the reader. Kantianism in ethics has many components that are often portrayed as more or less inseparable but that Fichte pries apart (sometimes self-consciously, sometimes without demonstrating any awareness of what he is doing) and reassembles in a way very different from the way they are assembled in Kant's texts. It seems to me that there is something to be learned about these components, and about Kantianism in ethics, by looking at this different way of fitting them together.

1.3 Scope of the Project and Overview of the Text

This book is aimed in part, of course, at scholars of classical German philosophy. The picture of Fichte's ethics that I present here aims to fill a yawning gap in existing scholarship; and the reading I defend is by no means uncontroversial. But the book is also aimed in part at those ethicists and political philosophers who would be interested in Fichte's thought if they knew anything about it. This second audience informs the scope of my discussion in several ways.

My focus will be on explaining and defending those parts of Fichte's project that seem to me both to require defense, and to be defensible and interesting in a contemporary context. This means that I will leave out discussion of many aspects of Fichte's ethical thought that are at least as interesting as the ones I do discuss, from the perspective of a historian of the period, but that are more difficult to motivate from a contemporary perspective. (For example, Fichte takes himself to have to provide a transcendental argument for the proposition that moral agents are embodied. This is a fascinating argument, and there is a substantial literature dedicated to understanding it. But since my focus is Fichte's ethical theory and since I take it that readers will be willing to grant him the premise that the moral agents we typically theorize about are embodied, I discuss his argument for it only very briefly.)

It also means that I will not try to explain, much less to defend, the broad features of Fichte's philosophical system taken as a whole. In fact I will do my best not even to refer to them. This is in an effort not only to spare the sensibilities of the general reader (though the general reader should, in fact, be grateful for it), but also to combat the belief, pervasive in the community of Fichte scholars, that one cannot begin to interpret Fichte's ethics without a definitive understanding of his transcendental philosophy (and of the 1794 *Wissenschaftslehre* in particular) already in hand. This belief is erroneous, both because Fichte's practical philosophy is perfectly comprehensible on its own, and because there is good reason to think that by 1798 the practical portion of Fichte's system had itself acquired a foundational status (and that the 1794 *Wissenschaftslehre* in particular had by then been entirely superseded). It is also pernicious, because the conviction that one either understands the whole of Fichte or none of him has surely been the chief reason the *System of Ethics* has until now received so much less hermeneutic attention than it deserves. So I will confine my investigation almost entirely to Fichte's ethical and political writings, and indeed to those from the period between 1794 and 1800. (Fichte's thought underwent a fairly radical transformation after 1799, and even the 1800 *Vocation of Humankind*, on which I rely at a couple of points, is at some other points inconsistent with the *System of Ethics*.) The hermeneutic challenge presented by these works is quite sufficient on its own.

The main task faced by an interpreter of Fichte's ethics is to say what material independence or self-sufficiency amounts to, and why it should be thought a constitutive end of rational agency. The first step in discharging that task is to give an account of what rational agency is for Fichte. Chapter 2 is devoted to this. Fichte defines rational agency as the disposition to form intentions spontaneously on the basis of concepts of ends. He takes this disposition to rest on a set of component capacities and dispositions that depend in various ways on the agent's interaction with her environment. The disposition to engage in practical reflection requires the possession of empirical knowledge; it requires a set of given ends (in Fichte's theory, a set of natural drives) from which the process of reflection begins and upon which it operates; it requires the capacity to expend mental effort in deliberation; it presupposes a conception of oneself as causally efficacious, which in turn rests on some empirical experience of the exercise of one's causal powers on an environment external to one's will; and it requires the disposition to develop second-order attitudes, to take oneself and one's states and dispositions as objects to be understood and manipulated, which according to Fichte is the result of the form of social interaction he calls a 'summons.' It is from the account of these components, and of their material conditions of possibility, that Fichte's account of material self-sufficiency will be drawn.

The next step is to provide an interpretation of Fichte's account of self-sufficiency as a substantive moral end. This is the task of Chapter 3, in which I argue that we should understand this as the end of procuring and securing the material conditions of excellent practical deliberation, and expanding the potential domain of that deliberation through the broadening of possibilities for rational planning. What Fichte calls the 'material' (or 'objective') condition on the moral correctness of actions is met when an action is part of the series of actions at whose limit one would arrive at the state of absolute independence in this sense.

In addition to having a material or substantive aspect independence also has, on Fichte's theory, a formal aspect: decision-making should, in addition to being oriented toward the correct end, also obey certain procedural constraints. Chapter 4 spells out these constraints. This 'formal' (or 'subjective') condition on the moral correctness of actions is met when the agent performs the action that is dictated by the conviction that issues from the sufficiently energetic application of her reflective capacities in a given situation, and performs it because it is so dictated. The formal condition is, I argue, independent of the material condition on Fichte's view: an action can be formally correct (that is, conscientiously undertaken) without being, objectively, the action in the circumstances most conducive to the moral end; and conversely an agent may rashly (and so unconscientiously) perform an action that is objectively the correct one in the circumstances.

If interpretations of Fichte's ethics have typically paid little attention to his account of self-sufficiency as a substantive end, that is usually because they have taken the account of the formal condition of moral correctness, which he treats in earlier sections, to exhaust the account (or to exhaust the salvageable part of the account) of the content of moral requirements. That this is not the intended role of the relevant sections of the *System of Ethics* is best grasped with an account of the material content of morality on Fichte's view already in hand. So in my exposition I reverse Fichte's own order of presentation, approaching the interpretation of the formal condition (in Chapter 4) only after developing an account of the substance of moral duty (in Chapter 3).

By the end of Chapter 4 I will have explained Fichte's claim that the conjunction of material and formal independence is a necessary end of rational agency; and I will have presented the textual evidence for attributing these views to Fichte. I will also have given (in Chapter 3) an overview of the normative ethical theory he builds upon this foundation. The final part of the interpretive task is to give an account of why, in Fichte's view, any rational agent (as construed in Chapter 2) must have satisfaction of the material and formal conditions of moral correctness (as construed in Chapters 3 and 4) as his or her end.

Having as one's end the fulfillment of the formal condition is just having as one's end the full exercise of one's agency in the moment of deliberation—undistorted by bias, wishful thinking, otherwise sloppy reasoning, or capitulation to external pressure. That this should be a constitutive end of rational agency is a claim that has been well explored and ably defended, and is assumed across a wide swath of philosophical literature. Of course some have doubted that there is or could be a constitutive end of agency or of practical reasoning; but against such doubts I see no uniquely Fichtean considerations to bring forward. In any case I assume Fichte's view that formal independence is a constitutive end, and in Chapter 5 focus on defending his more controversial thesis that independence in a material sense is also a constitutive end of rational agency.

For a given agent in the moment of deliberation, whether her reasoning is conscientious and whether she acts on her conviction are matters that are, on Fichte's theory, in her own hands. That is why it is possible for him to treat the formal condition as independent of the material one in the case of an action taken in isolation. But the actual degree of rationality her deliberative process displays, including the truth of the premises on which it operates, is by no means entirely in the agent's hands at the moment of deliberation. It depends on somatic and external factors that affect her ability to deliberate well (like adequate nutrition, sleep, peace and quiet), on her moral upbringing and the social expectations that have shaped her practice of deliberation and her subjective standard for its conscientiousness, and above all on the adequacy of her empirical beliefs. Looking beyond the present instance of deliberation, an agent can see that the decisions she makes—their substance, not the procedure she has used to arrive at them—themselves affect the degree of practical rationality possible for her, and for other agents, in the future. Since an agent with an interest in the excellent exercise of her rational capacities must also have an interest in its necessary conditions, and since these include certain relationships with her social and natural environment, such an agent must have an interest in these; and since rationality requires that differences in treatment be justified by relevant differences in individual situation or characteristics, this interest must extend to conditions necessary for others' exercise of their rational capacities as well.

I spell out Fichte's argument for this conclusion in Chapter 5. After showing that a moral distinction between limitations on material independence placed (illegitimately or unnecessarily) by other people and those placed by natural obstacles is not defensible on Kantian grounds, I reconstruct Fichte's argument in a form suitable for the broadest audience to which I think it can appeal, articulating and defending the additional premises on which he relies in reaching his conclusion. I conclude by offering responses to the most common and plausible objections that have been raised by audiences over the years in which I have been presenting the material from which this book is drawn.

2

Rational Agency

2.1 Spontaneous Self-Determination

Fichte defines rational agency as the disposition to form intentions spontaneously on the basis of concepts of ends. It is neither the activity of forming spontaneous intentions nor the mere capacity to do so, but the 'tendency' or disposition to do so—a 'tendency to determine itself absolutely, without any external impetus' (IV: 8–9; cf. IV: 30, 32, 37, 38, GA 4-1: 11). This disposition is activated whenever an agent puts aside immediate inclination and acts on temporally remote ends, whether from the motive of duty or from prudential or other motives (IV: 162, 184–91). The capacities that underlie it are, collectively, the basis of moral responsibility (IV: 125–6).[1]

Fichte has no fixed term to refer to this disposition, calling it variously 'formal freedom,' 'freedom' unmodified, 'self-determination,' 'the essence of the rational being,' and 'the will.' The reader should bear in mind that what is at issue in this chapter is the disposition and the capacities—the psychological properties of moral agents *qua* moral agents—in abstraction from agents' physical or social circumstances or their success or failure in carrying out the intentions they form. Since my eventual aim is to evaluate Fichte's argument for his moral principle, and since that argument depends in part on claims about the connection between agency on a narrowly psychological character-ization and the environment in which such agency is exercised, it would be question-begging to describe agency in a way that prejudges that connection, or that elides the distinction between agency and its external exercise. Caution is warranted because some of Fichte's terms (notably, 'freedom,' 'formal free-dom,' and 'self-determination') can refer both to rational agency construed narrowly and to the successful exercise of, or even to opportunities to exercise, such agency in the world.

---

[1] A discussion of the relation between Fichtean and Kantian conceptions of formal freedom that differs in some details from this one can be found in F. Neuhouser 1990, pp. 146ff. An earlier discussion of mine—which also differs in some details from the one here—can be found in M. Kosch 2013.

Fichte takes rational agency to be a sort of causality, a causality of the will upon itself, and he follows Kant in claiming that its exercise is spontaneous, 'an absolutely free, conscious transition from indeterminacy to determination' (IV: 158) which is not reducible to or explicable as the outcome of any non-rational natural causal process (IV: 134–6; cf. IV: 112, 158–9, 182). This part of Fichte's characterization recalls Kant's claim that free will would have to involve 'a causality... through which something happens without the cause of [that something] being itself determined according to necessary laws by a further antecedent cause—that is, an *absolute spontaneity* of the cause to begin, *of itself*, a series of appearances that [then] proceeds according to natural laws.'[2] But behind this surface similarity lies a very different account of the free will's place in nature.

Kant accepts both the causal closure of the physical and determinism about the empirical world. He reconciles his view that spontaneity is required for moral responsibility with this commitment to empirical determinism by distinguishing agents *qua* phenomena from agents *qua* noumena, the former but not the latter described by laws of nature. He argues in the first *Critique* that it is rationally permissible, and in the second *Critique* that it is practically required, to ascribe spontaneity to agents *qua* noumena. But he denies that such spontaneity is directly or indirectly accessible to inner or outer intuition. Though susceptible to demonstration from a practical point of view, freedom is for Kant empirically unobservable.[3]

Fichte, by contrast, denies the causal closure of the physical and rejects determinism entirely. Departing from Kant's view that although we cannot comprehend how organisms could be produced by mechanistic causality we must nevertheless assume them to be so produced,[4] Fichte simply denies that the behavior of organisms (even non-human ones) is determined by mechanistic laws (IV: 110–15). Instead he takes the behavior of organisms to be explained in terms of a drive toward organization (a *Bildungstrieb*) expressing itself in their development, in their internal articulation, and in their interactions with the environment (IV: 121). Fichte sees the *Bildungstrieb* as a force operating in nature alongside the forces described in Newtonian mechanics, posited to explain a set of phenomena in just the way the gravitational force had been, and no more mysterious in principle. (This position, rather than Kant's, was the one in conformity with the dominant contemporary theory of animal generation, that

---

[2] I. Kant 1900–, p. A446/B474; I. Kant 1998, p. 484.
[3] This is a condensed statement of a complex Kantian view that, moreover, evolved over time. For a more detailed discussion, see Kosch 2006a, ch. 1.
[4] See I. Kant 1900–, 5: 362–84; I. Kant 2000, pp. 235–55.

of J.F. Blumenbach.[5]) Determinism of the Leibnizean variety is thereby ruled out, for Fichte, though he holds that the operation of the *Bildungstrieb* in non-rational beings renders their behavior predictable, even if not in mechanistic terms.

The behavior of beings capable of thought, however, he takes to be unpredictable in principle insofar as it is explained by intellectual activity (rather than force or drive). Intellectual activity is, for Fichte, entirely spontaneous, not explicable in terms of any mechanistic or organic forces or laws:

Every link in a natural chain is predetermined, whether by the law of mechanism or that of organism....But what will occur in the I...is not predetermined and simply undeterminable. There is no law according to which free self-determinations follow and can be predicted, because these depend upon the determination of the intelligence, but this latter is as such simply free, pure activity.   (IV: 134; cf. GA 4–1: 48)

Although it is not reducible to other natural forces, and not predictable even in principle because essentially creative, thought is, for Fichte, a real and *sui generis* force acting within the natural world. This means that for him the physical (where this is defined so as to exclude the intellectual) is not causally closed, and the empirical world as a whole not deterministic.

So although Fichte follows Kant in emphasizing the free will's independence of determination by non-intellectual causes, and agrees with Kant that only creatures displaying such independence are moral agents, he describes the contrast between rational agents and non-rational organisms in ways that will seem unfamiliar to readers of Kant. Because he treats the transition from indeterminacy to (self-)determination as the object of introspective consciousness,[6] and because he treats the unpredictability of human behavior as non-introspective evidence that it involves some spontaneous causality, there is for him no special epistemological problem connected with knowledge of spontaneous causality.[7] His commitment to the uncaused spontaneity of the intellect puts Fichte on the

---

[5] See R. Richards 2000. For an alternative account that takes Kant and Blumenbach to be in basic agreement, see J. Larson 1979 or T. Lenoir 1980. I agree with Richards, and discuss Fichte's relationship to Kant and Blumenbach on this issue in work currently in preparation.

[6] For instance, he describes 'consciousness of my indeterminacy' as 'condition of the consciousness of my self-determination by free activity' (IV: 137). Cf. GA 4–1: 57.

[7] He of course recognizes that the existence of such causality is an object of philosophical controversy, and in fact he sees that controversy as unsettleable by argument because the two sides are informed by two incompatible basic assumptions. Those already committed to the universality of mechanistic causation ('dogmatists') will explain away the phenomenological and observational facts as illusions (IV: 25), but that explanation will appeal only to those who already share their assumptions. Those not so committed are able to take the empirical facts at face value. That they likewise have no knock-down argument that will convince the others is the idea behind Fichte's comment that one's stance on the spontaneity question is the object of a radical choice of philosophical disposition (IV: 26; cf. I: 429ff.).

incompatibilist side of the contemporary debate; but his account of rational agency reads very much like a contemporary compatibilist one, due to its emphasis on detailed description of the psychological dispositions and capacities that differentiate the self-determination of rational beings from the drive-based behavior of non-rational organisms. He can offer such an account because he lacks the Kantian commitments that preclude empirical observation of a will to which spontaneous causality could be attributed.

Another peculiarity of Fichte's account is that on it spontaneity enters only at the level of deliberation, not at the level of acting on the outcome of some deliberation. On his view, an agent's actions are determined by his reasons as he sees them; he can fail to act on them only if the reasons themselves are undetected or obscured (IV: 191–3). Spontaneity enters at the level of the exercise of the intellect itself, in practical reflection. In fact on this account responsibility requires spontaneity not because it directly requires alternate *action* possibilities (clearly a consideration that moved Kant, and that continues to move contemporary incompatibilists), but because it attaches to ends that are self-imposed through intellectual activity, and such activity is essentially spontaneous. Responsibility is thus tied directly only to the disposition to form intentions based on concepts of ends; spontaneity enters the picture only because forming concepts of ends is an exercise of thought, and spontaneity is, for Fichte, one mark of the mental.

The characterization of freedom as non-naturally-determined spontaneity is negative in that it asserts only that naturalistic explanations of human behavior are incomplete and that, even phenomenologically, consciousness of spontaneity is consciousness of being non-determined (IV: 137). But Fichte denies that unpredictability in the action of a cause suffices for attributing to that cause freedom in the sense required for moral agency (IV: 33). The transition from indeterminacy must be characterizable positively in a way that makes attributions of responsibility intelligible (IV: 36–8). Positive self-determination requires setting ends that are one's own, through conceptual activity ('through concepts' or 'through thinking'—IV: 35–8, 112). Such ends can be moral, as when one 'sets oneself an end that runs counter to all inclinations and is chosen nevertheless, from duty' (IV: 137). They can also be prudential: 'I choose with full freedom of will, for I choose with consciousness of self-determination, [even in cases in which] I by no means sacrifice enjoyment to morality, but only to a different enjoyment' (IV: 162). Fichte even allows for a third kind of case with no Kantian correlate, that of an amoral 'heroic' character who is able to subordinate all other motivations to a blind and lawless drive for individual (as opposed to universal) self-sufficiency (IV: 184–91). Whatever their nature, such ends are required for positive self-determination because they allow the agent to be motivated by something other than immediate inclination. So Fichte's positive characterization of formal freedom as self-determination through concepts of ends recalls another aspect of Kant's theory, namely his description of practical freedom as the 'capacity, through representations of that which itself is more remotely useful or harmful, to overcome the impressions on our sensible faculty of desire.'[8]

2.2 Reflection

The formation of concepts of ends of all kinds relies on what Fichte calls 'reflection.' He uses this term to refer to two intuitively distinct capacities, interrelated but independently variable, which I will call *minimal* and *evaluative* reflection. It has long been acknowledged that Fichte distinguishes two forms of self-consciousness: (1) the sort of immediate conscious awareness one has of what one is doing (or planning or wanting) in the moment of doing (etc.) it; and (2) the reflective self-consciousness of oneself-as-doing-this (or as intending-to-do-this or as having-this-desire) that takes the self (or its states or attitudes) as an object.[9]

Reflection in the minimal sense is the second of these two forms of self-consciousness, and Fichte calls this sort of self-scrutiny by both names: sometimes 'self-consciousness' (IV: 23, 29, 77, 89, 107, 161, 221), sometimes 'reflecting' or 'reflection' (IV: 30–43 *passim*, 57, 73, 100, 109, 112, 124–6, 130–40 *passim*, 144, 147, 178). Reflection in the minimal sense is simply taking oneself (especially one's actions, attitudes, and the connections between them) as an object of consideration. At several points Fichte seems to claim that what becomes an object of reflection in this sense comes, just in virtue of that, under the agent's control (IV: 125, 135, 140–1, 178–80; cf. GA 4–1: 12). This seems puzzling, since although reflective consciousness of some motive or capacity or deliberative pattern in oneself is plausibly necessary, it is surely not sufficient for intentionally controlling it. We do better to read Fichte as claiming that reflective consciousness suffices for responsibility assuming, as in the typical case, that the other components of agency are in place.[10]

---

[8]   I. Kant 1900–, p. A802/B830; cf. p. A534/B562; I. Kant 1998, p. 675; cf. p. 533.

[9]   Cf. D. Henrich 1967; F. Neuhouser 1990, ch. 3.

[10]   As an example, take the case of an otherwise normal adult whose decisions are influenced by an unconscious bias. If at some point she becomes aware of having it (if the bias becomes the object of reflective self-consciousness), the claim would be, she thereby acquires the ability to affect to at least some degree its influence on her decisions—assuming she has the standard repertoire of tools for self-regulation at her disposal. This more plausible reading turns out to be compatible with every passage in which Fichte appears to claim that reflective awareness is sufficient, *simpliciter*, for control.

Fichte also calls 'reflection' an activity that clearly goes beyond reflective self-consciousness to encompass rational evaluation of the consistency of attitudes—more particularly of motivations, intentions, and beliefs about matters of fact (IV: 111–31 *passim*, 159, 162, 165–72 *passim*, 185, 187, 191–2). Reflection in this evaluative sense requires minimal reflection, insofar as evaluating the consistency of attitudes requires having them in view. It also requires beliefs about how the world is and might be made to be (beliefs about facts, general causal laws, and one's own causal capabilities); and it presupposes the existence of some motivational material. Where he discusses it explicitly, Fichte describes such evaluative reflection in exclusively calculative terms.[11] It is means–ends or part–whole reasoning, always toward some end or other, but in the good case toward the moral end.

Since (for reasons I will explain in §3.2.3.3) pursuing the end of independence is possible only within a framework of interpersonal coordination, any actual instance of practical deliberation will involve determining which among the possible courses of action is permissible given the constraints of positive law and associative duties, and choosing the action most conducive to the end of independence from among the permissible ones. But where Fichte introduces his conception of practical deliberation he leaves those complications aside and characterizes it as a process of straightforward instrumental reasoning toward the end of material independence.

The moral law, in relation to empirical human beings, has a determinate *starting point*: the determinate limitation in which the individual (in which it initially finds itself) finds himself; it has a determinate (if never reachable) *goal*: absolute liberation from all limitation; and a completely determinate *way* along which it leads us: the order of nature. There is therefore for every determinate individual in any given situation only something determinate that is required by duty—and this, we can say, is what the moral law demands in its application to the temporal being. Call this determinate action or omission *x*.   (IV: 166)

The determinate action or omission *x* is required in virtue of being the proximal step on the path toward the goal of complete liberation.

This is a simplified picture depicting only a starting point, an end point, and a way the world is that constrains possible paths from the first to the second, in the deliberation of a single individual with only her own independence in view (although we see already in the odd parenthetical comment '(in which it initially finds itself)' that this location of reason in a particular individual point of view is

---

[11] Here by 'calculative' I have in mind roughly the sense defined in C. Vogler 2002.

provisional). The full picture will be complicated by the fact that the agent is one of many individuals working toward a goal that encompasses the independence of all of them, that the project requires the coordination of their efforts, that each individual involved in it has but limited knowledge of the order of nature, and that the project itself spans generations of creative effort and so is one whose end point cannot be fully specified in advance. Fichte devotes as much attention as he does to the requirement of due diligence in practical deliberation because such deliberation is complex and fallible, and because where the most that can be expected of an individual is that she do her best to figure out what progress toward the moral end requires, a clear specification of what doing one's best would amount to is in order. I will return to consideration of these formal constraints in Chapter 4. Still, it is clear that Fichte sees practical deliberation as guided by (a conception of) this goal of absolute independence, from which it follows that he sees that goal as sufficiently determinate—in any particular situation—to guide deliberation.

The fact that practical deliberation is entirely calculative for Fichte explains his remark that it belongs entirely to the theoretical faculty, to the 'power of reflecting judgment' (IV: 165). The moral principle, he explains, specifies only the moral end, leaving it to the theoretical power of judgment to seek that action x that, in the circumstances, is the one progress toward the moral end demands (IV: 166). Because 'the practical faculty is not a theoretical faculty . . . it cannot give this x; rather this x is to be sought through the (here freely reflecting) power of judgment' (IV: 166). Fichte appears to be referring, here, to the passage in the introduction to the *Critique of the Power of Judgment* where Kant distinguishes, within what we would call 'practical reasoning' in a loose sense (viz. deliberation about what to do), between a part that is properly practical and a part that is only 'technically practical' and that belongs, strictly, to theoretical reason.[12] By 'technically practical' Kant has in mind reasoning about what would bring about, or what would constitute the fulfillment of, a given end—calculative reasoning, in other words. He argues that such reasoning belongs strictly to the theoretical faculty, not to the practical, because it involves only causal and mereological judgments and concepts drawn from natural science (in a sense broad enough to include psychology), and these are theoretical.[13] Since for Fichte the reasoning we engage in to determine the action x that is the obligatory action in our situation

---

[12] I. Kant 1900–, 5: 171–3; I. Kant 2000, pp. 59–61.
[13] '[A]ll technically-practical rules (i.e. those of art and skill in general, as well as those of prudence . . .) . . . must be counted only as corollaries of theoretical philosophy' (I. Kant 1900–, 5: 172; I. Kant 2000, p. 60).

consists exclusively in the sort of reasoning Kant calls 'technically practical' it is, according to Kant's taxonomy, theoretical.[14]

Some have taken Fichte's remark that practical deliberation involves reflecting judgment to suggest a kinship to aesthetic judgment.[15] Fichte's talk of 'harmony' here also seems to invite comparison with Kantian aesthetic judgment. But on the whole the text does not support this conjecture. According to the distinction Kant draws in the third *Critique*, determining judgment is what we employ to place a given particular under a 'rule, principle, law' of which we are already in possession; whereas reflecting judgment extracts a universal from a group of given particulars.[16] Both determining and reflecting judgment are involved in theoretical inquiry, for Kant. So Fichte's reference to reflecting judgment does not on its own suggest that aesthetic judgment, or something importantly analogous to aesthetic judgment, must be at issue.

Others have taken the remark that practical deliberation involves reflecting judgment to be an effort on Fichte's part to say that practical deliberation involves only regulative principles, but no constitutive ones.[17] But while it is quite true that for Fichte the moral principle has the status of a Kantian *Idee* (IV: 65–6) and so is not a constitutive principle in Kant's sense, the distinction between the regulative and constitutive use of concepts cuts across the distinction between reflective and determining judgment, for Kant; so Fichte's description of practical deliberation as the exercise of reflecting judgment cannot be meant to indicate that it involves only regulative principles.

Given the sort of problem-solving Fichte thinks practical reasoning involves, it is no surprise that he describes it as employing reflecting rather than determining judgment. Although there is a sense in which it makes sense to say it begins from an a priori concept (INDEPENDENCE), far from being about whether the concept of a proposed action *x* is a determination of the concept INDEPENDENCE, practical deliberation is instead about determining what would amount to, or what would further, independence in a given area. This is often a matter of exercising creativity,

[14] Although Kant does not claim that the instrumental principle is itself a principle of theoretical reason, as some philosophers have done (see e.g. K. Setiya 2007), he does hold that all reasoning subordinate to it is theoretical. Fichte does not raise the issue explicitly, but it is likely that he simply follows Kant here in taking the instrumental principle to be analytic and so not a substantive principle of practical reason.

[15] e.g. A. Wood 2000, A. Wood 2015, and some audience members at the 2012 Boston University Workshop on Late Modern Philosophy who responded to the paper from which much of this subsection is drawn.

[16] I. Kant 1900–, 5: 179; I. Kant 2000, pp. 66–7.

[17] Several audience members at the 2012 Boston University Workshop on Late Modern Philosophy raised this point.

both because solutions to technical problems involve creativity, and because the moral end itself involves the creative expansion of action possibilities through artistic, conceptual, and other forms of invention. (Empirical concept formation, a paradigm case of reflecting judgment for Kant, is similarly creative.)

Wood objects to the characterization I have given of practical deliberation in Fichte, but as evidence against it has offered only a single page citation (IV: 57)—where, he claims, Fichte 'explicitly denies' that deliberation is a matter for technically practical reason.[18] But IV: 57 and the surrounding pages contain no explicit denial, nor anything that could plausibly be read as constituting an implicit denial, that the deliberation described at IV: 165ff. is exclusively a matter of technically practical reason. The question under discussion at IV: 57 is what it means to say that reason is practical, and whether there is anything puzzling or mysterious about the claim that it is (the background apparently being contemporary reactions to the Kantian version of it). Fichte explains that reason has long been acknowledged to be practical in the technical sense of supporting means–ends judgments, and that his view adds to that universally accepted sense of reason's practicality only the claim that reason is practical also in the stronger sense of setting an end (the end in question being the end of absolute independence). In addition to being '*technisch-praktisch*,' reason is also '*schlechthin praktisch*' (absolutely practical), and it is so because it also sets its own end, rather than being employed *only* to find means to ends set by natural need or arbitrary individual choice (IV: 57). Of course these comments are perfectly consistent with the account at IV: 165ff., on which absolutely practical reason sets only the end and it is left to technically practical reason (understood as a part of theoretical reason) to discover the x that is the proximal step on the path toward it for an individual in a given situation. Since this is just the account I have given, the source of Wood's objection is a mystery.

Understood in the way I have described, Fichte's account of practical reasoning differs strikingly from Kant's, at least on the usual understanding. For Kant, specifically moral reasoning involves the application of a constraint (consistency with universal legislation in a kingdom of ends) on the adoption of maxims whose initial formation is guided by an end (one's own happiness) that is essentially agent-relative and that moreover tends to set individual interests in opposition to one another.[19] The categorical imperative imposes a check on some ways of pursuing this agent-relative end.[20]

---

[18] A. Wood 2016, p. 175.   [19] Here I follow A. Wood 2001.

[20] I assume that at least one function of the universal law formulation of the categorical imperative is to rule out maxims whose universalization is collectively self-defeating. I take this

For Fichte, by contrast, specifically moral deliberation is distinguished from prudential deliberation only by its end. Prudential deliberation aims at the deliberator's overall well-being. But in a morally virtuous agent this end is replaced by the specifically moral end of reason's material self-sufficiency, regarded time- and agent-neutrally. Sometimes (perhaps ordinarily) pursuing one's own self-sufficiency is the best way to pursue the independence of rational agency generally; but where it is not, Fichte's position is that we have *no* reason to pursue our own before others', because he takes it to be a conceptual truth that considerations of the sort, 'y will happen in the immediate (as opposed to the farther) future' or 'y will happen to me (as opposed to someone else)' do not (all on their own) affect the sorts of reasons to which events like y give rise.

For Fichte's practical deliberator, then, there is no two-step process corresponding to the two-step process of maxim-formation and maxim-testing Kant describes. Fichte is careful to underscore this difference. Where he discusses 'the Kantian principle: act in such a way that you can think the maxim of your will as a universal law' (IV: 233–4), he concedes that the principle is correct insofar as, since '[t]he moral end of every rational being is...the self-sufficiency of reason generally,' we should all in principle agree about the right thing to do in a given situation (IV: 233). But he emphasizes that this significance is at most heuristic:

> But in my view we need to add...[that] this principle is only *heuristic* (I can very well use it to test whether I have erred in my judgment of my duty); but it is in no way *constitutive*. It is not even itself a principle, but only a consequence of the true principle, the demand for the absolute self-sufficiency of reason. The relationship of the two is not: because something can be a principle of universal legislation, for that reason it should be the maxim of my will; but instead the opposite: because something should be the maxim of my will, for that reason it can also be a principle of universal legislation.
>
> (IV: 234; cf. GA 4–1: 117)[21]

Fichte's point is that the result of the process of deliberation is a judgment that is presumptively universal in that it implicitly claims to be the one any rational agent in exactly this situation with exactly this set of background beliefs would, on sufficient reflection, come to. Disagreement is a sign that at least one party to it is in error, and to believe of one of my own judgments that it might not be the judgment of exactly similarly placed others just is to doubt its truth. Of course the

way of formulating it from D. Parfit 1984, ch. 2, but it is a component of orthodox Kantian interpretations as well—cf. C. Korsgaard 1996, ch. 3; S. Engstrom 2009, pp. 116–18 and 153.

[21] This position that the universality follows from the normativity, and not vice versa, is interesting because it calls to mind the position taken by many consequentialists, beginning with Mill, who have wanted to argue that their view is consistent with Kantianism. Cf. J.S. Mill 1985, chs. 1 and 5; S. Kagan 2002; D. Parfit 2011, vol. 1, chs. 16 and 17.

heuristic value of a universalizability test so construed would be limited. As Fichte points out, it is after all I who am making the judgment as to whether my maxim could be a principle of universal legislation (IV: 234).[22] He suggests that we do better to rely on actual rather than imagined agreement and disagreement as a heuristic. But even that has at most a heuristic, not a constitutive, status.[23] One upshot of this is that Fichte is committed to no controversial claims about constitutive principles of practical deliberation (like a universalizability requirement); his only controversial claim about practical reason is the one about its constitutive end of independence.

2.3 Necessary Conditions of Reflection

2.3.1 Empirical cognition

Not all action is basic action: sometimes agents do things by doing other things or by setting processes in motion. Fichte's way of drawing the basic/non-basic action distinction is to distinguish between immediate and mediated causal efficacy (IV: 98–9). He defines the body as the set of points at which one's will has immediate causal efficacy. (This set may be smaller (paralysis) or greater (some prostheses) than the set corresponding to the body in the ordinary biological sense.) Basic action is the action of the will upon the body. All mediated causal efficacy is mediated by the body; some is further mediated by interactions between external objects.

An agent can intend to exercise mediated causal efficacy only by employing an understanding of the physical nature of, and the laws governing, her body and the things on which it acts. Fichte concludes from this that empirical cognition is a condition of possibility of practical reflection. An agent needs to know what in her environment is contingent and so in principle alterable (IV: 68–9); to know something of her own individual causal powers (IV: 3, 79, 81, 83, 89–92); and so

---

[22] In discussing this passage Wood remarks that it contains no disagreement with Kant, because universalizability has a merely heuristic significance for Kant as well (A. Wood 2016, p. 213). This does not seem to me the correct reading of Kant; but that aside, it is clear that Fichte, at least, takes there to be a disagreement here, since he explicitly characterizes the Kantian view as one on which the universalizability principle is constitutive rather than heuristic (IV: 233–4).

[23] Contra Wood, I see no evidence that actual agreement or disagreement ever has a more than heuristic function with respect to finding out the moral truth. The substantive requirement to seek consensus that Fichte discusses in this part of the text is never justified by the claim that consensus would be constitutive of truth, as Wood contends in likening Fichte's view to Habermas' (A. Wood 2016, p. 225). Instead it is justified as a necessary condition of reconciling individuals' aims (in the sense of A. Gibbard 2008) and overcoming the need for a coercive state apparatus (as e.g. at IV: 253). I will return to this last point in §3.2.3.5 below.

to be able to distinguish between what she has herself brought about and what has simply happened (IV: 70). The more complex the projects she takes on, the more detailed the instrumental reasoning she has to engage in, and the more she needs to know about physical nature and its laws (IV: 68, 70, 103, 109, and 166–72 *passim*). This is why Fichte thinks some degree of causal knowledge of nature predates reflection. All drive-based behavior requires this sort of knowledge, and before one can be a moral agent one must be an effective causal agent (IV: 101–10 *passim*).

It may seem odd to call the cognitive attitude that figures in reflection 'knowledge' or 'cognition' rather than 'belief.' 'Cognition' translates Fichte's '*Erkenntnis*,' which is the default German term for an empirical cognitive attitude. '*Erkenntnis*' picks out an attitude that is factive; and in fact there is no equivalent, in German, to the English 'belief.' This is because the German '*Glaube*,' like the English 'faith,' carries with it the suggestion that its object is not, and perhaps cannot be, an object of knowledge. So the mere fact that Fichte uses '*Erkenntnis*' does not indicate a self-conscious stance on the question of whether rational agency requires justified or reliably produced true beliefs, rather than mere beliefs, on which to operate.

But he does seem to want to say that true belief is essential not just for the ability to accomplish what one chooses, but for the ability to choose freely to begin with (e.g. at IV: 66–75[24]). And this is not implausible. Moral responsibility is typically taken to have epistemic conditions in addition to control conditions, insofar as non-culpable ignorance is taken to relieve an agent of responsibility even for an action that goes according to the agent's conscious plan. Might conditions for moral responsibility and conditions for rational agency diverge here, such that it is only our capacity to be rational (but not our capacity to be morally responsible, where these diverge) that can be the source of constitutive ends? I do not know what sort of argument could be offered for thinking that— nor, consequently, do I have any idea as to how to rebut the suggestion. But it is worth pointing out that some sorts of cognitive limitation (e.g. sufficiently subnormal working memory) are typically taken to undermine responsibility *by* undermining rational agency; and that although in the typical case of ignorance of some discrete empirical fact it does seem plausible to claim that rational agency survives ignorance intact, it is considerably less plausible to say that rational agency survives intact ignorance of all empirical facts across the board. (Surely complete ignorance of actually valid inductive principles cannot be

---

[24] Cf. also GA 4–1: 134 where Fichte lists 'truth,' life, and property as three conditions of possibility of freedom.

simply external to the exercise of rational agency; but whether principles of inductive reasoning are formal principles or substantive, empirically grounded assumptions is, I take it, an open philosophical question.) On the whole, then, it seems at best strained to say that an agent is free in forming intentions so long as she has some beliefs to operate with, however outrageously inappropriate those beliefs may be. Certainly, it is not unusual for contemporary philosophers to include full information (or at least the absence of false beliefs) among the requirements of formal rationality.[25]

The point is important because it is in this cognitive requirement for moral agency, and the use Fichte makes of it, that much of the very considerable interest in Fichte's ethics and political theory lies. Coupled with the claim that there is a dialectical interaction between knowledge and control of one's environment, this cognitive requirement plays a key role both in Fichte's political philosophy (as part of his justification for property rights (III: 113–19)) and in his ethics (as the justification for duties of truth-telling (IV: 282–8, 290), truth-seeking (IV: 291), and collective support for a specialized class whose vocation is basic research (IV: 344)). The argument for these first-order normative propositions is complicated if mere belief rather than knowledge is taken to suffice as a cognitive component of fully rational agency on Fichte's view. However, as I will show in §5.2.1, Fichte's argument can be made even with this weaker claim, since it is uncontroversial that any deliberating agent has an interest, *qua* deliberating agent, in true beliefs relevant to the matters about which she deliberates, and so acquisition of these is plausibly an end partially constitutive of practical deliberation and, assuming such deliberation is essential to rational agency, of rational agency.

2.3.2 Drive

Practical reflection does not operate in the absence of conative attitudes, and Fichte conceptualizes these in the terms offered by the biology of his day. He takes the behavior of organisms to be drive-based, and his moral psychology is likewise built around the notion of drive (*Trieb*).[26] That part of a rational agent which is given by nature and upon which reflection operates is a system of drives that Fichte refers to, collectively, as the 'natural drive' (IV: 212). The natural drive is the drive, in any organized product of nature, to keep its parts together in something like the order in which it finds them, to organize its relation to

---

[25] Cf. e.g. B. Williams 1981, pp. 101–13 and M. Smith 1994, pp. 156–61.

[26] Fichte's drive-based moral psychology is a matter of some interest in its own right; but I will constrain my discussion of it to what I need for my purposes here. For more, see, e.g. W. Jacobs 1967; S.F. Bertoletti 1990; P. Rohs 1991a; and P. Rohs 1991b, pp. 104ff.

the external world in a way that facilitates its own maintenance, repair, and reproduction, and to do so just for the sake of doing so (IV: 123). As an organized product of nature, a human being has this drive, and is prompted by it to interact with her environment in certain ways.

All human action has its basis in some modification of the natural drive, according to Fichte, because without it agents would not be moved to action to begin with, and because its content is an ineliminable source of determination for the end of independence. Still the idea of behavior based entirely in the natural drive is an abstraction from normal adult behavior, which is always in fact influenced by reflection.

Fichte distinguishes between the content and the end of the natural drive. Its content is the pursuit of the fulfillment of natural needs; its end pleasure or enjoyment (*Genuß*) (IV: 128). That is, in behavior based exclusively in the natural drive the expectation of immediate pleasure would be what motivates (pleasure is the 'end'); but what produces pleasure, at a given moment, depends on what needs are fulfilled by the action (these provide the 'content'). Pleasure is a sign that these needs have been fulfilled, and it operates as a motivator in place of any reflective consciousness of, and reasoned determination to act in response to, these needs—since reflective consciousness and rational deliberation are by supposition absent in such behavior.

Fichte describes a series of moral-psychological configurations that result from the modification of the natural drive by rational reflection and that constitute a developmental path from nature to fully rational self-determination. The default state (IV: 129–30) is one in which immediate pleasure rewards conduct in accordance with natural drives and so motivates future conduct by a sort of habituation. This drive–pleasure feedback mechanism does not take into account future consequences (IV: 130) and the first modification of it, the first application of reflection to the natural drive, takes these into account (IV: 180). An agent at this stage acts on the maxim of her own happiness, understood as the maxim of choosing what promises the most intense pleasure of the longest duration. Such an agent is 'an animal with understanding' (IV: 180).

A second modification comes when an agent accomplishes a sort of self-liberation from the end of pleasure, which Fichte describes as the product of an awareness of the presence within itself of a drive to independence or self-sufficiency for its own sake (IV: 184). Fichte does not say whether this drive to independence for its own sake is something unique to rational beings or is something present in other (non-rational) organisms. As a conscious aim it surely is unique to rational beings; but there is some reason to see the *Bildung-strieb* itself as an expression of it. The *Bildungstrieb* as Blumenbach characterized it is what explains the organism's original self-formation (as an embryo) as well as its self-reproduction (in nutrition) and self-repair (in the face of outer insults); and this could without distortion be described as a drive to the independence or self-sufficiency of the organism with respect to everything outside itself. Blumenbach's own willingness to expand the reach of this concept to human phenomena such as individual self-development and even the development of culture over history is consistent with this. And Fichte writes, of drives in general, that they must be understood in terms of self-determination, and that therefore 'my nature, insofar as it is supposed to consist in drive, is thought as determining itself through itself, since drive can be understood only in this way' (IV: 111). This is why, Fichte thinks, the idea of a natural drive can operate as a 'mediating term' between nature and freedom (IV: 115).[27]

On this reading the system of natural drives would be the expression, in nonrational beings, of a more fundamental drive to independence, which could also manifest consciously as a drive directed at the end of independence for its own sake. This is what Fichte seems to have in mind when he describes the 'pure drive' (a drive to independence for the sake of independence) and the 'natural drive' (the system of natural drives unified in the explanatory construct of the *Bildungstrieb*) as two manifestations of a single underlying drive to self-determination— an 'original drive' (*Urtrieb*) that constitutes the essence of the natural rational being (IV: 130).

That there be these two manifestations is, Fichte argues, a condition of possibility of freedom to choose between alternatives. In order for there to be alternate possibilities there must be another source (beyond the unmodified natural drive) of the (possible) material determinations of the will (IV: 138). 'Thus there must be present a drive to determine oneself independently of and contrary to the natural drive, to draw the matter of action not from the natural drive but only from oneself' (IV: 139).

[Formal freedom] consists in the entrance [into nature] of a new power, a new formal principle, without there being the least change in the material element in the series of effects. Nature no longer acts; the free being does. But the latter produces exactly what the former would have produced on its own, were it capable of acting. Freedom in the second respect [i.e. material freedom] consists in the fact that there enters not just a new power,

---

[27] This idea that the notion of drive can mediate nature and freedom, that this distinguishes it from the notion of force, and that Blumenbach's drive-based account of self-organization in biology was particularly groundbreaking in this regard, is an idea that is common to Fichte, Schiller (who takes the discussion of drive in Fichte's *Foundations of the Doctrine of Science* (1794) as a landmark in the application of the idea in moral philosophy), and (with modifications) Schelling.

but also a new series of actions with new content. Now intelligence not only produces effects; it produces effects completely different from anything nature would have produced. (IV: 139)

Fichte is here conducting a regressive argument: there could be no formal freedom without alternate possibilities, and so without the presence of a drive to go beyond nature in setting one's ends.[28]

While the natural drive has both a content (natural needs) and an end (pleasure), the pure drive has no content of its own, but only an end: 'absolute self-determination to activity for activity's sake' (IV: 131). This end is not mysterious, though the emphasis placed upon it is distinctive of Fichte's thought: it is the end of being the source of what happens within and around one, being spontaneous rather than reactive, creative rather than imitative, active rather than passive.

The fact that the pure drive lacks a determinate content of its own means that it must operate on the content provided by nature. This is how we must understand Fichte's statement that 'I can never do anything that is not demanded by the natural drive' (IV: 149), that 'every possible concept of an end is directed . . . toward the satisfaction of a natural drive' (IV: 148). But this does not mean that the substitution of the end of independence for the end of pleasure has no manifestation in behavior, as we see when Fichte describes the second modification to the default psychological configuration, at IV: 184–5.

This modification consists in the first introduction of the end of independence as a conscious end.[29] The individual at this stage aims at mastery of the outside world (including other people) and eschews the end of happiness. But in this first manifestation in consciousness the drive appears as just another contingent desire, not as essential to this sort of agent; and it appears as a 'blind drive' rather than as 'law' (IV: 184–5), a drive to 'limitless and lawless hegemony over everything outside of us' (IV: 186). Since it makes its appearance in a psychological ecosystem dominated by the maxim of prudential self-interest,

---

[28] The same point is repeated at IV: 148–9. Fichte makes the Reinholdian thought—'There is no will without *Willkür*,' where *Willkür* is the capacity 'to make a choice among several equally possible actions' (IV: 159)—consistent with his fundamentally naturalistic account of agency by splitting the *Urtrieb* in this way.

[29] Note that Fichte thinks the pure drive itself is not something that ever occurs in consciousness, but is instead an explanatory posit (IV: 152). Strictly, the same should be true of the natural drive (which is why I have said that the idea of human behavior based entirely on the natural drive is an abstraction). This was the role Blumenbach gave the *Bildungstrieb*: it is the posited explanatory ground of the manifest phenomena, occupying something like the role that gravity played for Newton (J. Blumenbach 1789, pp. 25–6). This seems borne out by Fichte's remark that the natural drive manifests psychologically only indirectly, as a feeling (IV: 106).

action on it appears irrational (IV: 186).[30] A character dominated by this drive, in its conscious but not yet rational form, could, Fichte tells us, be called 'heroic.'

The heroic character, however, is not yet the moral one; for that a final transformation is required. The drive toward independence embraced self-consciously as such must be brought 'to clear consciousness'—at which point it will, through reflection, transform itself into a 'law commanding absolutely' (IV: 191). Reflection is itself the product of the pure drive (IV: 130-1), and the disposition to reflect on the prompts of the natural drive, and to develop an ability to refrain from acting immediately upon them (IV: 126, 130), operates in the transition from the first to second stages of rational development. Like Kant, Fichte understands the exercise of reason in reflection as a form of self-activity (IV: 140), and he sees the pure drive as connected to 'reason's tendency to determine *itself purely through itself, as* subject of consciousness, as intelligence in the highest sense of the word' (IV: 130). So the aim of activity incorporates the aim of rationality, and of efficacious rational reflection upon one's motivations, behavior, and the relations between them. Since on Fichte's view full rationality involves full neutrality with respect to person and time, rational reflection tends to expand the scope of an agent's concern to encompass the future consequences, and the consequences for other agents, of a contemplated action. Once the aim of independence is brought to full consciousness, irrational biases (like the bias toward the near future, or toward oneself) are eliminated.

The resulting drive to further material independence in general, now and into the indefinite future, is what Fichte calls the 'ethical' or 'mixed' drive.[31] This drive takes its content from the natural drive, insofar as it is a drive to organize specific parts of the natural world in relation to the agent in a certain way, and it remains in that sense 'determined by the object' (IV: 131). But it takes its end from the pure drive, insofar as it aims at activity for the sake of activity; or, alternatively formulated, at 'absolute freedom, absolute independence of all of nature' (IV: 131; cf. IV: 39-57 *passim*, 59-60, 144-5, 149, 152-3, 209, 211-12, 229).[32] The ethical drive is the drive toward independence and self-subsistence of an organized natural product, stripped of its parochiality by practical reflection. It is no longer

---

[30] In the appendix on ascetics, Fichte suggests that these two drives can be combined, describing 'domination out of self-interest' as their combined product, as distinct from domination out of mere arrogance (XI: 136).

[31] The drive that motivates the 'heroic' character is also mixed, as it also takes its content, but not its end, from the natural drive.

[32] The formulation of the end shifts, from the pure drive's 'activity for the sake of activity' to the ethical drive's 'independence of all of nature,' because 'independence' is Fichte's blanket term for the conditions of possibility of exercised agency, and it is within nature that a natural being exercises its agency.

a drive to my independence in particular, but to the independence of rational agency in general, a drive toward the moral end (IV: 231).

Thus although, as Fichte explains, his natural and pure drives are successor notions to Kant's lower and higher faculties of desire (IV: 131), his account of their relation is quite different from Kant's, insofar as he emphasizes the absence of any fundamental conflict between them. That they can be reconciled and so are not fundamentally at odds is presupposed by his conception of the ethical drive as a 'mixed' drive resulting from their unification. Underscoring this difference with Kant, Fichte attributes his ability to elaborate a complete science of ethics to this conception of the ethical drive as a synthesis of lower and higher drives. 'If one looks only to the higher faculty of desire, one obtains only a formal, empty *metaphysics of morals*. Only through synthetic unity of this one with the lower does one attain a *system of ethics*, which must be real' (IV: 131). Though he does not say as much, Fichte also owes to this conception of the ethical drive as a synthesis of lower and higher drives his ability to offer a naturalistic account of the drive's emergence as the result of a psychological process that, though dependent at every point on the spontaneity inherent in reflective activity, is still recognizably developmental.

2.3.3 Energy

Practical deliberation on Fichte's account requires effort, and so the capacity to exert cognitive effort—a sort of reflective energy—is also a condition of possibility of moral agency. Fichte does not say that in so many words in the portion of the *System of Ethics* published during his lifetime. But in the posthumously published appendix to that work (which was written at the same time) he does use the term 'energy' to describe what the person with a generally moral disposition whose deliberation goes awry has failed to apply (XI: 127). In the *System of Ethics* itself he describes failures of practical reasoning as the result of laziness or inertia (*Trägheit*) in practical reflection (IV: 192–205). Since practical reflection is required for rational agency, whatever is the opposite of laziness must be required as well—and that is what I am calling 'energy.'[33] Fichte's view about the expenditure of deliberative effort seems to be that it is at best partially under an agent's conscious control, and something for which she bears at best partial responsibility. The ability to exert it depends in an obvious way on somatic factors; and the disposition to exert it depends, in Fichte's view, on social ones. That disposition

---

[33] For a recent summary of psychological literature describing the role of effort in reasoning, see D. Kahnemann 2011, part 1, and especially chs. 2 and 3. For a recent philosophical treatment, see R. Holton 2009.

can be influenced by the agent's own past actions; but more typically it is influenced by the demands of other agents in the past and present (IV: 201–5). This view complicates Fichte's account of moral blameworthiness, since the application of (a determinate degree of) effort to a given instance of deliberation cannot itself be something for which an agent is responsible on that very occasion, but is instead a precondition for acting responsibly on that occasion. An agent could be blameworthy for her own (degree of) deliberative sloth only to the extent that it is the result of some past action(s) of hers. But those actions would themselves be *pro tanto* irrational for that reason, and so have their source in failures of practical deliberation, and so in deliberative laziness, on Fichte's account. The point is never reached at which an agent is fully responsible for her own expenditure of deliberative energy. This means that she is not fully responsible for her own immoral actions (and neither is she morally responsible for her own lack of moral responsibility for them). I will return to this topic in §4.2.

2.3.4 Causal efficacy; embodiment

Forming a conscious intention requires seeing the will as a causal force, and on Fichte's view this is, for any given individual, an empirical realization. This means that the exercise of practical agency in deliberation relies on some past experience of (arational) causal efficacy. Fichte's argument for this set of claims appears first in the *Foundations of Natural Right* (III: 19–31), where he reasons that forming the concept of a determinate end requires having a determinate representation of the state of things that would constitute the accomplishment of that end (III: 19–21), and that this in turn requires having a representation both of how the world is in which ends are to be carried out (III: 23–4) and of oneself as a causal force within that world (III: 28–9). But a sense of one's causal efficacy in general is possible only as an abstraction from actual instances of its exercise (III: 31). So for a rational individual to be conscious of itself as capable of acting externally (and so for it to be able to form intentions to do so), it is necessary that it have been the case (at least once) 'that the object in experience that is thought of through the concept of the person's efficacy actually correspond to that concept; what is required, therefore, is that something in the world outside the rational individual follow from the thought of his activity' (III: 9).[34] Fichte reiterates the same points in briefer form in both the lectures on ethics of summer 1796 (GA 4–1: 26–30) and in the *System of Ethics* (IV: 88–93; cf. 101–10).

---

[34] For a more detailed reconstruction of Fichte's argument in this passage in the *Foundations*, see F. Neuhouser 2001.

If we add as a premise that if the will is to be externally causally efficacious, then there must be some part of the world upon which it is immediately causally efficacious (III: 56–9), we arrive at the conclusion that a rational agent must have a body, in Fichte's technical sense.

A further argument for the claim that external causal efficacy is a condition of possibility of self-consciousness is described in the context of the argument, treated in §2.3.5, establishing social interaction as such a condition (since social interaction is, unsurprisingly, a form of causal interaction with the outside world on Fichte's view).

2.3.5 Social interaction; individuality

Fichte argues in the *Foundations of Natural Right* that social interaction is a condition of possibility of reflective self-consciousness, and that the rational agent is therefore necessarily an 'individual' in the specific sense of being one among many of its kind (III: 30–40; cf IV: 178, 218). This argument against skepticism about the existence of other agents is part of the foundation of Fichte's practical philosophy as a whole, and he appeals to it again at *System of Ethics* IV: 218–21. (It replaces a weaker anti-solipsistic argument that had figured in the second of the *Lectures on the Scholar's Vocation* (VI: 302–6) and had occupied the same systematic role.)

The summons argument is much discussed in the literature on Fichte's political philosophy;[35] and I will discuss it, and its role in Fichte's conception of right, at greater length in §3.2.3.7 below. The precise role it plays in his account of right is to some extent an open question in the literature. The point that is relevant to my purpose in this chapter is only the relatively uncontroversial point that normal moral agency has the right sort of early socialization among its conditions of possibility.

The form of socialization at issue in the *Foundations*—what Fichte calls a 'summons to free self-activity' or, alternatively, 'upbringing' (III: 39)[36]—is a demand (or series of demands) upon the summoned to exercise her external causality in a way that does not interfere (directly) with the summoner's exercise of her own in a sphere that the summons itself defines (initially the body; later a set of action-possibilities in the shared external world), a demand conveyed in a way that likewise does not interfere (directly) with the external causality of the

---

[35] A few examples (there are many more): P. Rohs 1991b, pp. 86ff.; F. Neuhouser 2000; A. Honneth 2001; S. Darwall 2006, pp. 20ff., 252ff., *et passim*; A. Wood 2006.

[36] 'The summons to free self-activity is what is called upbringing. All individuals must be brought up to be human beings, and would not become human beings otherwise' (III: 39).

summoned. The typical locus of this sort of interaction is the practical education of children, though it is of course possible among adults as well. Such a demand is the origin, on Fichte's view, of both reflective self-consciousness and the disposition to form second-order evaluative attitudes and so to impose normative demands of any kind upon oneself. In other words, both minimal and evaluative reflection depend upon the summons interaction.

In explicating Fichte's *Foundations* argument, Neuhouser emphasizes the idea that for a finite rational agent to be conscious of itself as such it must be able to be conscious, not only of its own finitude nor only of its own agency, but of the finitude *of* its own agency.[37] For it to be able to see this, it must experience the space of possible action as divided amongst agents, with its own possibilities occupying only part of that space. The summons interaction is one in which an agent experiences the space of freedom as divided in this way, because to take a summons as a summons is to take it as a demand from another rational agent making a claim to some part of the space of possible action.

It is clear why this idea of the finitude of rational agency is important for political philosophy, which would have no subject matter if the space of free activity were not divided in this way; what is less clear is why a rational agent cannot be conscious of itself as such without at the same time being conscious of this specific sort of limitation—not physical or causal limitation, but limitation as free being, something only the existence of other free beings could establish. When he approaches the topic of individuality in the *System of Ethics*, Fichte refers the reader to the relevant sections in the *Foundations of Natural Right*; but he also restates the argument in what he takes to be a different form, different because 'derived from a higher principle' (IV: 218). The higher principle, I take it, is the idea of an I engaged in practical reflection. This accounts for the emphasis in these pages (absent in the *Foundations*) on the idea that the summons is a condition of possibility of *reflection* in particular.

The discussion begins from a general fact about objects of reflection: that they must be determinate, and are made determinate only by having limits:

Everything that is an object of reflection is necessarily limited just in virtue of being an object of reflection. The I should be an object of reflection, and therefore necessarily limited. But the I is characterized by free activity as such, and thus that free activity must also be limited.... In short, the I can attribute to itself no free activity at all without this latter being a quantum, and therefore must in the same thought posit other free activity that does not belong to it, since each quantum is necessarily limited.
(IV: 218–19)

---

[37] Cf. F. Neuhouser 2001.

Fichte then considers why other *actual* individuals must be involved in order for the I to represent itself as limited in the relevant way. Why could the I not posit a merely possible (ideal) activity outside itself (IV: 219)? His answer appeals to a principle concerning knowledge of mere possibles mentioned already in §2.3.4 above: 'I can posit something as *possible* only in contrast to something *actual* that is already known to me. All mere possibility is grounded on abstraction from known actuality' (IV: 219). If I am to posit a merely possible free activity outside of myself, then, I must already be aware of an actual free activity. So the proposal that I might find my freedom limited by the mere idea of a possible other freedom fails because it is circular. Instead, 'I must originally *find* myself as a determinate object, and since I am only I insofar as I am free, I must *find* myself *as free*' (IV: 219). The question, then, is how this is possible, and the answer will be the same as the one given in the *Foundations*: I find myself as free because my freedom is presented to me as such by the other's demand that I limit my exercise of it in some way.

Fichte here distinguishes between merely engaging in an activity to which I am prompted, as a natural being, by the natural drive (which already involves a sort of causal reasoning) and explicit conscious reflection on that activity as something I am doing. This latter is the conscious, minimal reflection described in §2.2 above. I have said that for Fichte such reflection requires an awareness of one's own status as a particular cause within nature, and he reiterates that point here (IV: 218). The summons calls my attention to that status. It brings me from a state of immediate causal engagement with the world to a state of reflection upon myself-as-so-engaged. It does this by presenting the idea of a demand upon my use of that causal agency.

What the summons conveys, then, is a demand to exercise causal efficacy in accordance with some constraint; and if it is seen as such, the internalization of that demand on my own capacity to govern my behavior becomes the foundation of every second-order evaluative attitude I will go on to have. I am in this way 'determined to be self-determining' by another rational being (III: 33; original in italics).[38]

---

[38] Fichte emphasizes that self-determination cannot be presented to me as a *fact* in the summons situation—for only I can exercise it, and I must do so spontaneously if at all. Instead it must be presented to me as a *concept*—a concept to which I can either conform my spontaneous activity or not, by either grasping the summons as such or not (IV: 220) (a claim that will make sense if we recall that spontaneity is for Fichte one of the distinguishing features of conceptual activity). Fichte emphasizes in both the *Foundations* and the *System of Ethics* that his claim that self-determination relies for its possibility on a summons does not contradict his view that self-determination is spontaneous in a sense that precludes causal explanation. Even where self-determination occurs in response to some external stimulus it is not causally explained by that stimulus (IV: 179; cf. IV:

Later in the *System of Ethics* Fichte expands upon this idea and argues that moral agency relies not only on upbringing, but also on continuing social interaction of the right sorts, for its persistence and perfection, emphasizing our reliance, as moral deliberators, on the demands made by others and the example they set. It is on this basis that he argues for the existence of a moral duty to set a good example, both in general (IV: 313–25), and for those occupying the particular social roles of parent (IV: 338) and religious leader (IV: 204, 352); and for a moral duty to correct others, to be open to correction by others, and to debate and try to reach consensus in cases of disagreement (IV: 233–53 *passim*).

Since the concept of my voluntarily constrained free activity can be presented to me only by a being capable of concepts—a rational being, like myself—and since the summons is an empirical experience, it involves the empirical experience of another rational agent, and with that the information that I am one among many, an individual. It is on this basis that Fichte concludes that 'The human being becomes a human being only amongst human beings ... The concept of human being is thus by no means the concept of something singular ... but rather the concept of a type' (III: 39).

2.4 Variability

Uncontroversially, there are differences among normal adults in many of the dispositions and capacities just described: in the quantity and quality of their empirical knowledge, in their capacity for exerting mental effort, in their degree of reflective self-awareness, in their proficiency at evaluating the consistency and means–ends coherence of their sets of beliefs, desires, and intentions. Such variability is based in part on native psychological differences and in part on social conditions.

Fichte's view accommodates this set of facts. Every rational agent has, *qua* member of its kind, the same capacity for freedom; but not every rational agent has the opportunity to develop that capacity to the same degree. This commitment is explicit in the discussion of the developmental psychology of freedom (IV: 177ff.), where Fichte distinguishes between the rational being 'considered primordially,' which has 'everything that belongs to a rational being entire and without lack,' on the one hand, and empirical individuals, who fall short of this ideal of agency to varying degrees, on the other (IV: 177–8).

125, 220). The summoned's first reflection takes place in these circumstances as a purely spontaneous act, 'through absolute freedom' (IV: 179).

What accounts for most of the variability, on Fichte's view, is not native psychological differences but rather differences in agents' environments.[39] Their social circumstances are, he thought, particularly important. There are some social and cultural circumstances in which people's agency is more highly cultivated, and in these circumstances agents are able to be more rational, and morally better, than they could in other circumstances:

[W]e are only cultivated for the possibility of the use of our freedom through upbringing in the widest sense, that is, through the influence of society in general upon us. If we do not raise ourselves above the cultivation we have thereby received, that is the end of it. If society were better, we would be too; but for us [this would be] without merit. The possibility of individual merit is not thereby cancelled; it begins only at a higher point.

(IV: 184; cf. GA 4-1: 87)

The impact the actions of each agent have on these aspects of the agency of her fellows explains many of our moral duties to one another, on Fichte's picture. These are not only episodic (refraining from actions—like deception—that might undermine the integrity of a single decision (IV: 283)); they are also more global (contributing to others' knowledge (IV: 282–3, 290–1) or providing moral example and inspiration (IV: 317–25)). There are parallel self-regarding duties, appropriately describable as duties to improve one's own rational agency, by increasing the quantity and quality of one's theoretical knowledge (IV: 282), putting more energy into practical reflection (IV: 155, 178, 180–5), and correcting it by intentionally subjecting it to criticism from other agents (IV: 234–53 *passim*). These can correctly be described as duties to increase the degree to which rational agents are responsible for what they do. For, as the quotation above suggests, Fichte also takes his view to admit degrees of responsibility varying with degrees of development in an agent's reflective capacities (IV: 137, 178, 180).

This consequence of Fichte's account coincides with some ordinary intuitions: we often seem willing to admit a spectrum of degrees of moral responsibility among normal adults, an intuition also captured by compatibilist accounts of free will that cash that notion out in terms of psychological capacities and dispositions. But it marks a further departure from Kant, who, while accepting that an agent's circumstances can mitigate her responsibility for some individual actions,[40] seemed

---

[39] That is, what M. Vargas 2013 calls their 'moral ecology.'

[40] Cf. e.g. I. Kant 1900–, 6: 228; I. Kant 1996a, p. 382. But cf. I. Kant 1900–, 5: 30; I. Kant 1996a, pp. 163–4, for the example of the man threatened by the sovereign with immediate execution if he refuses to 'give false testimony against an honorable man whom the prince would like to destroy' and who must know that he is able to resist this threat.

committed to denying that moral agency, viewed as an agent-characteristic, can come in degrees. Combined with the Kantian idea that rational agency is that in virtue of which human beings have a dignity that is beyond price, it looks hard to reconcile with a commitment to the equal dignity of moral agents as such. Certainly, if equality of moral status is taken to rely on equality of responsibility, Fichte cannot both accommodate it and defend in the way he does both the importance of material independence as a moral ideal, and the importance of material equality in the political sphere.[41] Of course it is not clear that Kant himself was committed to this (or any) account of a link between equal responsibility and equal dignity; and many contemporary Kantians do not accept an account of this form (in part because every effort to defend the moral status of animals, infants, and the severely cognitively impaired on a Kantian theory seems to depend on its rejection or modification). What is certain is that on a theory like Fichte's, in which equality of responsibility is connected to equality of circumstances, it is an ideal to be striven for rather than something assumed given.

2.5 'freedom—for the sake of freedom'

I said in Chapter 1 that Fichte's ethics is a form of constitutivism founded on the idea that the rational agent has, in virtue of her rational agency, the constitutive end of *independence*. The main task for an interpretation of Fichte's normative ethics is to say what 'independence' means and how the end of independence guides action. The best place to start, in coming to grips with that task, is the summary statement of the moral principle Fichte offers at the end of the second division of the *System of Ethics* (after he has outlined his conception of agency and as he is about to move on to his normative ethics proper):

The ethical drive demands *freedom*—for the sake of *freedom*. Who does not see that the word freedom has two distinct senses in this sentence? In the second occurrence it denotes an objective state that is to be brought about: the absolute final end of complete independence of everything outside of us. In the first [occurrence it denotes] an action as such, something subjective, not an actual existence. I should *act freely* that I may *become free*.

But even in the concept of freedom as it occurs in the first instance there is a further distinction to make. Of free action one can ask *how* it must happen in order [for it] to be free, and what must happen; about the form of freedom and its material.

---

[41] Kant can mount at most a weak defense of egalitarian institutions (cf. T. Pogge 2002, 153ff.). Fichte has a stronger basis than Kant on which to argue that some measure of socio-economic equality is a requirement of right (cf. A. Wood 2008, ch. 11). But that basis comes with this cost, which to some might seem too high (cf. S. Shell 1986, p. 156).

But the material of it we have already discussed: the action must lie in a series through whose continuation to infinity the I would become absolutely independent. We will now take a look at the *how* or the form.

(IV: 153; cf. IV: 60, 149, 153, 209, 211–12, 229, GA 4–1: 72)

These paragraphs summarize the project of the third division of the *System of Ethics*, in which Fichte first explains in a general way the formal (§§14–16) and material (§§17–18) conditions on the moral correctness of actions, and then (§§19–33) elaborates a systematic doctrine of duties.

The moral principle states that 'I should *act freely*, that I may *become free*.' The freedom at issue in 'becoming' free is the moral end *qua* 'objective state that is to be brought about: the absolute final end of complete independence of everything outside of us' (IV: 153). What an agent *should* do is not simply bring about this end by any mechanism whatever, but rather produce it by 'act[ing] freely.' What is it to act freely? It is not simply to exercise rational agency in any way whatever: Fichte is here describing a normative constraint. He tells us that acting freely has two senses or aspects: '*how* it [*sc.* the acting] must happen...and what must happen.' To these components correspond 'formal' and 'material' conditions of the 'freedom' of an action (freedom in a substantive normative sense that denotes an action's moral correctness). The 'formal' (alternatively, 'subjective') condition requires that the action be done from the motive of duty (§§15–16). The 'material' (alternatively, 'objective') condition requires that the action be the one duty demands (§§17–33).

The material condition ('what must happen') requires that the action be part of a series at whose (infinitely distant) end one would arrive at the moral end *qua* state of affairs. As I will argue in Chapter 3, materially correct actions promote the material conditions of the perfection of the exercise of practical reason; and they maximize the scope for possible rational plans of action, which involves overcoming external limitations from two sources: those due to nature (in the form of disease and natural disaster, but also the general resistance of the forces of nature to human plans, insofar as knowledge and technology are capable of overcoming it); and those due to other human beings (in the form of acts of aggression and other interference, intentional or unintentional). Natural scientific research and the development and application of technology are the correct response to the first limitation; self-understanding and the development of social technologies (of which the most fundamental is the political state) are the correct response to the second. The state of maximum achieved progress on these fronts is an idea in the Kantian sense (IV: 65–6): an infinitely distant end, one that can be approached but never attained (IV: 229, 131, 149–50, 153, 209, 211, 231, 253, 261, 350).

The formal condition ('how it must happen') imposes a sort of due diligence constraint on the pursuit of the moral end. It requires that the agent know what she is doing and why she is doing it, that the answer to the 'why' question be 'because it is the required action,' and that the agent be sufficiently subjectively confident in her judgment that it is in fact the required action. Fulfillment of the formal condition is itself an exercise of independence: the independence of practical deliberation from the psychological impediments and external pressures that threaten to undermine or distort it in the moment of deliberation (e.g. intellectual laziness, self-deception, submission to external authority or threat, or capitulation to the demands of the most immediately pressing desire).

Independence in the formal sense is a constitutive end for rational agents in virtue of being the end of exercising their rational agency fully and well in the moment of deliberation. That rational agency has formal independence, so defined, as its constitutive end is a familiar idea. Independence in the material sense, as I will argue in Chapter 3, is a constitutive end for rational agents in virtue of promoting the necessary conditions for the fullest and most perfect exercise of rational agency's characteristic activity of practical reflection to take place and for it to have its characteristic point: intentional action in the world.

Fichte himself explains the formal component first and, unfortunately for the later reception of the *System of Ethics*, describes it in a way that invites the reader to believe that it is the only determinant of moral worth. The widespread disregard of Fichte's discussion of the material component in the second and third sections of the third division (§§17–33, IV: 206–365) is thus the result of an understanding of the formal component on which that entire discussion is— despite the fact that it takes up nearly half the text—strictly redundant. My order of presentation will be the reverse of Fichte's, and my aim in presenting his theory in this way is to end this history of neglect of Fichte's substantive normative ethics.

So I turn first, in Chapter 3, to Fichte's account of the material condition on the moral correctness of action, and only in Chapter 4 to his account of the formal condition. After that, I turn to an examination of the derivation of these constitutive ends of rational agency from the necessary conditions of rational agency introduced in this chapter.

3

Material Independence

Fichte tells us that the material condition on moral worth of actions ('what must happen') is met when an action is part of the series of actions at whose limit one would arrive at the state of absolute freedom from all limitation (IV: 39–60 *passim*, 59–60, 144–5, 149, 152–3, 209, 229, 253, 275, 361–3). No interpretation of the *System of Ethics* can do without an understanding of this claim; but the project of elucidating and defending it has not been a popular one, even among scholars of Fichte. Some prominent interpreters do agree that the texts support an interpretation on which Fichte's moral philosophy is teleological and the moral end is independence of nature in some material sense.[1] But not all of these find that idea intelligible, or intelligibly spelled out.[2] More commonly, interpreters have denied that Fichte even aims to articulate an account of the material content of moral requirements, taking his view to be that these cannot be specified in any general way apart from the conscientious decision of an agent in a situation.[3]

---

[1] Most notable here is Peter Rohs, whose reading is the one closest to my own. Cf. Rohs 1991a; 1991b, ch. 8.

[2] Neuhouser, for instance, refers to it as 'one of Fichte's more outrageous ideas' (F. Neuhouser 1990, p. 141). Arguing that Fichte fails in his stated project of deriving a doctrine of duties from the end of substantive independence, he offers a reconstruction on which for Fichte the end, in a piece of practical deliberation, is a matter of individual choice, constrained only by a norm of authenticity (F. Neuhouser 1990, pp. 131–66).

[3] Wood, like Neuhouser, doubts that material independence is a notion sufficiently determinate to guide action, though unlike Neuhouser he sees this not as a failure but as a success, even by Fichte's own lights. Wood emphasizes the indeterminacy of Fichte's moral principle mainly for the purpose of denying that Fichte can have been a consequentialist: to be a consequentialist, one must have a sufficiently determinate conception of the moral end; Fichte does not have a sufficiently determinate conception of the moral end; therefore he cannot have been a consequentialist (cf. A. Wood 2016, pp. 175–6, 180, 224). This seems to me a poor reason for insisting on the indeterminacy of Fichte's normative principle; and in conjunction with Wood's willingness to take seriously and literally Fichte's account of universal moral requirements (cf. pp. 185ff.), and his denial that Fichte was a 'particularist' (p. 244), it renders Wood's account of Fichte's normative theory fundamentally incoherent. Others, including Wood in earlier work, take Fichte's view to be that the individual's conscientious decision determines the objective content of her duty. Cf. D. Breazeale 1996 and 2012; G. Beck 2008; J. Schneewind and A. Wood 2012; G. Zöller 2012. I outline the problems with this type of reading in Chapter 4.

Since the very idea that Fichte defends a substantive normative ethics built on the end of material independence is a matter of dispute, I will begin this chapter with an extended survey of the textual evidence for that claim (§3.1) before reconstructing his normative theory in more detail (§3.2). My aim in this chapter is to formulate an understanding of the end of material independence that is both consistent with the texts and plausible at least in the minimal sense of being capable of guiding action in ways that are at least approximately in line with moral common sense. The more ambitious task of defending the claim that it is a constitutive end of rational agency I leave for Chapter 5.

3.1 Textual Evidence

3.1.1 Evidence in the System of Ethics

Toward the end of the first division of the *System of Ethics*, whose purpose has been to provide a deduction of the moral principle, Fichte summarizes that principle in this way:

> The principle of morality is the necessary thought of the intelligence that it ought to determine its freedom according to the concept of self-sufficiency, absolutely without exception.... The content of this thought is that the free being *ought* (for *ought* is just the expression for the determinacy of freedom); that it ought to bring its freedom under a *law*; that this law is no other than *the concept of absolute self-sufficiency* (absolute indeterminability by anything outside itself); finally, that this law is valid *without exception*, for it contains the original vocation [*Bestimmung*] of the free being.   (IV: 59–60)

The task of the second division is then to deduce the principle's applicability: to show that the principle can be used to guide action by the sort of agent to whom it is addressed.

The usual response, in the literature, to the suggestion that Fichte means seriously the proposal that material independence is an obligatory end points to this section, whose deduction (it is thought) does not yield any conception of independence determinate enough to guide action. An important passage is the one in which Fichte takes up the question of how the pure drive can be manifested in action, given that it has no content of its own but must take its content from the natural drive. There, he begins by floating an idea that he will immediately reject, namely that the pure drive acts as a mere check on actions motivated by the natural drive, forbidding some of them:

> The natural drive is directed toward something material, exclusively for the sake of the material, at pleasure for the sake of pleasure. The pure drive [is directed] toward the absolute independence of the agent as such from that drive, at freedom for the sake of

freedom. If it has causality, this can provisionally be thought in no other way than [this:] that through it, what the natural drive demands does not take place; accordingly, that simply and solely an *omission*, but no positive *action* at all, can follow from it, beyond the inner action of self-determination.   (IV: 147)

Fichte accuses some (unnamed) moral philosophers of being taken in by this provisional answer to the question, and of arriving at an ethics of self-denial on its basis:

Everyone who has treated ethics purely *formally* would, had they proceeded consistently, have had to arrive at nothing other than a permanent *self-abnegation*, an utter annihilation and dissolution...   (IV: 147)

He does not mention Kant in this passage, and perhaps he does not find Kant to have been actually guilty of this; but the accusation echoes criticisms of Kant that were common in the 1790s. In any event, Fichte denies that this conclusion is justified by the assumptions.

Instead, he argues, if my obligation is to posit myself as free, this must be an obligation to posit my freedom 'as something *positive*, as the ground of an actual action, and by no means a mere omission' (IV: 148). But if I (as subject) am to determine myself (as object) then something objective must be thereby produced; and this means that some natural causality must be exercised. As Fichte goes on to argue, since my will draws its causal efficacy from the natural drive, everything that I will must be something that could in principle be an object of that drive:

All actual willing is necessarily directed at some action; but all my action is action upon objects. In the world of objects, however, I act with natural power; and this power is given to me only through the natural drive, and is nothing other than the natural drive itself in me—the causality of nature upon itself, which it no longer has in its own power, as dead unconscious nature, but rather that I have got under *my* (my intelligence's) power through free reflection. Therefore the most immediate object of every possible willing is necessarily something empirical: a particular determination of my sensible power, which is conferred upon me by the natural drive, therefore something demanded by the natural drive... Every possible concept of an end is directed, therefore, at the satisfaction of a natural drive. (All actual willing is empirical. A pure willing is not an actual one, but a mere idea, an absolute from the intelligible world, that can only be thought as the ground of explanation of something empirical.)

After all that has been said up to this point, it will be impossible to understand us [as saying that] the natural drive as such brings forth the will. *I* will, not nature; but materially [*der Materie nach*] I cannot will anything except something that [nature] also would will, if it could will.   (IV: 148)

From this line of reasoning it would seem to follow that the drive toward absolute material freedom cannot have any causality (IV: 148–9). 'The *drive* to absolute material freedom is not, indeed, thereby cancelled [*aufgehoben*], but its *causality* is entirely cancelled. In reality there remains nothing left except *formal* freedom' (IV: 148–9).

But Fichte goes on: 'Now however the causality of the pure drive may not be cancelled; for only insofar as I posit such [causality] do I posit myself as an I. We have fallen into a contradiction...' (IV: 149). The contradiction can be resolved, Fichte suggests, in this way:

> The material of the action must be at the same time and in the same action in accordance with the natural drive and the pure drive. The two must be unified....
>
> This can be understood only in this way. The intention, the concept of the action, is directed at complete liberation from nature; but that the action nevertheless is and remains in accordance with the natural drive is not the consequence of our freely contrived concept of it, but rather the consequence of our limitation. The sole determining ground of the material of our actions is [the drive] to put an end to our dependence upon nature, irrespective of the fact that the demanded independence never occurs. The pure drive is directed at [*geht auf*] absolute independence; the action is adequate to it if it is also directed at the same thing, that is, [if it] *lies in a series through whose continuation the I must become independent*. Now the I can, according to the above proof, never become independent as long as it is to remain an I; therefore the final end of the rational being lies necessarily in infinity, and it is indeed one that cannot be reached, but one that [the I] must according to its spiritual nature continually approach.   (IV: 149)

How is this resolution of the contradiction supposed to work? Notice, first, that the denial that the pure drive can have, on its own, material causality (in the passage on IV: 148) amounts only to the denial that rational agents have *non-natural material* causality. This would be the sort of causality a god who could create *ex nihilo* would have. We who are not gods act only in nature and through nature, by setting natural force against natural force. We do not act *materially* independently of nature, although we strive to do so.

But we have seen that, on Fichte's account, reflection—itself an exercise only of 'formal' freedom, as Fichte here notes—modifies the natural drive in beings like us. Its exercise opens up new possibilities (both new ends and new ways of accomplishing existing ends) and thus the possibility of choosing amongst different courses of action (IV: 138–41). This means that our natural causality, as a matter both of physical and of motivational possibility, is not limited to a single course of action in a particular circumstance, as it would be if we were not reflective beings. (This is one upshot of Fichte's view of mental causation explained in §2.1 above: it is a cause acting *within* nature, without being a cause arising *from* nature. What Fichte here adds is that it acts within nature only by harnessing the natural drive.)

Not all of the courses of action whose possibility reflection uncovers need be (equally) consistent with the end of absolute independence dictated by the pure drive.

At each moment something is in accordance with our ethical determination [*Bestimmung*]; that thing is at the same time demanded by the natural drive...: but it does not follow that *everything* demanded by the natural drive is in accordance with [our ethical determination].   (IV: 151)

The pure drive, through reflection, creates a variety of action possibilities. At the same time it also points us toward the one most consistent with the end of material independence. 'Only in this way is the actual exercise of morality possible' (IV: 151).

The ethical drive is the product of the union of pure and natural drives (as we saw in §2.3.2 above). Fichte explains at this point in the text that although it usually comes to consciousness as the drive to take a particular action, 'when the drive is brought to clear consciousness and the action it demands is inspected more closely, it becomes manifest that it lies in the described series [*sc.* the series at whose end lies absolute material independence]' (IV: 151–2). So the object of the ethical drive is the action, among those possible for an agent at a time, that is part of the series at whose limit would lie absolute freedom in a material sense.

One natural objection to this line of reasoning, Fichte worries, is that the impossibility, for us, of material freedom in the defined sense means that the transposition of this end into the ambit of activity open to natural beings like ourselves cannot be action-guiding. His apparent focus is on the fact that the end 'lies at infinity.' If that were in fact the concern, it would be misplaced, since many of the tasks that make up our moral lives are in some sense uncompletable, and do not for that reason fail to guide action.[4] But this does not seem to me to be the real worry here.

The worry, I take it, is that it would be possible to recognize an action as making *progress* toward absolute material freedom only if there were something it would be like for us to *have* absolute material freedom. But there is not anything that would be like. This is the significance of the contrast Fichte draws between the 'concept or principle of morality' and the 'concept of right' (IV: 64) in the introduction to the second division. The concept of right determines an at least possible empirical object, namely a state of right (IV: 64). But the principle of morality is not a concept that determines an empirical object, possible or actual.

---

[4] A simple (non-moral) example: counting from zero to the largest natural number is a task whose end lies at infinity, but were one to take it on there would be, intuitively, only one way to proceed.

Instead it is an 'idea' (*Idee*) (IV: 65–6) in the Kantian sense. ('Ideas are tasks for thought' (IV: 65).) Fichte concedes, then, that we are unable to project this end of absolute independence onto a concrete conception of a possible state of affairs; and so he must deny that we need to do so, in order to be guided by it.

It is helpful, I think, to compare the end of absolute independence in the context of Fichte's theory with the end of the greatest happiness for the greatest number in a theory like Bentham's or Mill's.[5] It is impossible to specify in advance the state of affairs in which this would be achieved, because happiness has no determinate intrinsic limit, and its extrinsic limits are contingent and depend on unknowable facts about the future. (Indeed on a view like Mill's, which admits both the existence of qualitatively different forms of pleasure and the possibility of inventing new forms through experiments in living, we cannot even predict all of the forms *pleasure* will take in the future, much less what the state of affairs in which they are jointly maximized would look like.)

Fichte's theory is no worse off than other theories of its form on *this* question. He is not obliged to specify in advance what the state of absolute independence would look like, in order to give content to his principle. He need only specify what counts as *more* or *less* independence, as he points out:

My goal lies at infinity because my dependence is infinite. The latter, however, I never grasp in its infinity, but only comprehend within a determinate scope; and within this ambit I can without doubt make myself more free.   (IV: 150)

The claim is that although my independence may lie at infinity, my dependence has a determinate form at every moment, and there is at every moment some way things would need to change in order for me to overcome some current limitation. To say that we cannot act on nature with anything but the force of nature is not to say that we cannot act in a way that gives us more (or less) control over nature, or that puts more (or less) of the material capacity to pursue future ends under our control.

What is it, then, to make oneself 'more free' in the material sense? It cannot be to make oneself more able to exercise non-natural material causality (since that has been ruled out); nor can it be to make oneself more able to refrain from acting on the natural drive (since that also has been ruled out, as the false solution of a

---

[5] Bentham was Fichte's rough contemporary, and Bentham's most influential works had been published, and were being discussed in Germany, by the time Fichte was developing his ethical theory. Bentham's *Defense of Usury*, first published in 1787, was published in German translation already in 1788, with J.A. Eberhard as its editor. His works were announced and discussed, sparely but regularly, in German academic publications throughout the 1780s and 1790s. Fichte never mentions Bentham by name, but he cannot have been ignorant of his ideas. I will discuss another of Fichte's consequentialist contemporaries, William Godwin, in §3.2.1.1 below.

merely formal ethics concerned with self-abnegation above all else). If absolute independence would be the complete absence of limitations on what it is (materially) possible to will, progress toward it would then appear to have to involve removing, sequentially, such limitations.

What it is materially possible for us to will is limited because it depends on what we know about the environment and what physical and psychological force we have at our disposal, and these are limited. To act with material freedom as one's end, then, would be to seek to broaden one's knowledge and to overcome limitations on one's (always natural) causal and rational powers. It would be to take as one's end *perfecting the exercise of rational agency*, by promoting the necessary external conditions of good deliberation in ourselves and others, and *broadening the scope of possible rational plans of action*, by increasing our ability to ensure that our plans are carried out if we undertake them, and by opening up novel possibilities for planning through technological innovation and creativity in ways of living, producing, and interacting.

Notice the distance between the end so characterized and the end suggested by a different (perhaps more natural) reading of the phrases 'independence of nature' and 'absolute self-sufficiency': the end of increasing our ability to do without nature. It is clear that independence in that sense of the term is just what is ruled out at IV: 148; and in fact independence in that sense is never at issue in Fichte's ethical and political writings. That is as it should be, since every success-ful exercise of a rational agent's causality depends on its embodied existence and on the continued operation of the laws of nature.

It is clear that Fichte takes the end of independence, so construed, to be suitable for guiding action, because it figures again in the specification of the formal condition, as the given end toward which practical deliberation is aimed (in a passage already quoted in §2.2 above):

The moral law, in relation to empirical human beings, has a determinate *starting point*: the determinate limitation in which the individual (in which it initially finds itself) finds himself; it has a determinate (if never reachable) *goal*: absolute liberation from all limitation; and a completely determinate *way* along which it leads us: the order of nature. There is therefore for every determinate individual in any given situation only something determinate that is required by duty—and this, we can say, is what the moral law demands in its application to the temporal being.   (IV: 166)

It is likewise clear that he takes it to be possible to derive distinctively moral content from this end, because it also figures at many points both in the general characterization of the material condition on the moral correctness of actions in the second part of the third division, and in the doctrine of duties itself in the third part of the third division.

In the second part of the third division, devoted to the systematic exposition of the material condition, Fichte writes:

The final end of the moral law is absolute independence and self-sufficiency, not only with respect to our will, for this is always independent, but rather with respect to our entire being. Now this goal is unreachable, but indeed a constant and uninterrupted approach [*Annäherung*—also approximation] to it takes place. There must therefore from the starting point [*von dem ersten Standpunkte*] of each be a constant uninterrupted series of actions through which one approaches [it].   (IV: 209)

The question for this part of the text to answer, then, is: 'What are the actions that lie in the described series?' (IV: 209).

The description of the moral end in the beginning of the discussion of individuality is more concrete still (indeed, exaggerated, for reasons I will explain in §3.2.3.1):

Self-sufficiency, our final end, consists, as we have so often noted, in everything being dependent on me and me not being dependent on anything; in what I will happening in my sensible world, simply and purely because I will it, just as it does in my body, the starting point of my absolute causality. The world must become like my body to me. Now this end is indeed unreachable, but I should indeed constantly approach it, and so work on everything in the sensible world that it may become means to the attainment of this final end. This approach is my finite goal.   (IV: 229)

In concluding this section, describing the common object of striving that would be shared by agents who had ordered their relations to eliminate conflict and disagreement, he writes, 'Each would, with his individual power, in accordance with the common will, and to the best of his ability, modify nature purposively for the use of reason' (IV: 253).

In the doctrine of duties proper, in the third part of the third division, Fichte likewise appeals to the moral end, so construed, at several points. In the overview of other-regarding duties he writes:

The final end of all of the actions of the morally good person in general, and in particular all of his outer efficacy, can be summarized in this formula: *He wills that reason and only [reason] rule in the world of sense.* All physical force should be subordinated to reason.
(IV: 275)

In discussing particular duties attaching to professional roles Fichte distinguishes between professions concerned with work on rational beings (scholars/teachers, priests, artists) and professions concerned with work on nature. Of the latter he writes that their vocation is 'to work immediately upon reasonless nature, for the sake of rational beings, in order to make the former suitable to the ends of the latter' (IV: 361). Moral progress depends upon technical progress, he explains, because moral progress depends ultimately on the subordination of nature (IV: 362).[6]

I will argue in §3.2 that the doctrine of duties as a whole is guided by the application of the moral end as here construed to the situations in which human agents find themselves, even in parts of the text in which it is not mentioned explicitly as it is in these passages. But first I would like to describe further evidence for this characterization of Fichte's view drawn from other texts of the period.

3.1.2 Evidence in other texts of the Jena period

In the *Lectures on the Scholar's Vocation* (1794), a sort of prospectus of the Jena practical philosophy, Fichte presents the same general picture. While he there begins from an articulation of the moral principle that sounds quite Kantian— 'Act in such a way that you can think the maxim of your willing as an eternal law for yourself' (VI: 297; original in italics)—within four paragraphs he has spelled this out so as to encompass, explicitly, the end of material independence as described so far in this chapter.

The first step is a reformulation in terms of agreement or harmony (*Übereinstimmung*) of the I with itself: 'The final determination of each finite rational being is therefore absolute unity, constant identity, complete agreement with itself' (VI: 297). Fichte often describes the moral principle as demanding harmony or agreement of the I with itself (or of the empirical I with the pure I). This is true in the *System of Ethics* as well. The first presentation of the moral principle is often this minimal one; and this is the only way Fichte describes the moral principle in the *Foundations of Natural Right* (1796–7): as 'absolute agreement [*Übereinstimmung*] with oneself' (III: 10–11).

The source of this language of *Übereinstimmung* is likely the ethics of the Wolffian school. Wolff himself consistently described morality as demanding the harmony or agreement of an agent's actions with one another and with the agent's character, both at a time and over time.[7] But here as elsewhere Fichte goes on to explain that what harmony requires is (1) removing the irrational in oneself from

---

[6] Fichte's otherwise puzzling characterization of the 'final end' of objects in §17 should be understood in this light. There he explains that the actions in the series grasp the totality of the final ends of the objects involved in them, and use those objects appropriately according to their final ends (IV: 210). It is natural to read the passage as suggesting that objects have some final end of their own, quite apart from our purposes, and that correct actions must take that end into account. But Fichte goes on to say that acting in accordance with the final end of an object just means using the object in the ways in which it can be most efficaciously used for our purposes. 'I should be a self-sufficient I: this is *my* final end; and all that through which things help me to promote this self-sufficiency, that is *their* final end' (IV: 212; cf. VI: 299).

[7] C. Wolff 1752.

any influence on one's conduct, and (2) removing the resistance of irrational nature to one's rationally formulated plans. He continues: since the empirical determinations of the I depend in part on things outside, things not immediately dependent upon the will, if the I is to be at one with itself in this connection, it 'must strive to work immediately upon the things upon which the feeling and the representation of the human being depends; the human being must seek to modify these, and to bring them into agreement with the pure form of the I' (VI: 298). These modifications are made possible by the acquisition of skills ('culture') whose object is the control of both recalcitrant nature outside and the desires within that the unhindered influence of these outer things tend to produce:

The acquisition of this skill, in part to suppress and extirpate the erroneous inclinations that arose in us before the awakening of our reason and of the feeling of our self-activity; in part to modify things outside of us and to alter them in accordance with our concepts—the acquisition of this skill, I say, is called *culture*. . . . Culture . . . is the final and highest means for the final end of human beings (regarded as rational sensible beings), [namely] complete agreement with themselves, and is itself the final end, when the human being is regarded as a merely sensible being.   (VI: 298–9)

The final result of the development of culture is the harmony of everything outer with the concepts of ends formulated by rational beings:

The perfect agreement of the human being with itself and—in order that it may be able to agree with itself—the agreement of all things outside of it with its necessary practical concepts of them—the concepts that determine what [the things] *ought* to be—is the final highest goal of humankind.   (VI: 299; cf. VI: 316)

Fichte concludes: 'To subject all irrational nature to itself, to rule over it freely and according to his own laws, is the final end of humankind' (VI: 299).

In these *Lectures*, as in the *System of Ethics*, he presents this end as an unreachable one, the actual vocation of any concrete human being as the 'unceasing approximation' to it (VI: 300). Likewise, here as in the *System of Ethics*, he presents it as a collective endeavor possible only within a well-ordered society:

The goal of all cultivation of skill is to subject nature . . . to reason, [and] to make experience, insofar as it is not dependent on the laws of our faculty of representation, agree with our necessary practical concepts of it. Thus reason finds itself in an everlasting struggle with nature; this war can never end if we are not to become gods; but the influence of nature can and should become ever weaker, the domination of reason ever stronger; the latter should win one victory after another over the former. Now an individual may well struggle successfully with nature at his own points of contact with it, while perhaps all others are, by contrast, irresistibly dominated by the same. Now [however] society stands together, and stands as one man: through united force, all will be capable of what the individual could not do. Each struggles individually, indeed, but the weakening of nature through the common struggle and the victory that each wins individually in his part is received by all. (VI: 316)

Note that, far from contrasting with the end of control, 'harmony' simply describes abstractly the aspects of independence of nature that Fichte goes on to describe more concretely later in the *Lectures*. This means that there is no plausible way to present harmony as an alternative substantive moral principle, distinct from independence, to which we might look in understanding Fichte's ethics (as Wood, e.g., contends[8]).

The end of avoiding disagreement between one's practical concepts and their objects admits, in principle, two strategies: curtailing one's plans, and expanding one's capacities and opportunities to carry them out. On the first—perhaps Stoic—vision of the path to independence, technical mastery is held fixed and moral progress is taken to consist in the refinement of desire and the modification of ends so that they are less dependent on conditions that might fail to present themselves.[9] On the second—more modern, Baconian—vision of the path to greater independence, technical mastery is not held fixed and the scope of plans and projects is allowed to expand with and beyond it.[10]

That it is this second model that Fichte has in mind is evident in Fichte's every discussion of the vocation of scholars and of the working classes: we do not progress toward independence by merely raising the ratio of successful to unsuccessful attempts, nor by merely becoming better predictors, but instead by expanding of the set of possible projects through the development and application of technology and the exercise of creativity in every area of human life.

It is stated explicitly in the Mirbach notes of Fichte's lectures on ethics of summer 1796, where the moral principle is described in this way:

Liberate yourself only ever further; expand your limits. Expand your sphere of efficacy. (One sees that it is impossible that the moral law could contain a command to limit oneself ever further; instead [it] rather [contains] the command always to expand one's limits.) (GA 4–1: 25; cf. GA 4–1: 19)

---

[8] A. Wood 2016, pp. 152–3, 157.

[9] Baumanns seems to describe Fichte's view in these terms (though the text is not unequivocal): 'The inner system of limitation [*Begrenzungssystem*] of the original drive is a system of de-limitation [*Entgrenzung*] of the I. The I has to reflect, to concentrate on what continually brings it closer to its vocation to infinity.... To act in accordance with I-hood means, then, to live in consciousness of nature [*naturbewusst leben*], to adapt one's factical empirical I to the ideal order of nature and therewith, out of such self-reflection on the law of one's own being, to bring about a world of objects that corresponds to the objective essence of the I or the original drive: Act in accordance with nature [*Handle naturgemäss*]' (P. Baumanns 1990, p. 147).

[10] It scarcely needs saying that Bacon looms large in the background of Fichte's thought here, as he did in the thought of so many other 18th-century philosophers—among them Kant, who drew the epigraph of the B-edition of the *Critique of Pure Reason* from Bacon's *Great Instauration*, a quotation reproduced by Fichte in the 'First Introduction to the Wissenschaftslehre' of 1797 (I: 419).

In these lectures as well Fichte freely uses the language of 'independence' and 'liberation' with respect to nature (GA 4–1: 54, 69, 71), often in turns of phrase that will be repeated near-verbatim in the *System of Ethics*.

For a final source of textual evidence, we can turn to the *Vocation of Humankind* (1800), where, because it is a popular work, Fichte actually provides examples. There progress toward independence or self-sufficiency is depicted (in part) as progress away from a situation in which 'our species derives its sustenance and persistence in a struggle against recalcitrant nature' (II: 266), in which 'all its thoughts and desires and all its efforts must be directed toward the soil which nourishes it' (II: 267), in which those efforts are hindered by a constant struggle with disease and premature death, and in which even the most successful of them are unpredictably reversed by natural disasters. It is depicted as progress toward a situation in which 'the sacrifices that the lawless violence of nature has extracted from reason . . . exhaust . . . and appease that violence' (II: 267), in which 'nature's . . . pace can be calculated and safely reckoned upon, and [nature's] power maintains undisturbed a determinate relation to the power destined to master it (that of human beings)' (II: 268), in which 'science . . . penetrates into nature's invariable laws, surveys [its] whole power, and learns to calculate its possible developments,' in which 'nature becomes ever more transparent' and in which 'armed with these discoveries human power will effortlessly master it . . . ' (II: 268), and finally in which 'no greater expenditure of mechanical labor will be required than the human body requires for its development, fitness and health, and this labor will cease to be burdensome' (II: 268–9).

In these pages in the *Vocation*, Fichte plainly has in mind a relation to those aspects of the natural environment that stand in the way of human projects, by being powerful enough to disrupt our plans, and unpredictable or ubiquitous enough that they cannot effectively be planned around. One is independent insofar as one is free from such interference, and more independent the more free one is. There are aspects of the human environment that pose the same dangers, and Fichte goes on to describe them in gruesome detail—tribal warfare, cannibalism, state warfare, slavery, and genocide—in the paragraphs that follow (II: 269–71). Human aggression is presented as the same sort of threat as natural disaster, the same sort of insult to the same human capacity, though much more destructive. ('It is not nature but freedom itself that causes the most and the worst catastrophes' (II: 269).) So progress toward material independence must involve the right ordering of people's relations to one another as well as the right ordering of their relation to non-human nature. To the extent that the state and other social technologies function as they ought to, they function to increase individuals' independence in relation both to one another and to the natural world. They are thus related to the other technologies Fichte discusses in these pages—technologies with natural forces as their objects—by having the same end, the end of independence, which is the same whether the threat to it comes from natural or human sources. (I will return to this topic in §3.2.2.3 and §5.1 below.)

The progress of reason in Kant's *Critique of the Power of Judgment* and his essays on history—where he characterizes reason as a natural being's 'capacity to extend far beyond natural instinct the rules and aims of the use of all of its powers'[11]—is clearly discernible in the background of Fichte's thinking here. Kant takes it to be an empirical fact about rational end-setting that it tends to outstrip current knowledge, technology, and social organization and to force advances in those areas and so to expand its own reach; and he takes it to be clear that we cannot explain human history without seeing that mechanism at work.[12]

---

[11] I. Kant 1900–, 8: 18; I. Kant 2007, p. 109 (translation altered).

[12] In fact Fichte's characterization of the moral end in the *Lectures on the Scholar's Vocation* echoes rather strikingly a passage from the third *Critique* in which Kant describes, not the moral end of human beings, but rather nature's end for them:

> In order, however, to discover where in the human being we are at least to posit that **ultimate end** of nature, we must seek out that which nature is capable of doing in order to prepare him for what he must himself do in order to be a final end, and separate this from all those ends the possibility of which depends upon conditions which can be expected only from nature. Of the latter sort is earthly happiness, by which is meant the sum of all the ends that are possible through nature outside and inside of the human being; that is the matter of all of his ends on earth, which, if he makes them into his whole end, make him incapable of setting a final end for his own existence and of agreeing with that end. Thus among all his ends in nature there remains only the formal, subjective condition, namely the aptitude for setting himself ends at all and (independent from nature in his determination of ends) using nature as a means appropriate to the maxims of his free ends in general, as that which nature can accomplish with a view to the final end that lies outside of it and which can therefore be regarded as its ultimate end. The production of the aptitude of a rational being for any ends in general (thus those of his freedom) is **culture**. Thus only culture can be the ultimate end that one has cause to ascribe to nature in regard to the human species (not its own earthly happiness or even merely being the foremost instrument for establishing order and consensus in irrational nature outside him).
> ... The culture of **skill** is certainly the foremost subjective condition of aptitude for the promotion of ends in general; but it is still not sufficient for promoting the will in the determination and choice of its ends, which however is essential for an aptitude for ends. The latter condition of aptitude, which could be named the culture of training (discipline), is negative, and consists in the liberation of the will from the despotism of desires ...
> Skill cannot very well be developed in the human race except by means of inequality among people; for the majority provides the necessities of life as it were mechanically, without requiring any special art for that, for the comfort and ease of others, who cultivate the less necessary elements of culture, science and art, and are maintained by the latter in a state of oppression, bitter work and little enjoyment, although much of the culture of the higher class gradually spreads to this class. But with the progress of

Fichte's view differs from Kant's in that Kant's claim is a descriptive rather than a normative one, and he ascribes this end to nature rather than to human beings themselves. The question of whether and why this is a valid normative claim will be taken up in Chapter 5. In the remainder of this chapter the focus will be on Fichte's application of it in his normative ethical theory.

3.2   Material Independence in the Doctrine of Duties

It is clear from the passages quoted in §3.1 that Fichte's ethical principle is teleological:[13] it tells us to strive to bring about a certain outcome ('complete independence of everything outside of us'); and it judges actions (substantively or objectively) morally correct when they lie on the path that leads toward that outcome. It is also clear that it enjoins maximizing such progress. This is implicit already in the statements about the ethical vocation of finite individuals, but Fichte also states it explicitly: 'Each individual is commanded to further the independence of reason so far as he can [*so weit er kann*]' (IV: 258). The language of maximization (*so weit er/ich kann*) occurs at a number of points in the text (cf. also IV: 218, 245); and there is additionally much indirect evidence that Fichte's is a maximizing consequentialism, which I will discuss in due course.

But what exactly does it tell us to do? 'What are the actions that, *materially* [*ihrer Materie nach*], lie in the series approaching absolute self-sufficiency?' Fichte asks in §17 (IV: 210)—pointing out, correctly, that his characterization up to that point in the text has been insufficient to answer the question. The idea of absolute independence is initially 'unlimited' and therefore indeterminate; for it to acquire content, and so become able to direct action, its scope must

> this culture (the height of which, when the tendency to what is dispensable begins to destroy what is indispensable, is called luxury) calamities grow equally great on both sides, on the one side because of violence imposed from without, on the other because of dissatisfaction from within; yet this splendid misery is bound up with the development of the natural predispositions in the human race, and the end of nature itself, even if it is not our end, is hereby attained.
> (I. Kant 1900–, 5: 431–2; I. Kant 2000, pp. 298–9)

[13] 'Teleological' is used in two ways in contemporary ethics. First, it is used to describe views on which values are foundational and duties derived from values. Second, it is used to describe views on which acts (or rules, dispositions, etc.) are evaluated according to what they promote/aim at promoting/tend to promote/if followed would promote, etc. (where what is to be promoted is typically some end beyond the act itself). Fichte's theory is teleological in the second sense, but not in the first. It is, to use Cummiskey's language, a normative consequentialism ('one ought to promote certain ends, and there are no basic agent-centered constraints on the promotion of those ends, nor is there any basic priority of negative over positive duties') without being a foundational consequentialism ('only the goodness of ends can justify a normative principle'). Cf. D. Cummiskey 1996, ch. 1.

be limited. Fichte reasons that, since the only limitations reason imposes on itself are those that follow from the fact that the rational being is necessarily an I, the material content of the moral law should be derivable from the synthetic unity of the concept of I-hood and the concept of independence (IV: 211; cf. GA 4–1: 104).

What limitations are imposed by the fact that the rational agent is an I? I have described these in Chapter 2 in the order that seemed to me most perspicuous. At the point in the text at which he asks this question, Fichte has already described them as well (in the first and second divisions of the *System of Ethics*, in which he derived the moral principle and its applicability). In §18, he presents them in the following order: The reflecting I must be conscious of itself as such (IV: 212). This requires that it be given to itself, that it have a nature, and this nature takes the form of a system of drives (IV: 212–13). It requires that it be conscious of its efficaciousness, which must be that of a natural (if spontaneous) cause; but this means that it must have a material body set in motion by its will (IV: 214–15). The drive toward independence can be satisfied only through action; but action is possible only through the body, and so the sustenance and perfection of the body are part of the moral end (IV: 216). The reflecting I must also be an intellect, and duties concerning the intellect's cultivation are founded in this (IV: 217). Finally, an I must be an individual, one among many, with a limited quantum of external freedom (IV: 218–22). This means that each individual's drive for independence is conditioned by the fact that there are other individuals similarly driven. The independence of others is a further limitation of the drive to independence, and so another material determination of morality (IV: 221).

The content of the end of material independence is, then, derived from the concept of an I 'synthetically unified' with the concept of independence (IV: 211), where the concept of an I is spelled out in the way just summarized. Fichte has at this point already provided a series of arguments (in the *Foundations*, and reiterated in the *System of Ethics*) for the claim that any rational being must be an I in this sense. The division of duties into three categories in §18—those concerning the preservation and development of the physical powers, those concerning the preservation and development of the intellectual powers, and those concerning the coordination of individual spheres of activity—is based on this characterization.

In division three part three, where Fichte presents the doctrine of duties itself, he further divides duties into, on the one hand, 'universal' duties (those had by all) and 'particular' duties (those had in virtue of occupation of certain natural and social roles); and, on the other, 'conditioned' (self-regarding) and 'unconditioned' (other-regarding) duties. The organizational scheme that comes from overlaying those two sets of divisions is complex, and in places it masks Fichte's most interesting insights. I will summarize the roles of these distinctions in Fichte's theory in §3.2.3.9, but will structure this second part of the chapter according to the simpler scheme of §18.

Two other traditional distinctions have no role in the theory, as one would expect given what I have said about its structure. Although Fichte does draw a distinction between negative, positive, and limitative duties, the distinction has an organizational role only, and no substantive upshot. In particular, negative duties have no priority over positive ones. The distinction between perfect and imperfect duties makes no appearance at all in the *System of Ethics*, as the grounds on which these are usually distinguished have no place in the theory.[14] There are relations of priority amongst duties; but these correspond not to the traditional distinctions between negative and positive or perfect and imperfect duty, but instead to the relative importance of different conditions for the exercise of rational agency.

3.2.1 Embodiment and causal efficacy

Fichte's account of duties concerning the preservation and cultivation of the body, and part of his account of duties concerning property, are motivated by the idea that a rational agent must be embodied (that is, that there must be some sphere in which its will is immediately causally efficacious) and that this body must be externally causally efficacious to at least some degree. Fichte justifies those propositions by arguing that embodiment and awareness of external causal efficacy are conditions of possibility of self-consciousness (as we have seen in §2.3.4 above). Coupled with the technically practical reasoning described in §2.2 above, the obligatory ends of physical existence and basic causal efficacy give rise to subsidiary ends—physical subsistence and preservation, cultivation of the causal powers of the body (e.g. of skills) insofar as these are instrumental to the ends an agent is likely to have, cultivation of the sphere in which, in society, these powers can be legitimately exercised (i.e. property)—which are likewise obligatory. Moral duties concerning embodiment and causal efficacy are duties to pursue these ends.

---

[14] For Fichte no duty, perfect or imperfect, admits exception in favor of inclination, as Kant suggests imperfect duties do (cf. e.g. I. Kant 1900–, 4: 421; I. Kant 1996a, p. 73); and since for Fichte all such duties are maximizing, and admit leeway only when two would further the moral end to the same degree, he cannot agree with Kant that perfect duties are distinguished from imperfect ones by the leeway the latter provide in ways of fulfilling them (I. Kant 1900–, 6: 390–1; I. Kant 1996a, pp. 521–2). In fact Fichte uses the terms *vollkommen* and *unvollkommen* only in the manner of other perfectionists, to refer to the development of aspects of our nature, and never in the manner of deontologists, to distinguish classes of duty.

3.2.1.1 PHYSICAL PRESERVATION

For Fichte morality demands self-preservation not only because one's own exercise of one's agency depends upon it and such exercise is its own end, but also because one's exercise of that agency is (when substantively morally correct) instrumental in the collective progress toward the end of greater independence of reason in general from everything outside itself. Fichte's emphasis on the instrumental value of individuals' activity, along with his repeated insistence that I should regard myself and everyone else as a 'tool' (*Werkzeug*) of the moral law (IV: 215, 223, 231, 236, 255, 259–60, 268, 270, 276–81, 283, 290, 295, 298–9, 302–4, 310, 311–13, 336), are among the more striking features of the *System of Ethics*. In introducing the topic of duties of self-preservation, Fichte writes:

Whatever I may realize in the sensible world, it is never the *final end* commanded by morality ([since] the final end lies at infinity) [but only] the means to approach it. So the proximal end of each of my actions is a new action in the future. But one who is supposed to act in the future must exist in it; and if he is to act according to a plan that has already been conceived, he must be and remain the same as he now is. His future existence must unfold from his present one in a regular way. Animated by a moral disposition I regard myself only as a tool of the moral law; thus I will to continue existing, and to continue existing only that I may continue acting. For this reason, *self-preservation* is a duty.   (IV: 261)

So the fact that the moral task is never finished itself forms part of the grounds for the duty of self-preservation.[15] This is one piece of indirect evidence that Fichte takes the duty to promote material independence to be maximizing.

Physical self-preservation requires, in the first instance, avoiding external dangers (IV: 262–3), and refraining from committing suicide (IV: 262–8). Like Kant, Fichte argues that suicide is morally forbidden because, by removing the subject of moral obligation, it removes some quantum of (at least potential) morality from the world, and at the same time amounts to a shirking of obligation on the part of its agent.

My life is the exclusive condition of the fulfillment of the law by me. But it is absolutely commanded to me to fulfill the law. Thus it is absolutely commanded to live, insofar as this depends on me. This command directly contradicts the destruction of my life by myself, which is therefore contrary to duty. I cannot destroy my life without withdrawing myself from the sovereignty [*Herrschaft*] of the moral law....I no longer will to live means: I no longer will to do my duty.   (IV: 263–4)

---

[15] This is in marked contrast with the account of the end of self-preservation given in the *Foundations of Natural Right*, as Fichte points out (IV: 259–60).

So expressed, the sentiment seems similar to the one expressed by Kant in the *Metaphysics of Morals*.[16] But Fichte's explanation of it differs strikingly from any Kant could have offered (on the dominant contemporary interpretations, at least), because it relies on the teleological structure of Fichte's moral theory.[17] Fichte argues that any given action is but a step on an unending path toward the moral end, that killing oneself would eliminate known opportunities to further the moral end, and that since no way of furthering the moral end can be cited to which suicide would be a means, these could never be outweighed in deliberation by other, better opportunities (IV: 264–6). Strikingly, not only is the prohibition itself justified instrumentally; all of the objections to the prohibition that Fichte considers and rejects point to ways in which suicide might be thought to minimize morally relevant harms (to self and others) that the agent might expect to cause by continuing to live. Every reason cited on either side is instrumental. If the moral worth of actions did not depend on their contribution to the production of some state of affairs beyond the action itself—indeed, if the moral law did not enjoin maximizing progress toward that end—Fichte could not offer arguments of this form.

Murder is prohibited in any rightful system of law, according to Fichte, and since rightful legal duties are morally binding (for reasons I will explain in §3.2.3), murder is morally prohibited as well. But Fichte offers an independent moral justification for the prohibition on murder, precisely analogous to his justification for the prohibition on suicide:

Just as premeditated suicide is under no circumstances consistent with a true moral disposition, the premeditated murder of another is likewise inconsistent with it, and on the same grounds. In either case a possible tool of the moral end is annihilated.   (IV: 279)

(The explanation for the prohibition on murder as a duty of right is quite different from this, as one might expect.)

---

[16] Cf. I. Kant 1900-, 6: 422–3; I. Kant 1996a, p. 547: 'A human being cannot renounce his personality as long as he is a subject of duty, hence as long as he lives; and it is a contradiction that he should be authorized to withdraw from all obligation, that is, freely to act as if no authorization were needed for this action. To annihilate the subject of morality in one's own person is to root out the existence of morality itself from the world, as far as one can, even though morality is an end in itself. Consequently, disposing of oneself as a mere means to some discretionary end is debasing humanity in one's person (*homo noumenon*), to which the human being (*homo phaenomenon*) was nevertheless entrusted for preservation.'

[17] Korsgaard argues that the best reconstruction of Kant's account of the impermissibility of suicide relies implicitly on his account of natural teleology (C. Korsgaard 1996, pp. 89–90). This seems plausible, and if correct offers another example of a general tendency of Fichte, mentioned already in §3.1.2, to transpose ends Kant attributes to nature into moral ends for human beings.

Fichte recognizes, as grounds for a possible objection, the consideration that one might, by killing a morally vicious person, bring about more moral goodness on the whole. He responds not by appeal to an agent-centered prohibition on murder, nor (though the text above might seem to suggest this) to the goodness of stable, context-insensitive dispositions to avoid violent acts, but instead to an argument meant to undermine the apparent instrumental attractiveness of such a course, coupled with an appeal to a duty of optimism about agents' goodwill and capacity for moral improvement that is a corollary of the duty to promote their improvement through one's own action. The form of argument is exactly similar in the case of murder and that of suicide on grounds of one's own vice.

In the case of murder, he argues as follows: everyone's life is a means to the achievement of the moral end. For a given individual, either I (the agent) take it to be possible for him to be such a means, or I take it to be impossible. But if I take it to be possible, then in killing him I destroy a possible means to an end that I, by hypothesis, have. And if I take it to be impossible, that belief is itself a moral failing on my part, for it is my duty to take his moral perfection as my end, and to work toward his betterment. To believe that he is incapable of improvement is to give up on that task (IV: 278). In the case of suicide out of despair over one's own vice, he argues: the conviction that I am morally hopeless is itself an immoral attitude, since what I do is under my control, and I am obliged to behave morally (IV: 266).

Fichte uses the same language in both cases: despairing of another's, or one's own future, capacity for moral improvement is an '*unsittliche Denkart*.' What is wrong with thinking in this way, it seems, is that the *belief* that I (or the other) will behave badly is inconsistent with the *intention* to behave well (or to help the other to behave well); and since the intention is dictated by duty, the belief has got to go (or at least cannot be allowed to figure as a premise of any piece of practical reasoning).

But Fichte does not in general think that beliefs can be prohibited solely on moral grounds, as we will see in §3.2.2.2. So there must be some epistemic consideration in play here that is not mentioned explicitly. One good candidate is the nature of human choice on Fichte's view of it, a view on which it is spontaneous and therefore unpredictable in principle. That someone will continue along his path of vice is, on the view laid out in §2.1, something that it is not possible to know, because there is (as yet) no fact of the matter to be known. Indeed Fichte seems to think that we are, strictly, entitled to no beliefs at all about how others will conduct themselves in the future. Our own future actions are similarly indeterminate and therefore unpredictable; and though we can determine these by our intentions, we are obligated to intend the good. This means that there can be, likewise, no rational grounds for pessimism about one's own future conduct.

This requirement of presumptive optimism about one's own and others' good will—the idea that everyone, even those who seem irredeemably vicious, should be given the benefit of the doubt so far as their future actions are concerned—is an expression of the same fundamental moral optimism that underwrites Fichte's account of moral evil (IV: 191–205), his refusal to take a retributivist line on punishment (IV: 279; III: 262–3, 265, 268–9, 282–4) and his confidence that consensus can eventually be reached in every moral disagreement (IV: 233–5). It also stands in the background of his treatment of duties of rescue, to which I now turn.

Fichte distinguishes between suicide strictly speaking (where I act with the primary aim of bringing about my own death) and morally permissible self-endangerment (where I act on a morally sanctioned aim, such as the aim of saving lives, knowing that this puts my own life at risk) (IV: 263, 304–5). He argues that, in general, the duty of self-preservation is lifted when others' lives are in danger, and that this is so regardless of the danger's source (IV: 281–2). There is no conflict between the duty of self-preservation and the duty of risky rescue, Fichte argues, because the same agent-neutral end—the life of rational beings—underwrites both. The lives of both myself and the person to be rescued 'are entirely equal, of equal worth, on equivalent grounds' (IV: 281). 'Before the moral law human life in general has equal value; as soon as one is in danger, all of the others, whoever they may be, have no right to remain secure until he is rescued' (IV: 282).[18]

This argument from equal status gives rise to a dilemma when two lives are in equal danger and at most one can be saved. Fichte's treatment of this topic begins with the case in which one of the lives is the agent's own. He had argued in the *Foundations of Natural Right* that the relation of right is cancelled in cases like the one described in the 'hallowed' example of the board that can support only one of two shipwrecked sailors ('which for their greater comfort has recently been transformed into a lifeboat with the same property' (III: 252–3)). The principle of right is silent in such cases, he argues; and so from the standpoint of right, any action is permissible in them. (I will explain his reasoning here in §3.2.3.8 below.)

In the *System of Ethics* he treats the case from the standpoint of morality, and concludes that the only morally permissible course is *inaction*, even if the

---

[18] In the discussion of self-defense in the Mirbach lecture notes the point is put more succinctly: 'From what has so far been said it follows that there is no duty of self-defense as a particular sort [of duty]; there is only a duty of defense of rational beings' (GA 4-1: 133).

predictable result is two deaths instead of one. Strikingly, this is the only point of the text that could conceivably be read as asserting the priority of a negative to the correlative positive duty (although that is not the correct reading of it, as I will show in a moment). Here is the passage:

> I cannot fulfill the command of the moral law to preserve myself without sacrificing the life of the other (according to the assumption); and the moral law prohibits this. I cannot rescue the life of the other without sacrificing my own; and the moral law prohibits this as well. In this instance each command of the moral law is opposed by a prohibition; accordingly both commands annul themselves. The law is entirely silent, and I, moved as I am only by it, should do nothing, but instead calmly await the outcome.   (IV: 302–3)

It is open to Fichte to present this simply as a conflict of two positive duties of life-preservation, and in fact that is how he initially characterizes it: I should preserve my life, because I am a tool of the moral law; and I should preserve the other's, on the same grounds (IV: 302). But instead of opposing the positive duties of preservation to one another, he opposes each to a negative duty of non-destruction which (this is what is not perfectly clear from the text) either balances or overrides it.

The fact that it is possible to take the text of this section as saying that the positive duty is overridden by the negative duty, rather than simply cancelled by a negative duty of equal weight, is the basis of my remark that this text could conceivably be read as asserting the priority of the negative duty. This is how Wood seems to read it.[19] But there is no reason that I can see (in the passage itself or its context) to prefer the 'override' to the 'balance' reading; and a glance at the corresponding passage in the Mirbach notes from Fichte's summer 1796 lectures on ethics confirms that the 'balance' reading is in fact the correct one:

> Here therefore prescription cancels prescription, prohibition cancels prohibition, and the moral law falls silent. Since I may not act when the moral law does not command, in this

---

[19] On Wood's reading the prohibition on killing is overriding. He writes: 'Although Fichte had never read any articles about trolley problems, I think it is clear that his principles entail certain judgments about them. These principles would permit you, and it [sic] might even require you, to let the trolley run over you in order to save others. But you would not be permitted to throw yourself into the path of the trolley, nor would it be permissible deliberately to set the switch so that it runs over either you yourself or even one other person; it doesn't matter how many other lives it might save. Finally, if only the lives of others are at stake, you would not be able to choose between letting it run over one person or over five people. In that case you must refrain from action and "calmly await the outcome"' (A. Wood 2016, p. 241). Wood offers no textual evidence for these claims, and indeed there is none he could offer: these are simply Wood's own views about trolley problems (cf. Wood's contribution to D. Parfit 2011, vol. 2). But since this is the *sole* passage in which Fichte, who was not in general an advocate of calmly awaiting outcomes, counsels that we must 'calmly await the outcome,' I conclude that Wood takes it as a basis for his conclusions in the quoted passage. I discuss the other apparent basis, equally inadequate, in the paragraphs to follow.

situation I am not permitted to act at all, and must await the outcome of the situation from the nature that brought it about.... Should we both die, I have done my duty.

(GA 4–1: 134)

In this text, it is the two commands to save that oppose one another, and the two prohibitions on killing that oppose one another. Since the prohibition on killing is not even *paired* with the corresponding command to save, it is clear that the point cannot be that the prohibition on killing *overrides* the corresponding command to save. The point is rather that the reasons balance one another out. There is no choice one could make on rational grounds in such a situation, and so one is prohibited from making any choice at all. This rules out Wood's understanding of the upshot of this passage, which relies on the prohibition on killing having priority.

What moves Fichte here is not a commitment to the priority of negative duties; instead it is the idea that since all moral beings are of equal worth, there is no basis for deciding between them in rescue cases, a point he emphasizes in the immediately following discussion, where he responds to the question of how I am to decide whom to save in a case where not I but several others are at risk and I cannot save all of them.

There, he argues that saving all is the only morally permissible aim, and that this may require attempting to save those in graver danger first, but does not allow saving first those meeting any criterion by which one might judge one human life more *worth saving* than another. Here is the passage:

A situation arises in which the lives of several of my fellow human beings are in danger; I should rescue; I cannot rescue all, or at least not all at once; on what basis should I choose?

My goal is and must necessarily be to rescue all; for all are tools of the moral law, and in this there is no distinction to draw among them. Now, if I want to rescue all, then I must help those first who are in most urgent danger, because these cannot survive any longer at all without someone else's immediate assistance, whether their danger be more urgent because of the state of affairs or because of their own weakness and helplessness, as for instance children, the ill, the aged. If there are amongst them some whose care and guidance is assigned to me in particular—*my own*—then these must have priority: but note well, not out of natural, pathognomic love, nor out of consideration of my own happiness—such motives are reprehensible—but because their rescue is my particular duty, and because the particular duty always precedes the general one. If such bases of decision are absent, then I rescue the one that I can rescue first, the one I first catch sight of. Sophistry about the greater importance of this or that life has no place here, for on this point I can know nothing.   (IV: 304)

Wood has suggested that Fichte's reasoning in this passage is incompatible with consequentialism and so evidence that Fichte's view is not a consequentialist one.[20] That is incorrect. Fichte does not here (or anywhere else) discuss different-number rescue cases in the style of the literature following Taurek (1977),[21] and so gives himself no opportunity to deny that numbers count. There is no way to extend his reasoning in the cases he does discuss to those. He certainly does not deny that in such cases one is obliged to save as many as possible. In fact it seems to fall directly out of his assertion that one's goal must be to rescue all, that one is obliged to rescue as many as possible.

So there is no evidence in this passage for Wood's claim. Still it is clear that Fichte does have some target in mind, some 'sophistry about the greater import-ance of this or that life.' The target appears to be William Godwin, and more specifically Godwin's notorious example of Fenelon and the chambermaid, which I reproduce here for comparison:

In a loose and general view I and my neighbor are both of us men, and of consequence entitled to equal attention. But in reality it is probable that one of us is a being of more worth and importance than the other. A man is of more worth than a beast; because, being possessed of higher faculties, he is capable of a more refined and genuine happiness. In the same manner the illustrious archbishop of Cambray was of more worth than his chambermaid, and there are few of us that would hesitate to pronounce, if his palace were in flames, and the life of only one of them could be preserved, which of the two ought to be preferred.

But there is another ground of preference, beside the private consideration of one of them being farther removed from the state of a mere animal. We are not connected with only one or two percipient beings, but with a society, a nation, and in some sense with the whole family of mankind. Of consequence that life ought to be preferred which will be more conducive to the general good. In saving the life of Fenelon, suppose at the moment when he was conceiving the project of his immortal *Telema-chus*, I should be promoting the benefit of thousands, who have been cured by the perusal of it of some error, vice and consequent unhappiness. Nay, my benefit would extend farther than this, for every individual thus cured has become a better member of society, and has contributed in his turn to the happiness, the information and improvement of others.[22]

Godwin goes on to argue, in the paragraphs that follow, that the chambermaid should in that circumstance sacrifice *herself* to save Fenelon; and moreover that the son of the chambermaid should likewise save Fenelon rather than *his mother*, because Fenelon's life is more worth saving, according to the two measures to which Godwin appeals in these two paragraphs.

---

[20] This is the other, equally inadequate, textual basis for Wood's speculations about Fichte's stance on 'trolley problems' in the quotation from Wood in footnote 19 above. Cf. A. Wood 2016, pp. 240–3.

[21] J. Taurek 1977.   [22] W. Godwin 1793, pp. 81–2.

I am aware of no direct evidence that Fichte knew Godwin's *Enquiry Concerning Political Justice* first-hand. He does not mention Godwin by name; and since there is no record of the contents of his personal library it is impossible to say with certainty that he was familiar with Godwin's book. But there is ample evidence that the book was an object of lively discussion in Germany at the time;[23] and Godwin's was certainly among the most controversial contemporary treatments of such cases. At any rate, the passage in the *System of Ethics* certainly reads like a response to a position very like Godwin's. But although Godwin was a consequentialist and Fichte does disagree with him point-for-point in this passage, none of the points of disagreement concern the truth of consequentialism.

Notice, first, that Godwin's appeal to broader consequences is only the second of two considerations adduced for saving Fenelon rather than the chambermaid. The primary appeal is to Fenelon's higher quality as a human being—the chambermaid lying somewhere between Fenelon and a 'mere animal'—and consequent intrinsic ability to *embody* greater utility. Godwin's primary aim appears, indeed, to be to show that his utilitarianism is consistent with class privilege, thus defending it from a predictable set of objections. Fichte by contrast was an often intemperate opponent of any sort of class privilege, and he begins the parallel passage in the *System of Ethics* by denying that there is any inherent difference in quality between human beings that could form the basis of a rational requirement to save one before the other: 'all are tools of the moral law, and in this there is no distinction to draw among them.'

Notice, second, that to Godwin's point about the broader downstream consequences of saving Fenelon, Fichte's response is not that *even if we knew* that one person would go on to do incomparably more good for humanity than another, that would not justify us in saving that person first. (That would be evidence of a rejection of consequentialism.) His response is instead that we *cannot know* this: 'on this point I can know nothing.'[24] Here again, as in the discussions of suicide

---

[23] The German philosophical world of the 1790s was highly attuned to literary events in Britain as well as France. Godwin's *Enquiry Concerning Political Justice*, from which this passage is drawn, is cited already at *Friedens-Preliminarien* 1793, 1:4, p. 357 and its German translation is announced in the *Allgemeine Literatur-Zeitung Intelligenzblatt* of October 1793. (Godwin's works are announced and discussed in the *Allgemeine Literatur-Zeitung* throughout the 1790s.) According to Mill's account of the history of utilitarianism in British moral philosophy, in 'Dr. Whewell on Moral Philosophy,' although Bentham was 'earlier than Godwin in date, [he] was later in acquiring popular influence' (Mill 1985, vol. 10, p. 170). If Fichte directly engaged with British utilitarianism, it will have been with Godwin's version rather than Bentham's.

[24] Of the two further points of disagreement—concerning the impermissibility of sacrificing oneself (were one the chambermaid), and concerning the priority of the particular duty to rescue 'one's own' (were one the chambermaid's son)—the first has been discussed above, and the second will be discussed when I turn to the place of particular duties in the *System of Ethics* in §3.2.3.9 below.

and murder of the depraved, the unpredictability of human agents, and the consequent opacity to practical deliberation of the effects of downstream agency, plays a clear role in Fichte's reasoning.

It is worth dwelling on this role for a moment, and placing it in the context of a larger interpretive question raised by the frequent juxtaposition, often in the same passages, of an admonition always to *view* others as tools of the moral law and a prohibition on *using* others as tools for our own (even morally motivated) ends. How are these compatible? I want to suggest, contra Wood, who sees the prohibition as evidence of Fichte's acceptance of deontological constraints, that it is motivated by two limitations inherent to the moral viewpoint as Fichte sees it, both arising from the fact that moral agents must be individuals: first, that it is always the viewpoint of an agent who must often rely on coordinated action with others (and on the conditions of possibility of such coordinated action, whatever these turn out to be) to achieve his ends; and second, that it is always the viewpoint of an agent whose knowledge of the future consequences of his actions is limited in principle by the existence of other free agents.

The first is by far the most important constraint, and it figures in the next sort of rescue case to which Fichte turns (at IV: 304–5; cf. IV: 288–9): the rescue of a third party from violent attack. There Fichte argues that interventions that might harm the attacker are justified, even if they risk harming the attacker more than the victim would be harmed otherwise, because they are motivated not only by the end of preventing harm to the victim, but also by the additional end of maintaining the system that coordinates the actions of multiple agents, that is, the system of right. I will discuss these cases at length in §3.2.3.2 below.

At this point let me direct the reader's attention again to the 'hallowed' two-person-one-lifeboat example discussed above, and to point out one striking feature of Fichte's discussion of it: his failure to reach for what might seem the best way out of the dilemma he describes, namely the use of a randomizing procedure (e.g. the equally hallowed drawing of straws). Straw-drawing itself is a decision procedure that can be implemented only by the joint action of several individuals. (It is not even a randomizing procedure if the person holding the straws is also the person drawing.) But its cooperative nature is also, plausibly, the source of our intuitions about its legitimacy. Certainly the intuition that in such cases it is permissible for one person unilaterally to implement some randomizing proced- ure is accompanied by an assumption that the various parties *would consent* to such a procedure, as a means of fairly maximizing the chances of survival of

---

Note, though, the complete absence of sympathy for the usual grounds of the 'nearest and dearest objection' (cf. F. Jackson 1991; and for one canonical source of the objection, cf. B. Williams 1973).

each.[25] Similar considerations apply in the many-in-danger-one-rescuer case. In both types of case, a scarce and non-divisible good must somehow be distributed amongst individuals. If such cases are to be decidable from the moral point of view there must be specifically *moral* grounds for making decisions about this distribution.

But Fichte's view is that there are no such grounds. The sharing of scarce goods among more than one individual is the kind of problem that can be solved only by collective action; but (rational) collective action is governed by the principle of right, which, Fichte claims, is not derivable from the moral principle.

I will return to this issue when I discuss duties concerning rational agents *qua* individuals, in §3.2.3. For now, though, notice that the reason that the moral principle is silent in the lifeboat case (and counsels only 'save all' in the case of the rescue of others—an intention that incorporates no intention to distribute any good) may be simply that, as cases concerning the distribution of scarce, non-divisible goods among individuals, these are cases in which the moral principle could not speak with its own voice. If that is correct, then the moral principle is silent in these cases *because* the principle of right is silent. (Why the principle of right must be silent in such cases is discussed in §3.2.3.8 below.)

That is the consideration arising from the first limitation inherent to the moral point of view: the fact that it is always the viewpoint of an agent who must rely on coordinated action with others (and on the conditions of possibility of such coordinated action, whatever these turn out to be) to achieve his ends. But in these passages Fichte appeals explicitly to a second, quite different sort of consideration, one that speaks against using other agents and their intentional activity as if they were ordinary objects whose causal powers could be manipulated to bring about, indirectly, one's own ends.

He sometimes seems to advance this as a point about responsibility: the fact that human actions have their source in spontaneous end-setting means that only their agents can be responsible for them and their sequelae. I cannot be liable for other agents' freely undertaken actions (and their consequences), even where my own actions were among their necessary conditions. This position—that downstream agency screens off culpability for an outcome to which one has contributed some causally necessary condition—is well represented both in the law and in the literature on moral responsibility.

The texts are not univocal on this point. In discussing whether there can be a moral requirement to commit suicide in order to avoid becoming the (passive)

---

[25] It is plausible to think that this intuition in fact depends on that assumption. T. Henning 2015 argues, convincingly, that no *moral* requirement is fulfilled by the equal distribution of chances of rescue. (His topic is duties of third parties, but the point is applicable here.)

object of another's vice, Fichte remarks that morality could not command this, because we are responsible only for what *we* do (IV: 267). But in discussing the moral wrong of lying Fichte adduces a quite different consideration: that I cannot *reliably* cause another to act in a way I intend through deception. Here the point seems to be that since human agents are unpredictable in principle, it is at worst pointless and at best irresponsible to try to bring about a state of affairs through a causal chain that has free human actions among its links.

This is a different point from the one about culpability, but one that also follows from Fichte's conception of spontaneity. It motivates the caution against using others' free actions as means to our ends by appeal to the instrumental irrationality of doing so. Such attempts are impermissible for the same reason that it would be impermissible to insert a randomizing device into a purely physical causal chain through which one proposes to bring about some morally good result. Fichte's emphasis on the impossibility of knowing what Godwin purports to know about the future conduct of Fenelon, his readers, and his chambermaid suggests that this is the consideration he has primarily in mind.

Whether this second sort of consideration involves merely a claim about instrumental rationality or also a claim about culpability, what is certain is that one who holds it is not in virtue of that committed to the denial of consequentialism.[26] This is a form of argument against Godwin's second consideration in favor of saving Fenelon—that his future actions will have better long-term consequences than his chambermaid's—that leaves the consequentialist assumption that Godwin and Fichte share perfectly intact.

But the fact that appeal to a constraint on knowledge occurs at all in these passages raises a further question, which it is worth taking a moment to answer at this point. Is the doctrine of duties really meant to be a straightforward application to the actions of individuals of the substantive criterion of moral worth as I have described it (namely, as an objective consequentialist one which an action meets insofar as it is part of the series at whose limit lies absolute independence); or is it instead meant to present a subjective derivative, a view on which the obligatory action is the one that is most conducive to independence for all the agent knows, or could reasonably be expected to know, at the time of action?[27]

---

[26] Cf. W. Sinott-Armsrong 2015 for the description of a form of consequentialism—he calls it 'proximate consequentialism'—on which, 'when voluntary acts and coincidences intervene in certain causal chains, then the results are not seen as caused by the acts further back in the chain of necessary conditions.' C. Sartorio 2009 offers a broader survey of ways in which different accounts of causation generate different versions of consequentialism.

[27] For canonical discussions of this move to a subjective derivative and the motivations for it in contemporary consequentialist theories, see F. Jackson 1991 and F. Feldman 2006.

Fichte could, after all, reason as follows: Individuals are obliged to satisfy the formal condition on moral worth, and thus to act only upon having achieved the subjective feeling of settled belief that conscientiousness in action requires (cf. §4.1.1 below). If practical deliberation that takes as premises speculations about the moral character of agents' future actions is defective because the premises cannot be known true, and if I am aware of that, then I must lack, with respect to any decision taken as a result of such deliberation, the feeling of settled belief that conscientiousness requires. Deliberation that takes such speculations as premises cannot fulfill the formal condition.

If this were a correct portrayal of Fichte's reasoning, the formal condition would indeed have a systematic substantive upshot (*pace* my denial of this in §1.2 above). But there are several reasons for thinking that Fichte's reasoning does not take this form, and that the answer to the question just raised must be negative.

The first is that Fichte never articulates anything like this line of reasoning, never speaks of what an individual ought rationally to do (as opposed to what morality commands) in these passages, never makes mention of the formal condition and its requirement of conscientiousness in discussing these cases.

The second is that appeals to the rational significance of ignorance in the doctrine of duties are strictly limited to cases involving downstream agency. There is no sign that Fichte had any appreciation of the more general problem that is the basis for one contemporary line of objection to objective consequentialist views, namely that the distant consequences of our actions are virtually completely unknown to us, and that therefore we almost never act rightly,[28] or 'can' almost never do so in the sense of 'can' relevant for moral responsibility.[29] The fact that Fichte does not take on this general problem explains why he never discusses a case similar in form to that of Jackson's doctor who must choose a treatment in the face of uncertain outcomes.[30] Decision-making under risk appears to have simply no place in his thinking. Instead he assumes that we can, given sufficient epistemic responsibility, for the most part if not exceptionlessly, know exactly what we are doing and what its effects will be.

Fichte is of course no stranger to the idea that individual actions can in aggregate have distant and unforeseen yet dramatic effects on the well-being of

---

[28] E. Wiland 2005.   [29] F. Howard-Snyder 1997.

[30] 'Jill is a physician who has to decide on the correct treatment for her patient, John, who has a minor but not trivial skin complaint. She has three drugs to choose from: drug A, drug B, and drug C. Careful consideration of the literature has led her to the following opinions. Drug A is very likely to relieve the condition but will not completely cure it. One of drugs B and C will completely cure the skin condition; the other though will kill the patient, and there is no way that she can tell which of the two is the perfect cure and which the killer drug. What should Jill do?' (F. Jackson 1991, pp. 462–3).

other individuals. But he takes protecting individuals from such unforeseen consequences to be a task of government—in particular, government control of the economy—and not a goal that could ever be addressed adequately at the level of a moral theory directed at individuals.[31] The distant consequences that figure in his moral theory and that cannot be so managed typically concern research or education, and he takes the overall positive consequences of any effort in these directions to be easy to foresee.

One's own and other agents' future actions are the sole exception to this rule. That suggests that there is something special about them; and it is true that these cases are not, on his theory, at all analogous to the case of Jackson's doctor. They are not cases in which the agent lacks knowledge, reasonably or not, that she might have had. Instead they are cases in which, because they concern spontaneous actions that have not yet taken place, there is (as yet) nothing to know. What rules out reckoning other agents' future conduct among the consequences of one's own actions in all these cases—lifeboat and rescue, murder and suicide—is not merely a subjective epistemic limitation of the agent, but a gap in the causal order of things.

These cases, then, offer no grounds for thinking that Fichte means, in the doctrine of duties, to shift to a subjective version of consequentialism. The view is not that, were I to save the young future mass-murderer from drowning, my act would be objectively wrong but subjectively right or at least blameless because I could not know at the time what the boy would go on to become. The view is rather that saving the boy would be *objectively* right, because the sufficient conditions of his future evil actions, and therefore of their awful future consequences, will not be in place until he makes those future decisions, and so his future actions (and their consequences) cannot *be* wrong-making properties of my act of saving him at the time at which I do it. Of course in saving him I am contributing to a causally necessary condition of those acts, namely his survival until the time of the murders. But were saving him forbidden on that basis, any act of saving any individual from drowning would be forbidden on the same basis, for any person saved could turn out, in the end, to be a mass murderer (where the force of that 'could' is not epistemic, but causal).

3.2.1.2 PHYSICAL CULTIVATION

A second set of duties in the first class distinguished in §18 concern physical cultivation and protection from damage to the body due to mismanagement.

---

[31] This is not to say that he does not think we have individual moral duties toward the poor where government fails to fulfill its function. I discuss these in §3.2.1.3 below.

Fichte divides these into negative (the physical cultivation of the body may not be treated as itself a final end, without regard to its usefulness in rational activity; nor may the enjoyment of its sensations be treated as a final end); positive (the body should be made fit, to the extent possible, for all the possible ends of freedom, which rules out dulling of sensation and desires and damping down of powers); and limitative (every physical pleasure unrelated to the development of the body to fitness is disallowed) (IV: 216). In §20 he derives from them correlative duties to avoid disruptions to natural development—through fasting, intemperance and, Fichte tells us, unchastity (IV: 262). Self-regarding duties in this class are, like the duties discussed in §3.2.1.1, justified by appeal to the agent-neutral value of the causal efficacy of rational agency, and are accompanied by a parallel set of other-regarding duties.

Other agents stand in a different relation to their bodies than I do, insofar as only their wills have immediate causal efficacy in their bodies. This relationship between the individual's will and his body is protected by duties of right. So duties concerning others' cultivation will be constrained, both by what is possible (I cannot simply go out for a jog on someone else's behalf) and by what is rightful (nor may I rightfully chain him to a treadmill). But where my options for promoting the physical protection and cultivation of others are not so constrained, my duties are the same as the duties I have in my own case. Negative duties of non-aggression (IV: 277–8) and positive duties to make the health, strength, and preservation of others one's end (IV: 280)—indeed, to do as much on others' behalf in this regard as one does on one's own behalf, insofar as it is within one's power (IV: 280)—are justified on the same basis as the corresponding self-regarding duties. The physical cultivation of others 'should be as close to my heart as my own, for the basis on which I will these is the same' (IV: 280).

3.2.1.3 PROPERTY

A third set of duties in the first class distinguished in §18 concern the protection and cultivation of the sphere of legally protected entitlements to act assigned to individuals by property law. 'Property' is a technical term for Fichte, denoting a fixed sphere of external action possibilities, under an agent's exclusive and enduring control, in which he may exercise his causal efficacy without threat of interference by other agents, and which is sufficient to provide his means of subsistence. (I will describe Fichte's account of rational constraints on systems of property allocation, as well as explaining what counts as 'property' and why, in §3.2.3.4.)

The moral justification of negative duties to respect others' property by not stealing or vandalizing it, as well as positive duties (in force only where effective state intervention is impossible) to help protect others' property from attack

(IV: 307–8) and from loss to natural causes (IV: 306–7), and to increase its usability (IV: 298), are justified in part by the fact that property supports both physical subsistence (insofar as a person's occupation provides their livelihood) and rational planning (insofar as exclusive and enduring control over some set of action possibilities promotes this).

> Property is an object of duties because it is a condition and tool of freedom. The morally good person has as his end that others have as much freedom—that is, power and causality in the world of sense—as possible, in order thereby to further the rule of reason.
>
> (IV: 298)

This is also the justification of duties to keep one's own property in good order (IV: 269), to protect it from similar threats (IV: 306) and enhance its usefulness (when one can do so consistent with right) (IV: 269).

Fichte takes it to be a moral duty to ensure, to the extent that it is within one's power, that every mature rational being has property sufficient to maintain himself (IV: 295). In the ideal case, one fulfills this duty by being a member of a rationally organized state. Those who lack that option because they belong to a dysfunctional state have a duty to provide others with property by sharing their own (IV: 296)—not by giving alms in the customary way ('a very ambiguous good work' (IV: 296)[32])—but by providing the propertyless person with the means to support himself by his own efforts (e.g. giving him a piece of farmland, or an education in a trade) and so the means to exercise his agency independently of the benefactor in the future (IV: 296–7). In keeping with the indifference between self and other Fichte claims as a general principle, he argues that beneficence may be limited only by the minimum property requirements for the benefactor's own engagement with her chosen occupation (IV: 297).

Duties concerning others' property are complicated, as Fichte notes (IV: 292), by the fact that property provisions are dependent on positive law, and all such duties are conditional on the obligation to abide by property law (IV: 292–8). In fact most duties concerning the positive protection of others' property are discharged by one's contribution to the state's power to enforce legal sanctions surrounding it. As a private person one must go out of one's way to protect another's property only in the special case in which agents of the state cannot effectively protect it (IV: 301). In a case in which both my own and a neighbor's property are simultaneously threatened by loss to natural causes, Fichte writes, I must save mine first, but only because it is my 'particular occupation' and

---

[32] Giving alms, according to Fichte, amounts to saying: 'I can't really help you, but use this to stay alive until you find someone who can' (IV: 296). A social practice of almsgiving and -taking that merely perpetuates dependence is morally objectionable (IV: 297).

because I assume that the other will do likewise (IV: 306). That Fichte is here describing not a privileged relation between an individual and her property, but merely the solution to a coordination problem, is clear from the conditions that follow: that I must be sure that this priority I give to saving my own property is motivated by duty and not by self-love; that I 'rescue what is mine not as mine, but rather as the common property [*Gemeingut*] of reason'; and that I am prepared to share what has been rescued with the other if he does not manage to rescue his own (IV: 306). Moreover, I may not protect my property against a merely possible danger when an actual danger threatens my neighbor's; and I may not protect mine by redirecting a threat toward my neighbor's.

Where the threat is not natural but human, my obligation is to act to prevent the robbery, again regardless of whether the property is mine or my neighbor's, 'which should matter equally to me [*welches mir gleich gelten soll*]' (IV: 307). Whether and to what extent I may put my own life or that of the would-be robber in danger in doing so depends on whether the state is in a position to prevent the crime or to make the victim whole after the fact. Where it cannot, I must intervene, even at the cost of danger to myself or the robber (IV: 308). This contradicts the principle that 'life goes before property' (IV: 307–8), but is required because in so acting I am effectively a surrogate of the state, whose coercive enforcement of the property contract is justified even where it causes harm to the lawbreaker or the agents of the law (for reasons I will examine in §3.2.3 below).

3.2.2 Good deliberation and true beliefs

As I said in the overview of §3.2, §18 of the *System of Ethics* divides duties into three categories: those concerning the preservation and development of the physical powers, those concerning the preservation and development of the intellectual powers, and those concerning the protection of individuality. I now turn to the second category, that of duties concerning the rational being *qua* intellect. These have a different and more fundamental status than duties of physical self-development, according to Fichte. The body is a tool for the outer realization of ends; but the intellect plays a constitutive role in practical deliberation, and is thus the condition of the 'whole existence and persistence' of the moral law (IV: 217). Moreover, insofar as practical deliberation requires that theoretical reason be the (independent) source of the empirical knowledge that figures in it, epistemic norms (in the narrow sense) will be independent of moral ones. Norms governing the interaction of members of specific intellectual communities, and the personal virtues conducive to different sorts of productive intellectual life, will constitute particular duties that precede universal ones in this sphere. The two components of the moral end that give rise to these duties—excellence in practical reasoning and in theoretical cognition—are for the most part separated in Fichte's exposition, and I will maintain that separation here.

3.2.2.1 CONSCIENCE

Self-regarding duties to promote excellence in one's own deliberation in the moment of deliberation are spelled out in Fichte's discussion of the formal condition on moral worth, and so are the topic of Chapter 4. In this section I will discuss only indirect duties to promote conscientious deliberation by influencing the rationality and completeness of others' practical deliberation, and the rationality and completeness of one's own at future times. There can be such duties because on Fichte's theory conscientiousness is something susceptible to outside influence (IV: 179, 184, 204–5). The end of exerting a net-positive influence is the source of what he calls duties to spread and promote 'morality.'

There is some ambiguity in that term as Fichte uses it in the third division. On the one hand, 'morality' is the term for meeting the formal condition; and Fichte sometimes contrasts the formal and material conditions, calling the former a condition on the 'morality' of actions and the latter a condition on their 'legality' (IV: 154, 275). But by 'legality' in that context Fichte means simply the substantive moral correctness of actions, looked at in abstraction from the motives behind them, not anything having to do with law or right; and he also uses 'morality' to refer to the substantive moral correctness of actions (so long as they are also conscientiously undertaken).

In the section in which he discusses duties to promote morality (§25), Fichte appears to have in mind both the narrower and the broader sense just described. Part of what we are supposed to try to influence, when we go about promoting others' morality, is the outer behavior they display. Fichte's suggestion that we can promote morality in others by setting an example of good conduct, and that we can do this by making both our own actions and the maxims[33] that inform them as public as possible (IV: 317–25; cf. XI: 125), makes little sense if we hope only to influence the conscientiousness of others' moral deliberation. Still, our efforts to promote good behavior in others must not undermine the integrity of their deliberation. This is the force of Fichte's remark that it would be absurd to try to promote morality in others by simply manipulating their outer behavior, by offers of reward or threats of punishment (IV: 314–16). These ways of influencing others' decisions preclude the target's acting from the motive

---

[33] Fichte uses the term 'maxim' here and in many other places, but so far as I can tell only in the colloquial sense corresponding to 'rule of thumb' and not in any specialized Kantian sense.

of duty. (That they warp the exercise of practical rationality is also part of the justification for prohibitions on attempts to move another's will through non-rational means like torture, imprisonment, and deprivation (the other part of that justification being, of course, that they are typically illegal (IV: 277–8)).

Setting an example of good conduct conscientiously pursued is the chief mechanism Fichte identifies for improving others' conduct without undermining their ability to make conscientious decisions. The mechanism he describes is inspired by Kant's discussion of the motive of respect in the *Triebfeder* chapter of the *Critique of Practical Reason*.[34] Respect for the example-setter causes the target agent to feel self-contempt (*Selbstverachtung*), and awakens in him a desire to replace it with self-respect. This is a spur to improvement both for those whose immorality is due to ignorance and for those for whom it is due to despair over themselves and their capacity for improvement (IV: 318–19; cf. 204–5).

In §18 Fichte suggests an additional non-coercive way of improving others' reasoning capacities: engaging in debate with them, rather than withdrawing or acting unilaterally, in cases of moral disagreement (IV: 233). Since there is but one true practical judgment about any given situation (IV: 155, 195), disagreement is a sign that one or both of the disagreeing parties has made a mistake, that the individual limitations of one or both of them has distorted their practical deliberation (IV: 245). Such mistakes are uncovered when disagreements are hashed out.

Engaging with others with a view to the mutual cultivation of convictions is one general function of society; and there are two sorts of social organization specifically devoted to it. The first is the church, the institutionalization of the moral community, united by a symbolic belief that forms the common ground of moral debate (IV: 236, 241). A set of learned societies, among them universities, takes on the same function for those individuals who cannot honestly declare their belief in this symbolic basis (IV: 248–50). Both sets of institutions have the function, not of inculcating belief and thereby imposing consensus from above, but instead of serving as fora for debate and thereby enabling the convergence of individual judgments on the truth.

Promoting others' morality is a general duty; but it is also the particular duty of parents (§27) and of religious leaders (§30). In addition to caring for a child's well-being (IV: 335) parents are obliged to educate the child morally (IV: 336), and part of this moral education is to cultivate the child's intellectual powers in a purposeful and productive way (IV: 336). The vocation of religious leaders is to promote others' more perfect exercise of their rational agency by enlivening and

---

[34] I. Kant 1900–, 5: 71–89; I. Kant 1996a, pp. 198–211.

strengthening moral feeling (IV: 350), helping people to apply general principles in particular cases (IV: 351), and setting a good example (IV: 352). (That this is the particular social role of religious leaders explains, together with Fichte's conception of the church as a forum for discussion aimed at reaching moral consensus, why Fichte singles out organized religion as the most important spur to moral improvement in his discussion of moral evil in §16.)

3.2.2.2 TRUE BELIEFS

In addition to duties (both general and particular) to improve practical reasoning itself, by causing individuals to become more reflective, more consistent, and more energetic in their application of their rational capacities to the deliberative situations they face, Fichte also describes duties (both general and particular) to preserve and augment the factual knowledge on which their practical reasoning depends. These duties concerning agents' knowledge are strikingly prominent in the third part of division three.

Duties of intellectual self-cultivation are again negative (never subordinate theoretical reason as such, but rather research without regard to anything extraneous to the topic, and without aiming at a conclusion favored by extra-theoretical motivations); positive (develop the cognitive faculty by studying, thinking, researching as much as possible); and limitative (relate all reflection formally to duty; be conscious of this duty in all one's investigations; research for the sake of duty, not for the sake of mere curiosity) (IV: 218).[35] Intellectual self-preservation and self-cultivation require regular mental exercise, the avoidance of inactivity and boredom, but also the avoidance of excessive strain, irregular activity, and one-sided development (IV: 262). Aesthetic experience (to which I will return in §3.2.2.5) has its place here as well (IV: 269).

Fichte emphasizes the immorality of intellectual dishonesty and the danger that threatens when belief-forming mechanisms are corrupted by desires and even by moral demands. He defends freedom of conscience in a very strong form, calling for academic communities to take the place of the religious community for those whose intellectual situation no longer permits literal religious belief (IV: 237ff.), and defending both individual freedom of thought and conscience (IV: 237, 248) and the independence of scholarly activity from interference by church or state (IV: 249–51). Theoretical activity, he argues, is governed materially by epistemic norms that are not themselves moral and that can in some situations conflict with what the moral end would otherwise require (as, for

---

[35] Curiously, this limitative category is missing in the case of duties regarding the intellect at GA 4-1: 108.

example, when lacking knowledge in certain areas would make someone more likely to behave dutifully (IV: 217)).

This independence of epistemic norms is consistent with the value of theoretical knowledge being limited to its usefulness in some form of practical deliberation at some point in the future, and indeed Fichte argues that the project of theoretical enquiry is not an end in itself but, as a whole, subordinate to practical concerns. This places constraints not on theoretical beliefs or epistemic norms directly (these are internal to a given branch of inquiry), but on the choice of areas of research, and on the amount of time and other resources devoted to it. (This is what Fichte means when he writes that the intellect should not be 'materially' subordinated to morality, but should nonetheless be 'formally' subordinated to it (IV: 217).) This, coupled with Fichte's observation that their activity is directed not at nature directly, but at other rational beings, suggests that the knowledge scholars produce is not itself (*qua* knowledge) part of the moral end of material independence, but becomes part of that end only when it is incorporated by individuals into rational plans of action.

As was the case with duties of physical cultivation, Fichte's account of duties to other agents *qua* intellects is mediated by his account of relations of right, and by the constraints arising from the fact that some positive self-regarding duties have no obvious other-regarding counterparts. Still, his discussion of duties concerning others' knowledge is strikingly detailed. He offers a double justification of such duties in this context, appealing to the value of true beliefs both for efficacious external agency (IV: 282–3) and for formulating rational plans of action (IV: 283–5). Someone factually mistaken can see results different from those intended (IV: 282), so the effective causality of one's fellow human beings requires knowledge of the sensible world sufficient for the type of causality they intend to exercise in it (IV: 283). 'I must will the conditioned, the free causality of my fellow human beings in the world of sense; therefore I must will the condition: that he have cognition of it that is correct and sufficient for his manner of causality' (IV: 283). But not only outer efficacy is at stake. Prohibitions on deceit and on 'speaking about things whose truth I do not know' (IV: 283, 287) are justified also on the grounds that they hinder others in their effort to *formulate* rational plans of action. If I bring about an incorrect belief in someone else and he acts upon it, Fichte argues, what follows is chosen not by him but by me (IV: 283). (In remarking that even if I thereby bring it about that the person does something substantively morally correct that he would not otherwise have done, I have not furthered the moral end because I have interfered with his ability to fulfill the formal condition on moral worth (IV: 283–4), Fichte indicates that he sees this as interference with the purely *internal* exercise of the person's rational agency.)

False promising receives the same treatment: it is wrong because it undermines rational agency by depriving it of knowledge on which it depends (IV: 285).

General positive duties to seek knowledge oneself (IV: 291), to volunteer useful information to others when one sees they are in need of it (IV: 290–1), and to contribute to the collective support of a class of individuals whose professional vocation is the production, preservation, and transmission of knowledge (IV: 291) are justified on the same basis; and the same principle—that the mind should be made fit, to the extent possible, for all possible ends— underwrites Fichte's support for universal general (not vocational) education to the age of majority (IV: 272).

3.2.2.3 KNOWLEDGE AND CONTROL: PROPERTY

Perhaps surprisingly, duties concerning property also fall under the general rubric of duties concerning knowledge (in addition to falling, as we have seen, under the rubric of duties to support subsistence and promote causal efficacy). The centrality of knowledge is reflected in the justification Fichte offers for the institution of property in the *Foundations of Natural Right*.

Although he takes subsistence for all to be a requirement of right on any property division, Fichte does not take the end of subsistence to justify the institution of property to begin with. He recognizes that there are many circum-stances in which individuals can fulfill their basic material needs in the absence of any social contract. Nor does he appeal to causal efficacy as a transcendental condition of possibility of self-consciousness in justifying the institution of property. Since neither basic nor causally mediated action requires any social institutions at all, awareness of one's external causal efficacy cannot require them. Moreover, while opportunities to exercise that efficacy may be enhanced by such institutions, they need not be. Since any given property regime prevents some actions even as it enables others, where property is sufficiently unequally distrib-uted the result will be a net reduction in things people, in general, are able to do.[36]

What a property regime does expand, simply as such, is the complexity of the long-term plans people are able rationally to undertake. It does so by coordinat-ing claims to means (to all kinds of ends) available in the shared external world. What such coordination enhances is not (or need not be) the amount or availability of such means; what it enhances is agents' ability to *know* what means will be at their disposal at what time. This is why both §11 of the *Foundations of Natural Right* and §23 of the *System of Ethics* link the function of property to the exercise

---

[36] Cf. G.A. Cohen 2011, chs. 7 and 8.

of rational agency through the medium of knowledge. Here is the passage in the *Foundations*:

The person has the right to demand that, in the whole area of the world that is familiar to him, everything remain as he has come to know it, because in his efficacy he orients himself according to his knowledge, and as soon as there occurs a change in it, he will become disoriented and the course of his causality will be halted, or else [he will] see results follow that are completely different from those intended. (This is the ground of all property right. That part of the world of sense that is known to me and subordinated, even if only in thought, to my ends, is *originally* (not *in society*, in which regard, indeed, still further determinations are to be found) my property. No one can influence this without obstructing the freedom of my efficacy...)   (III: 116)

Property in the 'original' (i.e. pre-social) sense is just the involvement of the world in our intentions, in grounding the beliefs that figure in them. In a footnote to this passage, Fichte gives this example:

Imagine an isolated inhabitant of a deserted island, who feeds himself by hunting in its forests. He has let the forests grow as they will; but he knows them, and knows all the amenities they offer for his hunting. One cannot move or cut the trees in his forests without rendering useless all the knowledge he has gained and robbing him of it, without checking his course in pursuing game, and so making difficult or impossible his acquisition of sustenance—and thus, without disturbing the freedom of his efficacy.   (III: 116n)

In justifying both duties to obey property law and duties that concern property but go beyond mere obedience to laws governing it in the *System of Ethics*, Fichte appeals to the same ideas:

If the rational being is to be free in his efficacy—that is, if what was thought in his concept of his end is to follow in experience—the condition [*Beschaffenheit*] of everything that is related to his end and influences it must remain continuously as the rational being has come to know it and has presupposed it in his concept of his end. If something on whose persistence success depends and is thereby conditioned is changed while the action is being performed, the effect will be changed as well, and what should have happened will not happen. (For further clarification of this in itself simple proposition I direct the reader to my *Natural Right* §11.) This [thing] related to my action as the premise of all of my action in the sensible world, from which [that action] proceeds and which it presupposes can, when I live among other free beings, be only a part [not the whole] of the sensible world. This determinate part of the world subordinated to my end, when it is recognized and guaranteed by society (this recognition and guarantee is *juridically* and *morally* required), is my *property*.   (IV: 291–2)

Notice that Fichte's emphasis, in all of these passages, is not on the mere availability of things that are related to and presupposed by an agent's end, but instead on the knowledge of their availability.

One function of the social contract is to reconcile different individuals' claims to 'original' property in the sense at issue in the first passage. But Fichte assumes that this can exist as a problem to be solved by multilateral agreement only if original property is a necessary end of rational agents simply as such; so it is his aim in that passage and the footnote to it to argue that this is in fact the case. He reasons as follows. Intentions rely on beliefs about what is possible in a concrete situation of action. If these beliefs turn out to be false, the intentions that rely on them may be causally impotent. If they are absent altogether, no intentions can rationally be formed to begin with. Knowledge of means at one's disposal, and so the ability to formulate plans that involve those means, typically depends on control of some part of the environment. Since an agent with an interest in her capacity to set ends must have an interest in the knowledge required by practical reflection, she must have an interest in such control, and in rights against others' possible interference.

The social institution of property licenses complex long-term plans by making possible rational beliefs about the means that figure in them. This agency-based justification of the institution of property does not itself favor any particular property regime. But Fichte himself was a socialist who advocated strong centralized control of the economy (in both the *Foundations* and its 1800 appendix, *The Closed Commercial State*), on the grounds that an unregulated market could lead to the curtailment, for some, of the very sorts of activity that give the institution of property its characteristic point. (I will return to the topic of Fichte's theory of property in §3.2.3.4.)

3.2.2.4 KNOWLEDGE AND CONTROL: RESEARCH AND TECHNOLOGY

Notice that, in Fichte's wooded island example, a forest fire would have exactly the same effect as an axe-wielding intruder. The example involves an intruder because the specific context in the *Foundations* is property rights, which, like all rights, govern only interpersonal interaction (III: 55). What Fichte does not assume is that there is any difference in kind between human and natural interference: if other individuals are more of a threat to our plans than natural forces, that is only because they are in principle unpredictable (III: 115–16). This parallel is close to the surface in the *Foundations*; in the *Vocation of Humankind* it is perfectly explicit. There, as I have said, Fichte follows his discussion of natural disasters immediately with a discussion of man-made disasters (II: 269). The latter are more destructive than natural disasters, because they are designed to be destructive, because the technological sophistication that tames nature also arms human beings against one another, and because unlike natural events human assaults are unpredictable. But these are differences in degree, not in kind.

The knowledge at issue in Fichte's wooded island example, and the kind usually facilitated by property rights, is knowledge of particular facts concerning means at an agent's disposal for carrying out whatever ends she may form. But there is another way in which control facilitates the knowledge required for planning: it facilitates the discovery of the empirical regularities on which causal reasoning is based. It does so at the level of individual inquiry (insofar as, for example, the scientist, if she is to have confidence in the outcome of her experiments, must also have confidence in her control of the space in which they take place and the processes which comprise them). More importantly, it does so at the collective level, where science and technology stand in a dialectical relationship: discoveries spur technology, making it possible to answer new questions experimentally, leading to new discoveries.

This dialectical interaction of scientific knowledge and technological control is not at issue in the *Foundations of Natural Right*, where the topic is the property rights of individuals against other individuals, the division of a sphere of action possibilities that is, for Fichte's purposes there, assumed fixed. But it is a prominent theme in the *System of Ethics*, where Fichte addresses the question of what the collective attitude toward non-rational nature as a whole, and toward the expansion of the sphere of possible actions, should be. There (for instance in this passage, which appealed especially to Feuerbach[37]) he explicitly underlines the relation between technological progress, knowledge, and what it is possible to will:

We can actually do everything we *can will*: just not straight away, most of the time, but only in a certain order. (For example, people say: a human being cannot fly. But why should he not be able to? Granted, he cannot do it immediately, in the way that, if he is healthy, he can walk immediately. But of course he can raise himself up into the air by means of an air balloon, and move around in it with a degree of freedom and purposiveness. And what our age is yet incapable of doing, because it has not yet discovered the means—who says that *the human being* is incapable of it? I hope that an age like ours does not take itself to be [all of] humanity.)   (IV: 94–5)

It is part of the essence of rational beings, as individuals but also collectively, to engage in ever more complex plans of action, to seek to expand the scope of their possible activity, and, subordinate to this, to seek to expand their knowledge.

This is a picture that was sketched already, as I have said, in the 1794 *Lectures on the Scholar's Vocation*, where progress toward independence of nature forms the basis of a defense of the division of labor in society, and of the conception of the scholar's vocation in particular. Fichte takes the division of labor to be a

---

[37] Cf. L. Feuerbach 1848, p. 101.

prima facie moral problem, because specialization requires the one-sided culti-vation of individuals' capacities and results in inequality (VI: 315–16). (Fichte's concern is not with economic inequality, since he does not think it a necessary consequence of the division of labor, but instead with inequalities amongst individuals in the development of the capacities themselves.) The problem is solved by the observation that the rate of such progress is increased by special-ization, coupled with the observation that the progress made by each in their own fields of specialization can be communicated to, and so shared by, everyone in society (VI: 319–21).

Each has the duty, not to want to be useful to society only in general, but instead to direct all of his efforts, to the best of his knowledge, toward the final end of society—toward the ever greater ennoblement of the human race, i.e. toward making it ever more free from the constraints of nature, ever more self-sufficient, ever more self-active—and so there arises from this new inequality [*sc.* the division of society into classes] a new equality, namely, a uniform progress of culture in all individuals.   (VI: 321)

The class of scholars furthers this project by contributing both a systematic understanding of human capabilities and needs, and a systematic understanding of how to develop and satisfy these (VI: 325–36). Their vocation is the 'highest survey of the actual progress of the human race in general, and the ongoing promotion of this progress' (VI: 328; original in italics).

So it is unsurprising that the end of independence of nature figures promin-ently in Fichte's account of the particular duties of the scholarly *Stand* in the *System of Ethics*. The existence of a class devoted to the production of knowledge of no immediate practical use is justified by the fact that the moral end concerns the independence of the entire human race into the indefinite future:

If one sees the human beings on the earth as a single family—as one should see them from a moral perspective, and as they will one day inevitably become in reality—then one can also assume that there is a single system of knowledge belonging to this family, which is expanded and perfected from age to age. Like the individual, the race becomes more clever over time, and develops itself through experience. The knowledge of each age should rise higher [than the last] and raising it is the purpose of the scholar.   (IV: 346)

Not only applied sciences, but every inquiry that contributes to the understand-ing of anything that could affect human capabilities at any point in the future is justified in this way (IV: 347). The function of educators, archivalists, and researchers in applied and pure sciences is to preserve, expand, and propagate theoretical knowledge (IV: 346–7). They seek 'truths that are only theoretical for an epoch or for most of the individuals in it' (IV: 291); and although their activity is ultimately justified by the expectation that such truths will turn out to be of practical significance in the future (IV: 291), that activity is governed by substantive epistemic norms that are distinct from moral ones, precisely because it serves its moral function only by aiming at the truth.

What is perhaps more surprising is the role of knowledge-production in Fichte's account of the particular duties of the laboring *Stand*, whose particular role is to 'work immediately on reasonless nature for the sake of rational beings, in order to make the former useful for the ends of the latter' (IV: 361; cf. IV: 345). Fichte emphasizes that the progress of humankind depends on their technical skill in bringing nature under control (IV: 362), and it is their particular duty not only to apply the results of scholarly research to their particular fields (IV: 363), but also to engage in autonomous technical innovation and skill-development of the sort that allows more to be accomplished with less time and less physical exertion (IV: 362). He remarks that the discoveries of the pure sciences have no greater importance in this progress than innovations made in pursuits such as agriculture (IV: 362–3). So the particular duties of the working class encompass not only work upon nature aimed at subordinating it to human ends, but also expansion of the possibilities for such work. To use Marx's language, they are to develop the material forces of production; and in Fichte's view, as in Marx's, science and labor work hand in hand in that process.

3.2.2.5 AESTHETIC EXPERIENCE

Although he does not devote very many pages to describing the nature of aesthetic cultivation in the *System of Ethics*, it is clear that aesthetic experience figures centrally in Fichte's account of moral and intellectual cultivation. The brevity of the treatment in the *System of Ethics* may be due in part to an intention, never carried out, to treat aesthetics in another work. It may also be due in part to the fact that in the Jena of 1797–8 there was simply no need to make this point at great length. Schiller had already made it quite adequately in his *Letters on the Aesthetic Education of the Human Being*. In any event, apart from the admonition (at IV: 269) that duties of intellectual self-development include a duty of aesthetic self-cultivation, Fichte discusses the function of aesthetic experience in the *System of Ethics* only in the section dedicated to the particular duties of the fine artist (§31).

The function of fine art, according to Fichte, and therefore the vocation of the fine artist, is to cultivate (*bilden*) 'not only the understanding (as the scholar does) nor only the heart (as the moral teacher of the people), but rather the whole unified human being.... the whole temperament in the unity of its capacities' (IV: 353). Aesthetic experience induces introspection (IV: 354); it also shakes a person loose from the given and sets him on his own feet (an idea that has an afterlife in Adorno's aesthetics: the idea of aesthetic experience as a liberation from the world as it is) (IV: 354). Finally, following the lead of Kant's *Critique of the Power of Judgment*, Fichte writes that art makes the transcendental point of view into the common one by allowing us to see nature not only as something that limits us but also as itself the product of our (transcendentally) free intellectual activity, offering a reconciliation of moral and natural order (IV: 354).

So aesthetic experience promotes the moral end by cultivating our intellectual faculties, reconciling us to the fact that our constitutive end of independence will never be fully attained, and stimulating us to leave the given behind and create ourselves anew. From this set of functions derive the duties of the fine artist.

Since the sensibility required for success in the endeavor of being a fine artist does not depend on the will and cannot be imparted by instruction, Fichte sees no positive duties here (IV: 355). But it is possible to hinder aesthetic cultivation by spreading tastelessness as if it were beauty. The duties of the fine artist derive from that fact, and are negative: no one should become a fine artist who lacks talent; and no one who does become a fine artist should sacrifice her artistic vision to current fashion for the sake of fame or money (IV: 355).

3.2.2.6 KANT AND FICHTE ON ENDS THAT ARE DUTIES

Fichte's justification of duties to cultivate one's fellows physically, intellectually, morally, and aesthetically differs from Kant's. As we have seen, Fichte justifies these duties by appeal to the perfection of rational agency and the broadening of its scope of activity as a source of agent-neutral reasons. One should try to further this end in others in the same way and to the same extent that one tries to further it in oneself, and for the same reasons.

Fichte remarks at one point that this is the intuition that underlies the Kantian universalization test (IV: 234); but most contemporary interpreters of Kant would disagree. Certainly Kant himself denies that the duties we have to preserve and develop our own capacities *qua* capacities—to 'cultivate [our] powers of mind and body so that they are fit to realize any ends [we] might encounter'[38]— can have other-regarding correlates, for he denies that we can (effectively) take others' perfection as our end.

In the *Metaphysics of Morals* Kant describes two components, natural and moral, of the individual perfection that it is a duty to make our end in our own case. Moral perfection is reliable motivation to act in accordance with duty from the motive of duty, 'to do [one's] duty *from duty* (for the law to be not only the

---

[38] I. Kant 1900–, 6: 392; I. Kant 1996a, p. 523.

rule but also the incentive of [one's] actions).'[39] '*Natural* perfection is the *cultivation* of any *capacities* whatever for furthering ends set forth by reason';[40] and the duty to cultivate it a duty 'to make ourselves worthy of humanity by culture in general, by procuring or promoting the *capacity* to realize all sorts of possible ends, so far as this is to be found in the human being himself... to cultivate the crude predispositions of his nature, by which the animal is first raised into the human being.'[41]

Where he justifies these duties in one's own case, Kant's reasoning often looks rather like Fichte's (as long as we understand the content of 'living in conformity with nature' in the quotation below to be spelled out by the account of 'rational nature' developed in Kant's writings on history):

The first principle of duty to oneself lies in the dictum 'live in conformity with nature' (*naturae convenienter vive*), that is, *preserve* yourself in the perfection of your nature; the second, in the saying '*make yourself more perfect* than mere nature has made you' (*perfice te ut finem, perfice te ut medium*).[42]

But Kant denies that the perfection of others, in either sense, can be an end for us.

So too, it is a contradiction for me to make another's *perfection* my end and consider myself under obligation to promote this. For the *perfection* of another human being, as a person, consists just in this: that he *himself* is able to set his end in accordance with his own concepts of duty; and it is self-contradictory to require that I do (make it my duty to do) something that only the other himself can do.[43]

Kant may seem here to be describing moral perfection only, but it is clear both from the context and from the schematic table offered some sections later[44] that others' perfection in general is what he means to rule out as an obligatory end.

In the case of perfection of the moral will this denial has some *prima facie* plausibility: in forcing, manipulating, or cajoling an agent to do the right thing one would ensure that his action has motives other than duty. As we have seen, Fichte was alive to this concern, but still saw what is clearly the case, namely that there are ways to promote another's moral perfection that do not ensure that his actions will have the wrong motivation (e.g. setting a good example, providing information, alerting someone to some unnoticed moral significance of a proposed action, or spurring reflection on motivations).

---

[39] I. Kant 1900–, 6: 392; I. Kant 1996a, p. 523.
[40] I. Kant 1900–, 6: 391; I. Kant 1996a, p. 522.
[41] I. Kant 1900–, 6: 392; I. Kant 1996a, pp. 522–3.
[42] I. Kant 1900–, 6: 419; I. Kant 1996a, p. 545; cf. I. Kant 1900–, 4: 430; I. Kant 1996a, p. 81.
[43] I. Kant 1900–, 6: 386; I. Kant 1996a, pp. 517–18.
[44] I. Kant 1900–, 6: 398; I. Kant 1996a, p. 527.

In the case of natural perfection, Kant's denial that we can make that of others our end has no even *prima facie* plausibility, as there is no contradiction in improving another's talents and intellect by coercion, manipulation, or cajoling. Indeed, the development of an individual's natural perfection is so clearly under the influence of those around her that it is hard to see what Kant could possibly have in mind in denying that it is a possible end for us. Still there is no doubt that Kant in fact held this view, and that on his picture our duties of mutual aid derive not from the end of others' perfection, but instead from the end of others' happiness.

What Kant means by the end of happiness is, roughly, the idea of a whole-life maximization of satisfaction of the agent's natural desires (as they arise in the agent's social setting).[45] Two features of his account are worth noting. First, for Kant the idea of happiness is a fundamentally comparative one: 'only in comparison with others does one judge oneself happy or unhappy.'[46] Second, although the end of happiness (characterized formally) is humanly universal, individual conceptions of happiness are idiosyncratic, because they depend on what individuals find agreeable, and different individuals find different things agreeable. There is, for Kant, no measure of human well-being that is in any sense objective or universal. So in furthering someone else's happiness in the right way, I start not from what I think would make him materially better off, nor even from what I think would make him happy, but only from what his own plan for a happy life requires (consistent with my and his perfect duties). To proceed from my own conception would be paternalistic, and so disrespectful; helpfulness compatible with respect requires making his aims my own, and since the aim of happiness is both subjective and indexed to social conditions and so variable, I must allow his actual conception to be my guide (insofar as this is an option for me).[47]

So for Kant the content of duties of beneficence is indexed to individual preferences and, through them (since for Kant conceptions of happiness involve

---

[45] Kant's concept of happiness is of course a matter of dispute in the literature; what I say here is, I hope, neutral with respect to the various positions. Cf. e.g. A. Wood 2001; A. Hills 2009a.

[46] I. Kant 1900–, 6: 27; I. Kant 1996b, p. 75.

[47] Kant asks, under 'casuistical questions' in the *Metaphysics of Morals* discussion, whether someone in a position of power over another could be justified, or could consider himself the other's benefactor, if he were to take care of the other in accordance with his own conception of happiness, ignoring the other's conception of happiness, and indeed robbing the other of his freedom to make himself happy in his own way. He sets this up as a conflict between the right of freedom and the duty of beneficence and asks whether the benefits could be so great as to outweigh the infringement on freedom (even in a case where the freedom is voluntarily given up). His answer is no. 'I cannot do good to anyone in accordance with *my* concepts of happiness (except to young children and the insane), thinking to benefit him by forcing a gift upon him; rather, I can benefit him only in accordance with *his* concepts of happiness.' I. Kant 1900–, 6: 454; I. Kant 1996a, pp. 572–3.

comparison), to social conditions. The account has some counterintuitive consequences. For instance, it appears that on it beneficence might in principle require helping another to do something the beneficiary finds overwhelmingly important but the benefactor sees as utterly pointless. It also absolves the benefactor of any duty to elevate the level of the beneficiary's health, education, nutrition, or what have you, above the beneficiary's own subjective norm, which will be indexed to local conditions that may be quite abject. It thus shares with other accounts of mutual aid based on (broadly) preference-satisfaction conceptions of welfare a susceptibility to an objection pushed forcefully by Amartya Sen against welfarist consequentialism. Preferences are idiosyncratic, and they adapt to circumstances (sometimes to make life bearable in unbearable situations); but we do not think that we owe less assistance to people who have lower expectations, whether because they are easily pleased or because their circumstances are more abject.[48] Sen argues that one virtue of his capabilities approach is that the shift in focus from welfare (on either a subjective state or a preference-satisfaction conception) to capabilities (understood as abilities and opportunities to exercise rational agency in a social setting), eliminates this problem. Sen's capabilities approach seems to me to be the contemporary approach closest in spirit to Fichte's account of duties of beneficence, in this and many other respects (although there are of course important differences as well).[49]

One of the striking features of Fichte's vision of technological progress, visible already in the Lectures on the Scholar's Vocation but most striking in the Vocation of Humankind, is that the evil that it allows human beings to avoid is not suffering, but powerlessness and the fruitlessness of their efforts. When Fichte discusses child mortality in the Vocation, for example, the worry is that the children's existence ends 'without fruit and consequence' (II: 267). When he describes the results to be expected from increased technical mastery, he describes not a 'happy' people, but rather a people that is 'healthy, industrious and artful' ('ein gesundes, arbeitsames und kunstreiches Volk'). The words 'happiness,' 'suffering,' and 'well-being' do not occur at all in these passages. In the System of Ethics he mentions 'happiness' in three contexts: in the moral psychological context, one's own happiness is the end

---

[48]   A. Sen 1999, pp. 62–3. Cf. A. Sen 1979.

[49]   Cf. A. Sen 1979, 1985, and 1999, chs. 1–4. Other important commonalities are the emphasis on freedom in a concrete material sense, and the importance of political rights. One important difference is that Sen, unlike Fichte, is willing to admit agent-relative values and thus some form of agent-centered constraints (A. Sen 1985). Another is that Sen is not engaged in the sort of foundationalist ethical project to which Fichte is so deeply committed (A. Sen 2009). But Sen agrees with Fichte—and disagrees with some other proponents of the capabilities approach—in not seeing the theoretical importance of a fixed list of capabilities rooted in some conception of human nature (A. Sen 2005; note the contrast with Nussbaum's Aristotelian capabilities approach in M. Nussbaum 1992, 2011).

set by the natural drive against which the ethical drive must struggle (IV: 180, 304, 315); in the context of ethical theory, the principle of happiness (together with the principle of perfection) are the sophistical contributions of certain recent German 'so-called' philosophers (IV: 183); and in the doctrine of duties, we find a description of a certain sort of weak-willed individual who seeks to justify his mendacity by claiming that the happiness of others is furthered by it (IV: 286).[50]

Contemporaries described this as the elimination of the last vestiges of Wolffian eudaimonism in Kant's moral philosophy, and so as a move toward a more rigorous and consistent Kantianism.[51] This seems to me a fair assessment. Some contemporary Kantians have already and quite independently moved closer to Fichte's picture here, justifying the duty to promote happiness as an indirect way of supporting the development and exercise of others' agency.[52]

3.2.3 Individuality

I now turn to the third essential determination of the end of independence outlined in §18 of the *System of Ethics*: the fact that the being whose independence is at issue is an individual, one of many of its kind.

The first two sources of determination (embodiment and intellect) are independent, and give rise to ends that can, in some circumstances, be at odds with one another. The beliefs that an epistemically virtuous agent would have are not in every instance the beliefs that would lead to the action most likely to further the moral end in that instance. Conversely, the production of knowledge might require sacrifices of health, strength, or opportunities. Fichte acknowledges both

---

[50] Fichte's view about the role of the end of happiness in moral theory appears to have evolved over the course of the 1790s. In the *Attempt at a Critique of All Revelation* (1792) he accepts happiness on a roughly Kantian understanding as a fundamental human end, and with it the existence of an antinomy of practical reason (V: 16–58). By the time of the *Lectures on the Scholar's Vocation* (1794) he has redefined happiness in terms of independence (as 'the agreement of things outside of us with our will') and emphasizes that 'the concept of happiness itself and the desire for it arise only from the ethical nature of the human being' (VI: 299). By 1798 he has dropped all non-pejorative use of the term 'happiness.'

[51] For more detailed discussion and citations see M. Kosch 2015b.

[52] Herman's account of duties of beneficence extracts something close to the Fichtean view from the Kantian texts. She argues that we are to attend to the well-being of others 'because and insofar as it is in and through the pursuit of happiness that persons create and sustain themselves as agents.... agency-related needs are the object of aid...' (B. Herman 2007, p. 228). The focus on happiness is instrumental: 'it is by means of our effect on the happiness of others that we tend to affect their rational condition and abilities' (B. Herman 2007, p. 267). (Cf. also B. Herman 1993, pp. 55–7.) Herman acknowledges that her account seems to depart from the Kantian letter in the merely instrumental role it gives to the end of happiness: 'It looks as though the end of correct willing and its material conditions are the only possible objects that the will gives itself' (B. Herman 2007, p. 262). Uleman's interpretation of Kant (J. Uleman 2010) is another example of the interpretive development of Kantian ideas in what seems to me a Fichtean direction.

sorts of conflict, at least implicitly. His acknowledgment of the first is an implication of his remark that one should not aim at not knowing certain things because knowing them would make one less likely to do one's duty (IV: 217). The prohibition would be pointless were there no such things to be known. His acknowledgment of the second is an implication of his remark that one should not overstrain oneself, in research, to the point at which it is detrimental to one's health (IV: 262). The prohibition would be pointless were it not possible to sacrifice one's health to one's research.

To be sure, there are in some cases clear priority relations. For instance, there is a clear priority relation between self-regarding duties concerning one's own deliberative capacities and those concerning one's own external freedoms: it would make no sense to sacrifice my deliberative capacities in order to expand my causal powers, for these are important only as powers to carry out plans, plans I would no longer be in a position to form. Still in most cases of conflict there will be nothing like a relation of lexical priority. In particular, there can be no lexical priority of the deliberative integrity of individuals to the causal efficacy of individuals across the board (such that no increase in scope of causal efficacy could justify any sacrifice of deliberative integrity), because that would require the separability of these, across the board; and although they are sometimes separable in a single case, they are not separable across the board.

So the components of the moral end so far discussed are for the most part tightly connected either constitutively or instrumentally, and Fichte treats the conflicts he discusses as easily soluble when one takes a sufficiently long view. But the same is not true of the third source of determinacy for the end of independence. If there is an antinomy of practical reason, for Fichte, it is fair to say that it arises from the fact that the rational being is an individual; and we learn a great deal about the structure of Fichte's theory by looking carefully at how he sets up this problem.

3.2.3.1 A CONFLICT OF THE MORAL LAW WITH ITSELF?

The basic problem (as it is laid out in §18.IV, IV: 229–30) is this: my end as a rational agent is to expand indefinitely the scope of my possible rational plans of action, which involves subordinating as much as possible of the outside world to my control. But the existence of other individuals, coupled with the fact that they also will have rational plans of action that require control over the outside world, requires that I limit the scope of my own activity so that they may also act. Notice that the conflict here is between the demand for indefinite expansion and the demand for limitation. Were a demand for indefinite expansion not part of the moral end, Fichte could not present the conflict as he does here. This is an important piece of indirect evidence of his commitment to the imperatives of progress (described in §3.2.2.4) and maximization (described in the introductory paragraph of §3.2 and in §3.2.1.1).

It is in the first paragraph of this section that Fichte makes his surprising remark about the end of independence demanding that the world become 'like my body to me' (in the passage reproduced in §3.1.1 above). The analogy ('like my body') is most likely motivated by Fichte's intention to underscore the *conflict* between the moral end as construed up to this point in the text and the determination that arises from individuality. The analogy is inapt in general: it suggests that the end of independence is that of expanding the scope of the will's immediate causality and shrinking the set of things done through the exercise of mediated causality. But as we have already seen, this is not at all what Fichte has in mind. Progress toward the end of independence involves the expansion primarily of mediated causal powers. However, the analogy *is* apt for the specific purpose of underscoring the conflict between the moral end as construed up to that point in §18 and the determination that arises from individuality. Fichte has argued in the *Foundations of Natural Right* that interaction between distinct individuals must involve the interaction of distinct bodies (III: 61–84 *passim*, especially 69). So the world could become 'like my body to me' only if I were the only person in it—only if I were not an individual.

The sub-section that follows (§18.V) begins with a further specification of the problem of individuality, which Fichte presents as an assumption that must be true if any solution is to be possible (though notice that it is not itself a solution or even a first pass at one). 'This contradiction could be resolved and the agreement of the moral law with itself established only on the basis of the presupposition that all free beings necessarily had the same end...' (IV: 230). The passage that immediately follows is one that interpreters have found puzzling,[53] but that is critical for understanding the structure of Fichte's ethical theory:

The contradiction could be resolved and the agreement of the moral law with itself established only on the basis of the presupposition that all free beings necessarily had the same end; in which case the purposive action of one would be at the same time purposive for all others, the liberation of one at the same time liberation for all others....

The drive toward self-sufficiency is a drive of I-hood, and has only that as its end: the I alone should be the subject of self-sufficiency. It is indeed, as we have seen, part of I-hood that each I be an individual—but only an individual in general, not the particular

---

[53] Verweyen admits this quite frankly ('Dieser Gedankengang ist verblüffend'—H. Verweyen 1975, pp. 148–9). Zöller gives it a reading that is patently incorrect, insofar as it contradicts Fichte's claim that individuality is an essential feature of I-hood and so an essential constraint on the end of independence (G. Zöller 1998, p. 651). Most commentators have simply ignored it.

individual A or B or C etc. . . . . . [S]o far as I-hood is concerned it is wholly accidental that *I*, the individual A, am in fact A; and the drive to self-sufficiency should be a drive of I-hood essentially as such, and so is directed not at the self-sufficiency of A [in particular], but instead at the self-sufficiency of reason in general. The self-sufficiency of all reason, as such, is our final end: and thus not the self-sufficiency of the reason of one, insofar as it is individual reason.

Now of course I, A, *am* as my person only insofar as I am A. A is my empirical self: only in it does that drive and that law come to consciousness, and only through A can I be effective in accordance with it, because it is only through [A] that I can be effective at all. A is, for me, the exclusive condition of the causality of the drive . . . .

Although the drive is directed at the self-sufficiency of reason in general it can only be presented *in* the individuals A, B, C, etc. and *through* them; and it is necessarily a matter of complete indifference to me whether I, A, or whether B or C presents it. . . . I will morality in general; whether it be *within* or *outside* of myself is a matter of complete indifference. I will it from myself insofar as it is up to me, and from others insofar as it is up to them; through the one or through the other my end is reached in the same way.

My end is reached, when the other acts *morally*. But he is free, and capable of freely acting immorally. In that case, my end is not reached. Do I not, in that case, have the right and the obligation to disturb the efficacy of his freedom?   (IV: 231–2; cf. GA 4–1: 115)

Fichte's point in the first two paragraphs is to forestall an interpretation of the problem of individuality that (we can assume) he judges likely enough to require forestalling. If the fact that rational agency must be distributed amongst distinct individuals required that the end of independence take the form, for each individual, of the agent-relative end of her *own* independence, then there could arise a conflict between the *ends* of distinct individuals simply *qua* rational individuals. In emphasizing that all agents in fact share the agent-neutral end of the independence of reason wherever it is instantiated, Fichte denies this (cf. also IV: 281–2). So the first thing he wants to rule out is that individuality is a problem because the demands of individual self-interest place rational limitations on the pursuit of what is impartially best. Individuality does not, in other words, make *partiality to self* rational.[54]

In the fourth paragraph, and the first sentence of the fifth, Fichte draws out what he sees as a consequence of the point in the first two: that the reasons agents have to further this end are likewise agent-neutral. If the fact that rational agency must take individual form required that reasons be agent-relative, then even if these were not reasons of self-interest they might nevertheless set individuals rationally at odds with one another.[55] In emphasizing that it is fundamentally a

---

[54] Fichte is not, then, moved by considerations of the sort articulated in e.g. S. Scheffler 1982 in defense of agent-centered prerogatives.

[55] Cf. D. Parfit 1984, pp. 55–62.

matter of indifference (to me as agent) *who* acts on the reasons the moral end gives us, Fichte denies this. My circumstances leave certain ways of furthering the moral end within my power and others within the power of others ('I will it from myself insofar as it is up to me . . .'). But it is as good, morally, from my perspective, that those others act on those reasons as it is that I act on them, in a situation in which not all of us can do so. So the second thing he wants to rule out is the existence of agent-relative reasons even of a moral variety.

This second point is important because it means that there is no place, in Fichte's theory, for what in the contemporary literature are called 'agent-centered restrictions.' These are restrictions on types of action (e.g. lying, intentionally killing) that are uncancellable even in cases where it is known with certainty that one violation (by the agent) now will prevent more than one exactly similar violations (by other agents, on some views even by the same agent) in the future. The rejection of agent-centered restrictions on this conception—along with the refusal to prioritize negative over positive duties, or indeed to recognize any deep distinction between the two categories of duty—is one of the watersheds that is taken to divide consequentialist theories from deontological ones.[56] Fichte's point in the fourth paragraph is therefore among the more important reasons for thinking that his ethical theory is consequentialist in structure.

In fact he remarks a few pages later that 'Who cares only for himself, from a moral point of view, does not care even for himself, for it should be his final end to care for all of humanity. His virtue is no virtue, but something like a servile, reward-seeking egoism' (IV: 234–5; cf. IV: 239). This remark looks very like one standard objection to agent-centered restrictions: that the emphasis on keeping one's own hands clean is an objectionable form of moral narcissism. Fichte argues, here, that a requirement to care differentially about one's own moral virtue *qua* one's own is as little dictated by the fact of individuality as is permission to care differentially about one's own independence *qua* one's own.

In both these ways Fichte's theory differs from Kant's on the interpretations dominant in today's literature—since on those interpretations Kant's theory is said to allow at least limited partiality to one's own well-being and more or less exclusive partiality to one's own moral virtue.

Fichte rules out these options because he takes them to be easy misinterpretations of his worry that individuality presents an apparent contradiction of the moral law with itself. This is a plausible concern, as the existence of agent-relative ends or reasons would indeed threaten to set individuals rationally at odds with one another. His point in the first sentence is that, were either of these the

---

[56] This is one of few points of consensus in this literature, but cf. e.g. D. Cummiskey 1996, ch. 1.

problem, it would be insoluble. But the worry that he actually sees is a different one, finally enunciated in the continuation of the final paragraph:

My end is reached, when the other acts *morally*. But he is free, and capable of freely acting immorally. In that case, my end is not reached. Do I not in that case have the right and the obligation to disturb the efficacy of his freedom?   (IV: 232)

If the answer were 'yes' there would be *no* apparent conflict of morality with itself. The problem arises because Fichte believes the answer must be 'no.'[57] Progress toward independence of nature is accomplished through the expansion of human powers and the suppression or manipulation of natural forces insofar as they threaten rational plans. The problem is that human beings can be at least as destructive as the non-human forces of nature; and Fichte resists the conclusion that the proper approach to them, in that case, is suppression or manipulation.

Why? To answer that question it is not enough, he writes, to appeal to the fact that progress toward material independence relies on all agents' causal efficacy, for by stipulation the situation is one in which the other agent does not (intend to) use his causal powers in a way that would further material independence. Furthering others' efficacy is a general duty, but that general duty cannot be appealed to on its own, here, because what is at issue is precisely an apparent counterexample to its generality.

3.2.3.2 THE PLACE OF RIGHTS IN THE MORAL PROJECT

One clue to the answer comes from the fact that it is clear, in this passage and in other passages that I will discuss in the next two paragraphs, that only the protection of *legal rights* is at issue. Although there is a general negative duty not to be an obstacle to others' free efficacy, and although there is a general positive duty to enhance it by assisting others when one can, these do not appear to be in force here. Fichte does not argue in this passage that I may not try to forestall or counteract the other's efforts in any way whatsoever; nor does he argue that, finding myself in the situation described, I must positively assist the other in his morally repugnant endeavors if I can. (He does not, for instance, foreclose the possibility that I may legitimately seek to distract the other's

---

[57] Notice how Fichte poses the question: do I have 'the right and the obligation' to interfere? He does not leave open the option that one might be neither required nor forbidden to interfere in such a case, because on his view there are no morally indifferent actions, no actions that are permissible but not required (IV: 155, 195). This commitment licenses an inference from 'It is not the case that I am obliged to interfere' to 'I am obliged to not-interfere,' and that is why he takes there to be a single question on the table in the discussion that follows ('Ought I to interfere or not?'). Readers with other commitments might see two questions here ('Am I permitted to interfere, or not? If I am permitted, am I obliged to interfere, or not?').

attention, or to interfere downstream with some process he has set in motion in order to achieve his immoral end, so long as I am not violating his rights in so doing; and he argues in the pages immediately following that I am obliged to try to forestall the action by rationally convincing the person of his error.) What is at issue is only an obligation not to interfere with that part of an agent's free efficacy that is guaranteed by law.

In Fichte's extended discussion of moral duties concerning threats to the life and property of others (IV: 300–10), we learn two important things about that obligation. First, it is in force only if the wrongdoer is acting within his (legal) rights. If he is instead violating my rights or those of a third party, and if the situation is such that the state cannot prevent or later remedy the violation, I am required to interfere, in ways that would constitute rights-violations (harming him physically, even putting his life at risk) were he not breaking the law (IV: 288–9, 301, 305–8; cf. GA 4–1: 135). Second, duties concerning others' rights are not in fact limited to negative duties of non-interference, but instead encompass positive obligations to protect the rights of individuals from violation by third parties. Rights give rise, not to agent-centered restrictions, but to patient-centered constraints whose violation the morally conscientious agent must seek to minimize even where he is not himself the cause of the violations in question.[58]

The question, then, is how rights acquire that status. One possible answer—that rights have a direct moral foundation, that is, that the moral principle, in addition to setting rational agents the end of independence, also sets limits on the pursuit of that end, in the form of individual rights—is ruled out categorically by the texts. Not only does Fichte provide no moral derivation of individual rights in the *System of Ethics*; he has already explained at several points in the *Foundations of Natural Right* that there can be no such derivation: the theory of right is a freestanding branch of practical philosophy, independent of ethics and not derivable from the moral principle (III: 10–11, 13, 54–5). That is why he instructs the reader, both in this section and in the doctrine of duties itself, to insert the results of the *Foundations* into the text of the *System of Ethics* at these points. What rights individuals have is not, on Fichte's view, a question that can be answered from the moral perspective.

Indeed, although Fichte takes rights to have a priori rational foundations in the sense that it is possible to articulate certain a priori *constraints* on possible

---

[58] I disagree, here, with Darwall, who sees these constraints as agent-centered (Darwall 2005, p. 96). I am convinced by arguments to the effect that no patient-focused theory can support agent-centered restrictions which are stronger than the sort of restrictions supported by consequentialism on other grounds (Cf. e.g. J. Brand-Ballard 2004), and it is clear that Fichte's account of right is patient-centered.

regimes of rights, even the *Foundations* itself is not a doctrine of 'natural rights' in the sense at issue in, for example, the *Declaration of the Rights of Man and of the Citizen* of 1789. Fichte denies that there are natural rights in this sense. Rights exist only within a commonwealth, and what rights individuals have depend on the positive law of the commonwealth to which they belong. '[I]n the sense in which people often take the word there is no *natural right*—that is, no rightful relation between human beings is possible except in a commonwealth and under positive laws' (III: 148; cf. 111–12). Individuals who lack membership in some commonwealth (or lose it, for example by being exiled for some crime) lack rights entirely (III: 260, 271, 274–5, 278–80). Morally, Fichte argues in the *System of Ethics*, we ought to be unwilling to live alongside anyone unwilling to join us in a commonwealth, precisely because in that condition he has no rights, and we must always fear we are treating him against his will (IV: 238).

There is, then, no moral analogue or substitute for positive law, on Fichte's theory. Moral concern for individual rights, in situations like the one described at IV: 232, must thus be a concern for their *legal* rights. One consequence of this is that moral concern with individual rights is not a direct concern with the rights themselves, since these have no existence outside of a commonwealth and will vary in profound ways among communities depending on the particular laws they have. The primary object of moral concern is instead the existence of an organized system in which individuals are assigned determinate rights by law. The moral obligation is to act in a way that is consistent with the maintenance of such a system where one exists, and to work toward the instantiation of such a system where one is absent (IV: 234–5, 245).

To answer the question of why, for Fichte, individual rights have the moral status that they do—why they have the power to check our pursuit of the moral end in some cases—we must then answer the question of what the good is, from the moral standpoint, of the existence of such a system. Why are individuals morally obliged to organize themselves in a way that gives them rights, and why are they obliged to support that organization not only negatively, by refraining from violations, but also positively, by acting as stand-in enforcers in extraordinary circumstances?

Interestingly, this is not a question to which the literature on the relation of right to morality in Fichte, or indeed any of the literature on Fichte's *Foundations*, offers a plausible answer. In fact some prominent accounts of the relation of right and morality in Fichte rule out even the possibility of an answer. On Neuhouser's proposal, for example, the good of the commonwealth, its function, and the function of the individual rights that structure it, is the furthering of a particular end that is not a part of the moral end, but is a purely political end: the end of individuality (in a substantive sense that subsumes protection of individual differences in tastes, goals, and beliefs).[59]

There is an obvious textual problem with this proposal, namely that Fichte never actually speaks of a 'value' of individuality or of individuality as an 'end.'[60] End-language rather than value-language is what we would expect, since Fichte rarely uses the language of value and favors the language of ends. But Fichte treats individuality as neither. Instead he treats it as a form of determinacy (just as he treats embodiment as a form of determinacy) and the question is always how the end of independence is made determinate by the fact that the agent is an individual (or embodied).

But quite apart from the textual problem, Neuhouser's interpretation would leave Fichte with no answer to the question posed at the end of the long quotation from IV: 231–2 reproduced in §3.2.3.1 above. That question is why individual rights have a moral status that allows them to place constraints on our pursuit of moral ends. Appeal to a distinct political value, one that by hypothesis has no place in Fichte's moral theory, cannot in principle answer this question.[61]

---

[59] 'Implicit in Fichte's later [sc. Jena] position is the view that the political realm has its own distinctive end, the fostering of citizens' *individuality*, whose value is not simply derivative of the value of moral autonomy' (Neuhouser 1994, p. 158; cf. pp. 163, 174–6).

[60] This is why Neuhouser describes Fichte's reliance on the value of individuality as 'implicit' in the quotation in footnote 59.

[61] Of course Neuhouser does not claim that it does; and he goes on to acknowledge that his interpretation raises a problem of systematicity for Fichte's practical philosophy (Neuhouser 1994, p. 158). He suggests that problem can be solved by appeal to the overarching notion of self-positing subjectivity at the foundation of Fichte's system. But the problem is more acute than he acknowledges, for if his interpretation of the independence claim is correct, the demands of right and the demands of morality come into all-things-considered conflict in every case in which someone proposes to act immorally and others can prevent this only by violating their rights. Surely such cases are exceedingly common. This sort of systematic conflict would threaten to render Fichte's practical philosophy internally incoherent. That it is incoherent in just this way was Hegel's charge in his *Differenzschrift* (G.W.F. Hegel 1986, vol. 2, pp. 80–94); and it is reiterated in some form in much contemporary secondary literature (cf. L. Siep 1979, pp. 26–35; R. Williams 2006). One way around the difficulty has been to interpret the *System of Ethics* in a way that restricts the scope of moral duty so as to exclude the actions that are governed by the principle of right, for example by taking morality to concern only the manner of deliberation, or to demand only conscientiousness or authenticity in action, and to have nothing to say about *which* (external) actions are to be performed. This seems to me one upshot of Neuhouser's 'individualist' interpretation of substantive self-determination in the *System of Ethics* (F. Neuhouser 1990, ch. 4), and it is implicit in his account of how the claims of the different branches of practical philosophy can be reconciled. Clarke has made this argument explicitly, writing: 'the sciences of right and morality have discrete, separate domains.... [The domain of the science of morality] is the "inner" domain of conscience which Fichte regards as cognitively inaccessible to other rational agents,' and the domain of right, Clarke writes (citing III: 55), encompasses only that which is externalized in the sensible world (J. Clarke 2009, p. 366). This seems to me a faulty inference from the passage at III: 55, where Fichte writes:

> Rational beings enter into interaction with one another only through actions, externalizations of their freedom in the sensible world. The concept of right therefore

In fact, though, Fichte believes not only that people can have rights to perform immoral actions, but also that others have a *moral* obligation to respect those rights. What is the basis of that obligation? I will argue in the next section that the good of the commonwealth, from a moral point of view, is that it is the presupposition of every form of coordinated action. The primary mechanism of coordination in the commonwealth is the assignment of rights to individuals. This is why rights are morally important. The points I make in the next section will be familiar to readers acquainted with the literature on consequentialism and coordination. They have never been applied to the *Foundations*; but once the importance of coordination in a theory like Fichte's is brought into focus, we find not only the answer to this question, but also the solution to a pair of perennial puzzles about Fichte's philosophy of right.[62]

3.2.3.3 COORDINATION

Imagine a group of individuals rationally benevolent according to Fichte's moral theory as just outlined; and consider a typical coordination problem members of such a group might face. One of them is a farmer who would like to raise the frame of a new outbuilding. With four sets of hands this can be done in a day. With less than four, given available technology, it cannot be done at all. The farmer's three neighbors, motivated by the end of furthering material independence in whatever ways available to them, are happy to help. Each believes that the frame-raising is more worthwhile than the other work the four of them could do, each on her own, on any given day. However all do have other useful work to do, and each would like to avoid going to their neighbor's farm, on a given day, unless all of the others will also show up on that day. Now imagine one of the neighbors, on a given morning, aware of the situation, unable to communicate with the others, and unable to discern anything special about the present day or any other that would make it the

concerns only that which is externalized in the sensible world. What has no causality there, but remains in the mind alone, belongs before another tribunal, namely that of morality. It is pointless therefore to speak of a right of freedom of thought, of freedom of conscience, and the like.

If the moral principle and the principle of right indeed covered non-overlapping domains, that would in fact eliminate the possibility of conflict between them. But that they do not overlap cannot be inferred from the passage Clarke cites, in which Fichte says *not* that the moral principle does not govern external action, but *only* that right does not govern what remains in the mind (and so thought, religious belief, and the like). In any case, the text of the *System of Ethics* rules out this strategy for reconciling these two sets of demands.

[62] What is at issue in the sections that follow is the coordination of action. To the coordination of opinion—what occupies Fichte in the remainder of §18—I will return in §3.2.3.5 below.

obvious day to raise the outbuilding.[63] What does Fichte's moral principle, as described so far, direct her to do?

The answer is that it does not, all on its own, direct her to do anything. In cases of this type, in which the efforts of multiple individuals are non-additive, what each individual (objectively) ought to do depends upon what others do.[64] Now it is easy to see that the efforts of multiple individuals are non-additive in the case of many impediments to independence in the material sense. Against many natural threats the efforts of a single individual are strictly pointless; and many morally important projects can be accomplished only by the coordinated action of some group of people.[65] Fichte points this out when discussing the moral justification for the division of labor in society, in the *System of Ethics*:

Each individual is commanded to promote the independence of reason as much as he can. Now, if every individual does, in this regard, whatever first occurs to him, or whatever seems most necessary to him, many things will happen in manifold ways, and much [will] not [happen] at all. The effects of the actions of several will mutually hinder and cancel one another, and the systematic furthering of the final end of reason will not take place. But it absolutely ought to take place according to the command of the moral law. It is therefore a *duty*, for everyone who grasps the obstacle just described (and everyone who reflects even a little grasps it quite easily), to remedy it. But it can be remedied only if the various individuals divide among themselves the various things that must happen for the promotion of this end, each assuming a particular portion for all the others, and conversely in a different respect giving his own over to them. Such an arrangement can arise only through a convention, through the assembly of many with the aim of [accomplishing] such a division. It is the duty of everyone who grasps this to bring about an assembly of the sort described.   (IV: 258)

Fichte here describes the social division of labor as a conventional solution to a set of coordination problems (conventional not in the narrow Lewisean sense, but in the somewhat broader sense of being a stable solution to a coordination problem that admits more than one possible solution[66]). Morally motivated agents will recognize that they have problems of this sort and must find a way to solve them, collectively.

They cannot rely on their moral principle to do this work, because an objective consequentialist principle, directed at individuals, is indeterminate in such cases.

---

[63] I assume not only no explicit agreement but also no difference between the days that would be salient to all of the neighbors because, as Schelling has shown, such clues can replace explicit agreement in many such games of coordination (cf. T. Schelling 1957, pp. 20–2).

[64] Cf. D. Regan 1980.

[65] No parallel claim will be true of formal independence: at the moment of deliberation, every individual is the sole custodian of his own conscience. This is indeed the upshot of the remainder of §18: there can be no regime of right where conscience is concerned.

[66] Cf. D. Lewis 1969.

Neither it, nor a generalized principle or rule derived from it, so long as it is directed at individuals and specifies only actions with no provisions for coordination, can guide agents in such circumstances.[67] Generalized principles or rules (of the sort offered by utilitarian generalization or rule-utilitarianism) are not sufficient to deal with such cases, in part because not all coordination problems are solved, as they are in the barn-raising case, by each person's doing the same thing that all of the others do. Some are solved only if each person does something different from what each of the others does.[68] Still others are solved only if individuals' efforts are distributed in more complex ways.[69] No moral principle directed at individuals can solve the various coordination problems that moral agents face. For that, they need conventions of the sort Fichte describes.

Note that, although objective consequentialist theories are indeterminate in such cases when directed at individuals, they may be perfectly determinate when directed at a group.[70] The neighbors (together) ought to raise the frame, since that is the best use of their (collective) time. The moral community (together) ought to promote the independence of reason as much as it can. The problem is that the group is not, or not yet, an agent. The agency is spread across several independent loci of practical deliberation and causal efficacy: the individuals. This is the significance of Fichte's claim that individuality introduces a distinctive dimension of limitation essential to rational agents. Coordination is a moral problem because, and only because, rational agents are individuals.[71]

But coordination is not a problem confined to specific tasks like barn-raising, nor to any other means toward or component of the moral end. The most

---

[67] This is what D. Regan 1980 is taken to have established. As Regan and others emphasize, coordination problems like the one described do not show that unsupplemented act-utilitarianism cannot be consistent with the best outcome in all cases—only that it cannot guarantee the best outcome. Cf. Regan 1980, chs. 3 and 4.

[68] This fact lies at the basis of a well-known class of counterexamples to Kant's formula of universal law. See, e.g. B. Herman 1993, ch. 7, p. 138 for a couple of canonical examples.

[69] For examples, see D. Parfit 1984, p. 53; D. Regan 1980, ch. 2. See D. Regan 1980, ch. 11 for a discussion of the limits of his own cooperative utilitarianism in dealing with this kind of case.

[70] Cf. D. Parfit 1984, pp. 72–3 and note 41 at pp. 510–11.

[71] That is, it is necessary because 'one of the basic facts about the world is that there is a multiplicity of moral agents' (D. Regan 1980, p. 144). Fichte does not use the language of 'coordination' in the *Foundations* (instead he uses the language of 'coexistence'); but he describes individuality as introducing a problem of coordination already in the *Lectures on the Scholar's Vocation*:

> The social drive…is a drive toward *reciprocal action* (*Wechselwirkung*), *mutual* influence, *mutual* give and take, *mutual* action and passivity: not a drive to pure causality, not to pure activity, toward which the other would have to relate only passively. The drive is to discover *free rational* beings outside of us and to enter into community with them; it is not a drive to *subordination*, as in the world of material things but a drive to *coordination*. (VI: 308)

fundamental coordination problem that rational agents who are individuals must solve is the problem of dividing the space of possible activity amongst themselves in a way that keeps each from attempting to do the same thing in the same place at the same time as any of the others. This is a problem that arises as soon as agents engaged in pursuing any rationally formed plans whatsoever have to live alongside other agents so engaged. Fichte calls it the 'problem of right.' His view is that solutions to more complex arrangements of individual actions, such as those involved in the division of labor, are possible only on the basis of the arrangement (the commonwealth) that solves this most fundamental problem.

Since they will need a mechanism for solving this most fundamental coordination problem, morally motivated Fichtean agents will need to be members of a commonwealth:

The agreement [concerning] how humans may mutually act upon one another, that is, the agreement concerning *their communal rights* in the sensible world, is called the *social contract* [*Staatsvertrag*]; and the community that has come to [such] an agreement [*die übereingekommen ist*] [is called] the state. It is an absolute duty of conscience to unite with others in a state. Whoever does not will this, cannot be tolerated in society, because one cannot enter into community with him with a clear conscience: because, since he has not declared how he wants to be treated, one must always fear treating him against his will and right.   (IV: 237–8; cf. III: 10–11, 54, 88; IV: 234–5, 245, 258)

The mechanism for solving the problem of existing alongside one another as rationally planning agents who are individuals is the assignment and enforcement of rights. This is the explanation for the moral importance of rights, and so of the obligation to respect others' rights, to protect those rights from violation by third parties, and to create rights where they do not yet exist.

The science of right is the science of the a priori rational constraints on possible stable, law-governed solutions to the problem of right. Its content is the set of normative principles governing the interaction of rational individuals with one another simply *qua* rational individuals (that is, the rational principles of strategic interaction[72] in the most general case, in which they are not constrained by existing political institutions). To say that it is independent of moral philosophy is to say no more than that those principles cannot be derived from

---

[72] By 'strategic' here and elsewhere I mean only that the situation is one in which what each ought to do depends on his expectations about what the others will do, which in turn depends on the others' expectations about what he will do, and so on. There can be strategic situations, in this sense, also where players' interests are perfectly aligned. Cf. Schelling 1958, p. 205: 'It is to be stressed that the pure-co-ordination game is a *game of strategy* in the strict technical sense. It is a behavior situation in which each player's best choice of action depends on the action he expects the other to take, which he knows depends, in turn, on the other's expectations of his own.' This will be important for what I say in §3.2.3.5 below.

the normative principles that govern rational choice in non-strategic situations (which, for Fichte, derive from the moral principle).

This is not a surprising or controversial view. Yet it suffices, all on its own, to explain Fichte's claim—much discussed in the literature on the *Foundations*—that the science of right is freestanding, independent of the science of morality and not derivable from it (III: 10–11, 13, 54–5). We are offered, in the existing literature on the *Foundations*, two alternative explanations for that claim, and it is worth taking a moment to discuss them here.

The first, due to Renaut, appeals to the fact that, for the Fichte of the Jena period, the problem of right must be solved without assuming the moral motivation of potential citizens.[73] Renaut sees an evolution of Fichte's views on this score between the 1793 *Contributions to the Correction of the Public's Judgment concerning the Revolution in France* (VI: 39–288) (in which Fichte treated political philosophy as a branch of ethics) and the 1796 *Foundations*. The change was motivated, Renaut argues, by a realization Fichte owed to Kant's *Toward Perpetual Peace* (1795), in which Kant wrote that the problem of right must be soluble 'even for a nation of devils.'[74]

Fichte does emphasize in the *Foundations* that the reasons agents have for entering into a commonwealth cannot be exhausted by their moral reasons for doing so (III: 44, 50, 148), and that even individuals motivated by self-interest alone must have reason to enter into a state and abide by its laws (III: 150–2). Likewise the discipline of politics (the applied science corresponding to the science of right, whose task is to make progress toward a more just constitution, starting from actual conditions) 'assumes only rational self-interest, without which a human being is not even capable of living among others' (XI: 123).

This is because, as Fichte explains both in the *Foundations* (III: 148) and in the *System of Ethics* (IV: 233–53), moral virtue is a result of cultivation, not at all a natural state of human beings. But cultivation is possible only through human interaction and so within some sort of society; and among the imperfectly virtuous, society can exist only within a state. (I will discuss Fichte's reasons for this last claim in §3.2.3.4 below.) This means that political philosophy cannot assume motivations exclusive to morally virtuous agents.

Now, Fichte's radically anti-Rousseauian view that the 'natural' human condition is one of ignorance and vice and that cultivation of human beings in society improves them morally is first systematically laid out in the fifth of the

---

[73] A. Renaut 1992; cf. F. Neuhouser 1994.

[74] I. Kant 1900–, 8: 366; I. Kant 1996a, p. 335. Kant's claim was a response to J. Erhard's 1795 'Apologie des Teufels.'

Lectures on the Scholar's Vocation (VI: 335–46); and since these were published already in 1794, that aspect of the view can owe nothing to *Toward Perpetual Peace*.[75] But the real worry for Renaut's interpretation is this: the mere fact that the motivations of unregenerate egoists must be accounted for in a normative account of law does not, all on its own, entail that principles of right cannot be derived from moral principles. For the question of motivation is distinct from the question of content: people may very well follow a single set of laws from either moral or prudential motives.[76] Indeed this is exactly what Fichte thinks they must do, as the existence of morally motivated people alongside egoists in the commonwealth (both groups motivated to obey the same law, even if for different reasons) is required for moral cultivation to take place. So a change in mind about the derivability of right from ethics cannot be explained *solely* by the breadth of the clientèle on which the principle of right must have a motivational grip.

Instead, as Neuhouser points out, Fichte clearly takes the independence of right from morality to derive from the nature of the principle of right itself, not the nature of citizens' motivations, as Fichte explains in this passage (which echoes Kant's language in *Toward Perpetual Peace*, to which Fichte also directs the reader):

A right is plainly something one can exercise or not; it follows therefore from a law that is purely permissive.... It is simply impossible to see how a permissive law should be derivable from an unconditionally demanding one, and therefore [to see how it should be derivable from] the moral law, which extends to every [action].   (III: 13)

Now, the obvious response to this line of thought, for someone who wanted to defend the derivability of right from the moral principle, is to insist that rights *do* take the form of universal commands—not commands directed at the individual whose rights are in question, indeed, but commands directed at other individuals. This is a response we find already in the literature to which Fichte is responding.[77] For an individual *a* to hold a right is just for all *other* individuals to be prohibited from interfering with *a* in defined ways. Since the prohibition on violating others' rights is, so construed, 'unconditionally demanding' and 'extends to every [action],'

---

[75] The idea that coordination is a distinctive practical problem also has its first articulation in that work—not, as Renaut supposes, only in 1796 (cf. Renaut 1986, pp. 236–43).

[76] For example, the principle of equal division among (rough) equals of a resource to which none has an antecedent claim has traditionally been seen as having an ethical ground (it is part of Aristotle's explanation of the virtue of justice, for example). But it has also been cashed out as a purely prudential principle in certain strategic interactions (cf. Skyrms 1996, ch. 1). Kant's example of the honest shopkeeper in the *Groundwork* is likewise supposed to be an example of a policy that can appeal to either moral or prudential interests (I. Kant 1900–, 4: 397; I. Kant 1996a, p. 53).

[77] We find it, for example, in K. Heydenreich 1794, pp. 110–11.

the explanation Fichte offers in this passage—taken on its own—seems to fall short, as Neuhouser points out.[78]

With what should we supplement it? Neuhouser argues that we should supplement it with the view that the political realm has an end distinct from the moral end: the end of promoting citizens' individuality.[79] This, then, is the second proposed explanation for the independence thesis. I have already described the textual and systematic difficulties it raises. Here let me just point out that if we supplement the passage at III: 13 with the understanding of the limitation of the moral principle I have offered in this section, it makes perfect sense even without the assumption that the political realm serves an end distinct from the moral one. For if by 'prohibited' we mean 'morally prohibited' and if what I have said in this section is true, what I have called the 'obvious' response is unhelpful. The only moral prohibition yielded by the obvious response is the prohibition on violating a's rights. But that in no way tells us anything about what rights in general, or a's rights in particular, are—since the sphere of actions permissible to a as a matter of right is not derivable from any moral imperative.

So we must conclude that right is independent of ethics not simply because the principle of right must appeal to a broader clientèle, nor because right and ethics have distinct, potentially opposed ends, nor (as Clarke has argued) because 'the sciences of right and morality have discrete, separate domains.'[80] (If they did, there could be no even *prima facie* conflict of the sort Fichte describes at IV: 232.) Right must be (able to be) a *part* of ethics. Fichte's claim is only that it is not a part that ethics is able to produce from its own principle.

3.2.3.4 FICHTE'S THEORY OF THE SOCIAL CONTRACT

Fichte describes the problem of right as a technical one in the most literal sense: solving it is a matter of engineering an arrangement that makes possible the unimpeded exercise of external causality on the part of multiple agents who are able to interfere with one another and who have an interest in avoiding such interference, an arrangement that can be implemented by multilateral agreement among a group of agents none of whom is able to impose any such arrangement unilaterally, and that is compatible with constraints imposed by the physical, rational, and communicative capacities of those agents. In this section I outline what I take to be the core features of such an arrangement, on Fichte's account.

---

[78]   F. Neuhouser 1994, p. 172.

[79]   'One's rights to those actions that morality condemns must be understood as serving some end other than that of moral autonomy, and it is an account of just this end that Fichte's conception of the person is supposed to provide' (F. Neuhouser 1994, p. 173).

[80]   J. Clarke 2009.

Since by hypothesis not all potential co-citizens are perfectly morally motivated, the technology that solves the problem of right must be one that functions for individuals with a wide range of ends. But Fichte does not think the problem of right is soluble for just any population in just any circumstances with just any interests and rational capacities. Agents who are potential co-citizens must have the degree of rationality required to direct actions with a view to future consequences;[81] and they must share certain fundamental interests.[82]

These are the interests described in the section of the *Foundations* on 'original right,' where Fichte outlines two sorts of claims that rational agents inevitably make on one another when they interact: the claim to bodily inviolability, and the claim to 'original' property. Neither of these claims is a claim to a right in the strict sense; instead they are articulations of the most fundamental interests of rational agents simply as such, interests that structure the problem of right and so to constrain solutions to it: 'An original right is...a mere *fiction* [*eine blosse* Fiction], but one that must, for the sake of the science, necessarily be thought' (III: 112).

The body, as we have seen, is defined by Fichte as that part of the world in which the will is immediately causally efficacious (III: 56–9; cf. IV: 214–15). Since all mediated causal efficacy is possible only on the basis of immediate causal efficacy, an agent with an interest in her causal efficacy has a privileged interest in the unimpeded exercise of her immediate causality. This is a defeasible, but very general, moral interest reflected in the fundamental division of duties in the *System of Ethics*; and it is also a defeasible, but very general, prudential interest. The agent presupposed in the *Foundations* is assumed to have this interest, and the original claim to the inviolability of the body as a matter of right is based upon it. But the demand itself is intrinsic to rational agency quite apart from the rules that structure the relations between individuals and so quite apart from the relation of right. It is part of original right because it is a demand rational agents cannot fail to make concerning a capacity with which other agents can interfere.

---

[81] Individuals at any of the stages of moral development Fichte describes in *System of Ethics* §16 (IV: 178–91)—beyond the first, in which behavior is basically instinctual—must be able to enter into a state of right and rationally abide by its requirements.

[82] It is important to see that Fichte does assume some constitutive ends of individuals capable of citizenship. Remarkably, this has been denied (cf. M. Baur 2006). But Fichte could construct no science of right without some such assumptions, because a commonwealth functions by structuring incentives in a way that produces voluntary compliance (at least enough of the time). It is likewise important that the agents that figure in the *Foundations* differ from those described in the *System of Ethics* only in that the constitutive ends attributed to the former are more spare. This also has been denied (cf. F. Neuhouser 1994, pp. 162–4; F. Neuhouser 2000, p. xxiv). But if participation in a state of right required interests not shared between morally motivated and solely prudentially motivated individuals, the moral developmental function Fichte attributes to society could not be fulfilled by it.

Property is defined by Fichte as the fixed set of action possibilities under an agent's exclusive and enduring control, in which she may exercise her mediated causal efficacy without threat of interference by other agents (with the added proviso that it be sufficient to provide her means of subsistence). That is, instead of viewing property as a relation between an individual and an object or set of objects, Fichte views property as a relation between an individual and a set of possible actions (III: 210).

Initially a sphere for his freedom as such is allotted to him, and nothing more. This sphere contains certain objects, determined by the freedom allotted to him. *His property right in the objects extends as far as the allotted freedom, and no farther.* He acquires them exclusively for a particular use; and he has the right to exclude everyone only from this use, and from everything that would hinder this use. The object of the property contract is a determinate activity.   (III: 210)

One's property, then, is one's entitlement to engage unimpeded in certain activities. Property includes control over objects (such as a piece of land or a set of tools) insofar as such control is necessary for engaging in those activities; but the control over those objects extends only to their use in those activities; and skills, access to raw materials, an economic niche, and the like are also part of an individual's property.[83]

The original interest in property is more complex than the original interest in bodily integrity, insofar as there are many ways in which the possession of a fixed sphere of action possibilities may be valuable to a rational agent simply as such. But most fundamentally, as Fichte explains in *Foundations* §11 and as we saw in §3.2.2.3, the interest in property is an interest in being able to construct the sort of complex long-term plans of action that are characteristic of rational agents, and to do so rationally.

The chief interest that is met by any property arrangement—in the ability to plan—gives rise to a presumption in favor of a property regime in which control is exclusive and permanent, because both permanence and exclusivity facilitate planning. But individuals who cannot maintain themselves in existence have no interest in planning, and so, Fichte argues, a constraint on any property

---

[83] For example, the holder of a right to exclusive use of a piece of land for hunting or farming may not prevent people from crossing this piece of land or using it in ways that do no harm to his hunting or farming activities (III: 197, 217–18). His right to use the land exclusively for one use cannot be exchanged by unilateral action for a right to use it for the other (III: 211, 214). He may, if he has a right to use a piece of land for agriculture, also have a right against, e.g. upstream diversions of water that would disrupt that activity. He will not simply thereby also have mineral rights to the land he farms (III: 218, 221–2), nor the right to leave it unused (III: 219) or to damage it in a way that renders it unsuitable for future use (a concern explicitly addressed only in the case of livestock (III: 226–7) but presumably generalizable).

arrangement is that it must allow each individual to survive by activity within the sphere allotted to them. This requirement may require redistribution should conditions change (III: 212–15, 218, 233, 259, 257 *et passim*; cf. *The Closed Commercial State* III: 402–5), and that in turn places restrictions on the permanence of any given property arrangement.

Subsistence for all is not offered by Fichte as the justification for the institution of property, as we have seen. Still Fichte takes subsistence to be a requirement on any property division, because physical maintenance is one of the fundamental interests that embodied rational agents have simply as such, and no individual can be presumed willing to uphold her end of a multilateral agreement whose purpose is to render consistent the free activity of multiple agents, when doing so would itself preclude the possibility of any free activity at all in her case.

> All property right is grounded on a contract of all with all, whose content is: all of us retain this [*sc.* what is ours] on the condition that we leave you what is yours. Thus as soon as someone cannot live from his labor, that which is absolutely his has not been left to him, and so the contract is entirely cancelled with respect to him, and he is from that moment on no longer bound by right to recognize the property of any person.   (III: 213; cf. III: 195)

Others have like claims to derive sustenance from their allotted sphere of activity, and his may likewise be curtailed to accommodate their need (III: 213). That is, the property contract is subject to renegotiation whenever rational multilateral buy-in can no longer be sustained, and the permanence of anyone's allotment is relative to that constraint.[84]

---

[84] All of this concerns property insofar as it is used in economic activity: property in land, labor power, skills, or tools, for example. Fichte also recognizes the legitimacy of claims to properly private property. Such property—what Fichte calls 'absolute' property (III: 219, 237–60 *passim*)—has several features that distinguish it from the 'relative' property that figures in economic activity. First, it is initially the product of the person's own economic activity (III: 219) (though it can be passed on through gifts (III: 257) or—if positive law permits this—through testament (III: 257–9)). It consists in goods, or wealth, of the sort that can in principle be kept on one's person or in one's house. 'House' is a technical term to designate a private sphere entirely exempted from public control or intrusion, and which can consist of one's rented room, a storage area for personal items in one's place of employment, one's baggage, or the like (III: 242).

> My house stands immediately under the protection and guarantee of the state, and thereby immediately does everything contained within it. The state guarantees it against violent intrusion. But the state does not and should not know what is in it. The individual objects, as such, therefore stand under my own protection and my own absolute dominion, as does everything I do within my house—assuming that the effects of what I do remain within its walls.   (III: 242)

But goods and wealth constituting 'absolute' property are entitled to such protection only insofar as they are not used economically. In a merchant's house, trade goods are not beyond the supervisory reach of the state (III: 244). Should one choose to trade one's absolute property for relative property— say, a part of one's inheritance for the license to practice a certain trade, or the use of a piece of

One additional constraint that Fichte at some points describes as applying to the property contract is likewise based in part on the fact that any property agreement will be the result of a process of negotiation. This is the presumption in favor of equality. Fichte argues that, given certain assumptions—that there is a fixed 'sum of possible freedom,' that each would want for themselves as much freedom as possible, and that each has an antecedently equal claim to possession of any item—it is plausible to think that people would agree only on an equal distribution of spheres of possible action:

If a million human beings are together with one another, each individual will want for himself as much freedom as possible. But if one were to unite the will of all into one concept, as in one will, the same sum of possible freedom would be divided into equal parts, if the aim is that all should be free together and that therefore the freedom of each should be limited by the freedom of the others.   (III: 106–7; cf. III: 127–8, 192, 195)[85]

Of course he also recognizes that the sum of possible freedom is not fixed in advance, but instead depends in part on how the division itself is arranged. Right divides a space of freedoms, and in dividing it usually expands it; but different regimes expand it in different directions and to different degrees, and some may even contract it. Dropping the fixed-sum assumption would lead Fichte to accept that departures from equality will often be justified by the aim of each to get for himself as much external freedom as possible. This is just what we find him arguing in the third of the *Lectures on the Scholar's Vocation*, where he defends the division of labor, and the resulting inequalities in the development of individual capacities and opportunities, by appeal to its utility in advancing the level of culture of humankind as a whole, and to the fact that such advances are communicated among *Stände* in a way that makes all, in the end, more free (VI: 312–23). The same will not be true of departures from sufficiency, and this may explain why sufficiency plays a greater role in Fichte's discussion of constraints on property arrangements—especially in the part of the *Foundations* that deals with applications—than does equality.[86]

---

agricultural land—the transaction must take place under state supervision (III: 255–6). The buyer of a piece of relative property must be in a position to use it (to have the relevant expertise), and can be constrained by the state to use it (III: 256). Further, the proceeds of the sale cannot be considered the absolute property of the seller in the proper sense if the relative property sold was her only source of livelihood. If that is the case, the state must intervene to ensure either that the seller retains some right to the further use of the item or, if not, that the proceeds are invested in the means to pursue another activity sufficient to support the seller (III: 256). Relative property can be passed to heirs by testament only in case positive law permits this and conditional upon the provision that all must be able to earn their living from the relative property in their possession (III: 257–9).

[85] As an empirical matter, this assumption seems to be correct. Cf. B. Skyrms 1996, ch. 1 and R. Sugden 2004, ch. 4.

[86] For more discussion of the extent of Fichte's egalitarianism, see N. Nomer 2005 and D. James 2011.

Like the original claim to bodily integrity, the original claim to property is intrinsic to rational agency quite apart from the rules that structure the relations between individuals and so quite apart from the relation of right. But where an agent coexists with other agents this interest in control over the environment becomes an interest in rights against others' possible interference. It is the inevitability and legitimacy of this concern that makes property an object of moral duties in the *System of Ethics* (cf. IV: 291–308) as well as of rights in the *Foundations*.

Property differs from bodily integrity on Fichte's view in that the former, but not the latter, is possible only by explicit collective agreement. Individuals have no need to negotiate the answer to the question of whose will is to have immediate causal efficacy in which body. So if a group of agents wills a state of affairs in which the immediate causal efficacy of each is unconstrained by the mediated causal efficacy of others, the only thing they need, apart from that will itself, is the ability to recognize other rational agents' bodies as such. Fichte argues that rational agents invariably have this ability (III: 74–82). This does not mean that there is nothing conventional about the notion or institutionalization of bodily inviolability, only that the conventional aspect of these rights is confined to the understanding of 'inviolability' and does not extend to the distribution of spheres once that meaning has been fixed.

Property rights, by contrast, are entirely conventional, since there is no naturally privileged connection between an agent and any particular outer sphere of possible activity. Such a connection is not forged by labor (III: 116n, 219); nor is it forged by intention alone, since two agents may independently form incompatible intentions involving the same activity (III: 124–6). Instead it is forged by the first and most fundamental element of the social contract, a multilateral agreement about the division of action possibilities among agents that Fichte calls the 'property contract.'

However, although such an agreement is necessary for the solution to the problem of right, it is not alone sufficient. The ends motivating original rights claims require not a mutual noninterference agreement, but instead the reasonable expectation of actual mutual noninterference; and Fichte argues that among agents of the sort he assumes in the *Foundations* the former does not suffice for the latter. Some will, by hypothesis, be moved by prudential considerations alone, and for these there will be gains to be had from some violations. But even agents fully committed to the agreement can be expected to make some mistakes. Violations are inevitable, and Fichte argues that an unenforced multilateral agreement could not survive these (III: 97–100, 137–9).[87]

---

[87] An unenforced agreement, he reasons, would rely on mutual trust; but trust would be undermined by violations, and could not be re-established in the absence of some coercive

What is required for the security and stability of the property agreement is an arrangement institutionalizing what Fichte calls the 'right of coercion' (III: 95–103, 137). Such an arrangement would, by threat of sanctions, eliminate any motive for violation (III: 141–2, 150–87 *passim*).[88] Fichte's assumptions about constitutive interests and minimal rational capacities enter here, again, as presuppositions of the possibility of any such incentive system. In considering how a right of coercion could be implemented, Fichte first rules out the possibility that each dispute could be adjudicated and remedied by the parties to that dispute themselves (III: 96–102, 146–9). To leave enforcement to the one whose rights are violated or to the violator or to both in conjunction would leave at least one of the parties a judge in her own case, and would typically leave no one with both the will and the power to enforce a remedy (III: 146–7).[89] The application of a law of coercion to a given case would require the intervention of some third party who would act as judge and enforcer (III: 101). A multilateral agreement to serve as that third party for one another where required would be a 'protection contract.'

Some contract of this second variety is required for the stability of the first, property, contract; but Fichte goes on to argue that such a contract is impossible in a state of nature (III: 148–9), and that it would differ in this respect from a

enforcement mechanism (III: 97–100, 137–9). The reason Fichte offers for thinking that this specific situation is one in which trust could not be re-established is that re-establishing it would require an infinite series of actions as evidence that the violator does not intend future violations. How are we to understand this? Here it is important to bear in mind the structure of interaction Fichte is describing. It one in which there is (at least sometimes) an incentive for an individual to renege on the agreement, and everyone knows this, but there is (as yet) *no* mechanism for punishment or reparation in place (not even a unilaterally applicable mechanism like tit-for-tat). Such a structure is one in which a self-interested agent not committed to abiding by his promise could be expected to renege (at least sometimes). The initial violation conveys important information, namely that the violator's commitment to keeping his word is not *always* stronger than self-interest where these conflict: that he has not made abiding by the agreement 'a universal law for himself' (III: 97). In saying that trust can never be restored in such a situation, Fichte is simply saying that this information, once conveyed, cannot be taken back by any finite chain of subsequent behavior on the part of the violator. It is very important to understand, though, that Fichte is here describing a situation in which reciprocity is not reinforced by any punishment of violators. Punishment is the province of the 'law of coercion,' which he is about to introduce.

[88] An institutionalization of the right of coercion would not be an arrangement that would physically prevent all possible violations, since that would be inconsistent with the purpose of the arrangement: a set of individuals confined to cages, however large, would not be 'coexisting as free' (III: 92–3). Where actual coercive intervention takes place, right has (by definition) been suspended (III: 260–85). Instead it would be an arrangement that would structure individuals' interactions by expectations of reward or punishment. Fichte describes a deterrent mechanism that would ensure ('with mechanical necessity' (III: 141–2, 150–87 *passim*)) that the 'opposite' of the violator's intended end would be the actual result of a violation.

[89] Fichte worries both that, in the ordinary case, the violator is in a stronger position than the victim (and so immune to the other's efforts to extract reparation), and that, where this is not the case, the victim will be liable to exact more compensation than the offense merits.

non-binding multilateral property agreement, which would merely be fatally unstable, but not strictly impossible, in a state of nature.

He argues that a protection agreement would require positive performance (righting wrongs done to others) rather than the mere noninterference required by the property contract (III: 148). This part of the text is not transparent, and the positive/negative performance language Fichte uses suggests an action/omission distinction for which he provides no argument and that has no obvious place in his larger view. But the explanation he goes on to offer suggests that the problem is instead that the protection contract would require agents to incur costs, and to do so intentionally and therefore knowingly. The mere noninterference required by the property contract could in principle be cost-free, or its (opportunity) costs unnoticed. Adherence could even happen accidentally, in the case in which no two people's plans ever happen to be jointly unfeasible (III: 148).[90] But the fulfillment of a protection contract could never be cost-free, and parties to it could never be ignorant of its costs.

He then points out that a simple multilateral protection contract would require that different parties perform their services to one another at different times, since it would extremely rarely be the case that the parties to such an agreement would play the roles of protected and protector simultaneously (III: 198–9). He reasons that no one motivated solely by considerations of maximizing his own individual well-being could be expected to repay past protection with (costly) present protection; and no one who assumed his fellows so motivated would provide protection to begin with, for he would know he could expect no repayment (III: 199). The result would be that no protection would ever be provided, and Fichte concludes that a protection contract by multilateral agreement would be 'intrinsically void' (III: 200).[91]

The stability of a property arrangement requires a third, 'unification' contract, whose (sole) function is to make it possible for the parties to bind themselves to the fulfillment of the protection contract. Each individual contributes to the constitution of a coercive power distinct from each of them individually: the coercive power of all of them together, exercised by a state apparatus (III: 201). Where no one knows in advance who will benefit from, or be harmed by, the exercise of this power, it is possible for each to view entry into it, and their contribution upon entry, to be in their own self-interest (III: 202)—as in the

---

[90] This is in fact the only case in which the maintenance of an unenforced property contract can be firmly counted on: when it imposes no costs, or at least no costs that they are aware of, on the parties to it (III: 148). Its instability is due to the rarity of that situation.

[91] The situation described looks like the familiar inability of transparent rational egoists to make certain agreements, in the absence of an external enforcement mechanism. Cf. D. Parfit 1984, p. 7.

aggregate it is. It is this unification contract that brings them out of a state of nature and into a commonwealth.

In uniting themselves, Fichte argues, members of the commonwealth also tacitly agree to a fourth, 'subjection' contract, according to which each individual's freedoms (bodily integrity and property) are forfeit if he violates the agreement (III: 206). Expulsion (*Ausschließung*) from the community is the default response to violations according to Fichte (III: 260–1; 262–85 *passim*), because, strictly, any violation is a sign of inability or unwillingness to remain a cooperative member. Since the relation of right must be reciprocal if it is to be instantiated (for reasons I will explain in §3.2.3.7), this deprives an individual of citizenship and of any protections enjoyed in the state (III: 260, 271, 274–80). In the eyes of others, such a person takes on the status of non-rational being—a wild animal ('set free as a bird...[but] his security as little guaranteed as a bird's' (III: 260)), a 'piece of livestock' (III: 278–9), a 'force of nature' (III: 280).

The threat of expulsion functions as the deterrent that ensures voluntary compliance with the law (at least in the typical case: sufficiently 'untamed' or imprudent individuals cannot be deterred and so cannot be citizens (III: 273–4)). But since 'if a state and the neighboring states are rationally organized, expulsion is the most horrible fate that can befall a person' (III: 273), the parties may in addition agree to a fifth, 'expiation' contract, which would provide for a set of punishments short of total forfeiture to stand in as deterrent (III: 261). One such punishment is internment, which Fichte sees as a form of temporary internal exile (III: 274–7).

Such punishments have no moral justification, and their legal justification is exhausted by their ability to bring about voluntary compliance (III: 262). Fichte endorses the principle of proportionality, but only conditional on deterrence being achieved through the loss of something proportionate to what one stands to gain by breaking the law (III: 263). He explicitly denies that proportionality is a principle of *justice* in punishment, indeed denies that there are any such principles (III: 265, 268–9, 282–4). The only purpose of punishment is security; and this is likewise the only basis for determining a punishment's severity (III: 265). But by the same token, exile is always an option that can be chosen by the criminal (III: 272–3) because membership in a state is, on Fichte's view, at every moment voluntary.

3.2.3.5 IDEAL AND NON-IDEAL COMMUNITIES

I began this section (§3.2.3) by asking what reasons a morally motivated Fichtean agent has to enter a commonwealth and abide by its laws. It may seem at this point that I have gotten away from that question, since Fichte's argument that an institutionalized enforcement mechanism is required for the stability of any property contract might seem to require (and not merely to permit) that individuals' interests be at odds. Given what I have said about Fichte's specification of the problem of individuality at IV: 230–2 (viz. that it is soluble only on the assumption that morally motivated agents share an agent-neutral end), it might seem to follow from this that the individuals on whose motivations Fichte bases the arguments in §3.2.3.4 above cannot be morally motivated.

This is not the case. It is true that Fichte's argument for the necessity of a protection contract (and thus of the unification contract that makes it possible) requires that individuals' proximate ends be imperfectly aligned. But individuals' ends can be imperfectly aligned for a number of reasons. One instance is where individuals seek, immorally, to promote their own well-being before that of others. But another instance is where individuals embrace the agent-neutral end of furthering the material independence of rational agency wherever it exists, but disagree about the factual question of what would promote it in some instance.[92]

This is plausibly why Fichte moves seamlessly, in the pages following IV: 230, from a characterization of the problem of individuality as the problem of what to do when another agent proposes to act immorally and one could prevent this by violating her rights, to a characterization of it as the problem of what to do in the case of moral disagreement:

> But here arises the further question: which use of freedom is against the moral law, and who can be the judge of that in a way that is universally valid? If *the other* claims to have acted according to genuine conviction, and *I* act differently in the same situation, then *I* act just as unethically according to *his* conviction, as *he* does according to *mine*. Whose conviction should be the guide? Neither conviction, so long as they are contradictory; for each should absolutely act according to *his* conviction, and the formal condition of all morality consists in that.   (IV: 233; cf. GA 4–1: 116)

On a first reading the passage might seem to suggest that Fichte is advocating a form of moral relativism in which the rightness of an action is indexed to the subjective convictions of its agent; and its location might seem to suggest that Fichte is offering up this sort of moral relativism as a way out of the 'conflict of the moral law with itself' that is the problem of individuality, which he has just set up at this point in the text. But relativism would be inconsistent with the overall form of Fichte's moral theory and with the content of the third main part

---

[92] In showing that agreements would be possible in a society of act utilitarians incapable of binding themselves, Gibbard assumes a number of conditions, one of which is that the parties agree on the expected benefits of the relevant courses of action, which requires agreeing not only on the end of maximizing utility, but also on the facts that bear on how a given course of action will affect the total utility. Cf. A. Gibbard 1978, pp. 107–9 and A. Gibbard 1990, pp. 195–6.

of the *System of Ethics*, which assumes that there are non-relative answers to moral questions; and in any case he presents this as a 'further question' rather than an answer to the question already posed.

On reflection we can see that the passage is indeed simply an elaboration of the initial problem: individuals who share an end but disagree about means sufficient to bring it about find themselves in the same strategic situation as individuals whose interests are only partially aligned for any other reason. For such agents, agreement on the division of the sphere of possible activity is not a game of pure coordination; and it is to such agents that Fichte's claim that the property contract as an unenforced multilateral agreement is fatally unstable is meant to apply.

Moral disagreement, and how to overcome it, is a central theme in the treatment of individuality in *System of Ethics* §18, because the finitude of rational agency is manifested not only at the level of causal efficacy, but also at the level of deliberation. Fichte takes disagreement even among morally conscientious individuals to be the default state. This is because moral judgment, on his view of it, is complex and fallible. It depends on factual knowledge that can be difficult to obtain and on inferential reasoning that can be effortful, and it is therefore easily undermined by ignorance and cognitive laziness. Different agents come to any decision situation with different life experiences, which give them different stocks of background knowledge, different habits of reasoning, and dispositions to regard different features of the same situation as morally salient. They come with different capacities for problem solving, different levels of creativity, and so forth. So Fichte thinks it should be no surprise that they often disagree in their practical judgments. But even perfectly morally *motivated* agents will find their proximate ends at odds unless they agree about all relevant matters of fact. This is the justification for the specific moral obligation to engage in debate aimed at reaching consensus about moral and other matters (IV: 233–5).

Assuming full consensus (counterfactually, because perfect consensus is as much an idea in the Kantian sense as is the moral end itself (IV: 234)), no coercive enforcement mechanism—no state—would be required for individuals to coexist as free:

The final goal of all social action is that all human beings should agree; but all agree only on the purely rational, for that is the only thing that is common to them. Assuming such an agreement, the distinction between learned and non-learned public falls away. Church and state fall away. All have the same convictions, and the conviction of each is the conviction of all. The state *as legislating and constraining power* falls away. The will of each is actually a universal law, because all the others will the same; and no force is needed because everyone wills what he ought of his own accord.... This goal is unreachable—but if we imagine it being reached, what would happen? Each would, with his individual power, in accordance with the common will, and to the best of his ability, modify nature purposively for the use of reason.   (IV: 253)

This passage echoes remarks to the same effect in the second of the *Lectures on the Scholar's Vocation*, where we are cautioned against confusing 'society in general,' characterized as multilateral interaction, influence, and coordination,

with the particular, empirically conditioned sort of society we call the state. Life in the state does not belong among the absolute ends of human beings...but is only under certain conditions an available *means toward the formation of a perfect society*. Like all human institutions that are only means, the state aims at its own annihilation: *it is the aim of all government to make government superfluous*.   (VI: 306)

These passages should not be taken to mean that every problem of coordination would disappear in a world of morally and epistemically ideal agents.[93] Perfectly rationally benevolent Fichtean agents in full agreement about the morally rele- vant facts would still plan; and their plans would still require a conventional reconciliation (IV: 230). Theirs would be a problem of pure coordination, their interests being perfectly aligned. They could maintain a conventional solution to it by unenforced multilateral agreement, since they could rationally adhere, and expect one another to adhere, to its terms (if not exceptionlessly then at least enough of the time).[94] But so long as they remained numerically distinct sites of practical deliberation and action, they would still need some agreement defining individual spheres of activity. In such circumstances the moral obligation to respect rights to bodily inviolability and property would remain; only provisions for coercive enforcement would fall away.[95]

Although Fichte never says this explicitly, there is some reason for thinking that the property arrangement of such ideal agents would differ from the one

---

[93] Düsing takes the *System of Ethics* passage to assert that individuality *itself* would disappear in a condition of total consensus (E. Düsing 1991). But in neither passage does Fichte say anything that supports that conclusion. The mistake may be due to the fact that Düsing—like Neuhouser (1994, 2000)—understands 'individuality' in a thicker sense than the one that seems to be at issue in Fichte's political thought. In fact qualitative differences between persons (for instance, differences in what they want or believe) play no role whatsoever in Fichte's argument for the necessity of the relation of right. Only the fact that they are quantitatively distinct loci of agency plays a role, and there is no reason to think that individuality in *this* sense would disappear in a condition of total consensus.

[94] Gibbard argues that although agents committed to promoting the impartially best outcome and agreeing about how to bring it about would sometimes face situations like the one faced by Parfit's hitchhiker, since their future compliance with any agreement would be predicated on their belief, at the time of compliance, that compliance would produce the best outcome overall, such situations would be rare. Cf. A. Gibbard 1990, pp. 232–3.

[95] This would be the 'humanly impossible but logically possible' scenario Raz describes at J. Raz 1999, pp. 158–60.

described in the *Foundations*, since the justification he offers for the equality constraint on distribution of property relies in part on the assumption that individuals' ends are not perfectly aligned. The situation of perfect moral agents in perfect agreement would be different, insofar as they would have a shared criterion of efficiency to apply. They would favor an arrangement of social resources that maximally promotes the exercise of rational agency in general and expands the scope of human action possibilities into the indefinite future, while protecting for each the conditions necessary for deliberative integrity and so ability to fulfill the formal condition on moral worth. Whether those ends are best served by institutions obeying egalitarian distributive principles is an empirical question. Where they are not, morally motivated individuals would have no interest in equality per se, and might agree multilaterally on very unequal distributions, so long as these were maximizing. (It is worth noting that any sacrifices made by individuals for the collective good in this scenario would always be voluntary, since there would by hypothesis be no coercive institutions in it.)

3.2.3.6 RIGHT AS A SYSTEM OF HYPOTHETICAL IMPERATIVES

The account I have given so far, on which the value of coordination and so of political institutions is instrumental, squares with Fichte's characterization, in the *Foundations*, of the principle of right as having 'hypothetical validity' and the choice of whether to become or remain a member of a commonwealth an 'arbitrary' one:

It is not possible to indicate any absolute reason why someone should make the formula of right (viz.: limit your freedom so that others beside you can be free as well) into the law of his will and his actions. We can see that no community of free beings as such could exist unless each is subject to this law, and that whoever wills the community must necessarily will the law as well—in other words, that it has hypothetical validity. The law of right must have validity, *if* a community of free beings as such is to be possible.   (III: 89)

It is necessary that each free being assume [the existence of] others of its type beyond itself; but it is not necessary that they all persist alongside one another *as free beings*. The thought and the realization of such a community is therefore something arbitrary.... [B]ecause the thought and the task of such a community is, thought as a practical concept, arbitrary, it is merely technically practical. That is, if the question is, 'according to which principles can a community among free beings as such be instituted, were one to want to institute one?' the answer must be: according to the concept of right. But it is by no means thereby stated that such a community ought to be instituted.   (III: 9–10)

The science of right is independent of ethics, but it is not an independent source of categorical obligations (III: 54). This is another set of commitments we find expressed already in the *Lectures on the Scholar's Vocation* (VI: 306–7) and reiterated in the Mirbach lecture notes (GA 4–1: 119).

Fichte takes the moral and prudential reasons to enter, or remain a member in good standing of, a political community to be, in most circumstances, overwhelming. From a moral perspective, the interest that motivates cooperation is just the agent-neutral moral concern with the material independence of rational agents generally.[96] Since moral progress requires interaction, I must interact with (willing) others (IV: 235). Since my aim is the independence of rational agency wherever it exists, I must do my best to ensure that that the interaction be such as to allow all of its participants to coexist as free (IV: 238-9). Since individuals can coexist as free only in a state that assigns them determinate rights (III: 9-10, 92-3; IV: 230, 300), part of the moral end is the existence of a state and the protection of the rights it assigns to individuals.

From a narrowly prudential perspective, self-interest offers similarly powerful motives for cooperation. Other rational beings are uniquely placed to facilitate, or undermine, my plans; and I am likely to be harmed if I ignore them, if only because they also see that I am likewise uniquely placed to facilitate or undermine their plans (III: 115-18). So even if I do not expect to call on others' help, but seek only to pursue my own projects unmolested, I am better off as a member of a commonwealth.

This account is consistent with there being some commonwealths membership in which will not further these interests (or will not do so on the terms offered to some individuals in them). So (unsurprisingly) Fichte endorses no absolute duty to obey the law. In the *System of Ethics*, he explains that it is contrary to morality to try to overthrow the state unless I am firmly convinced that doing so is the will of the whole community (IV: 238-9), and that absent such conviction it is my duty to work to improve the state within the confines of the law (IV: 239, 296-7). It is a clear implicature of these remarks that there *can* be cases in which I morally ought to take direct action aimed at overthrowing the government (and so cases in which I may break the law as part of an effort to reform it). This was presumably the case for the French working

---

[96] Fichte sometimes describes this interest in terms that suggest a direct instrumental connection between others' freedom and the agent's own, as here:

> My I-hood and self-sufficiency in general is conditioned by the freedom of the other; *my drive to self-sufficiency* can therefore not at all be directed toward the annihilation of the *condition of its own possibility*, namely, the freedom of the other.... Therefore there lies in this curtailment of the drive an absolute prohibition on the disruption of the freedom of the other, a command to regard him as self-sufficient and absolutely not to use him as means for my end.... I may not be self-sufficient at the cost of the freedom of others. (IV: 221-2)

But we do best to understand the concern as the agent-neutral concern with the maximization of material freedom generally—which, as we have seen, is indeed furthered by coordination.

classes, whose overthrow of their existing regime Fichte defended.[97] It is the case for those believing their government sufficiently corrupt (III: 182–4; cf. VI: 13), and for those to whom no right to property is acknowledged or who lack property sufficient to support themselves independently (III: 195; IV: 296).[98] In both the *System of Ethics* and the *Foundations*, the only criterion of institutional legitimacy Fichte admits is the ongoing support of the governed (III: 14, 107, 152, 164–5, 174, 182–5).[99]

Many interpreters have taken at face value Fichte's denial that there is any duty to claim or recognize rights that is independent of the instrumental value of the community in which they are assigned and enforced.[100] But others have seen a tension between this denial and Fichte's claim to have derived the principle of right from conditions of possibility of self-consciousness. The worry is motivated textually, at least in part, by the line of argument in §§3–4 (that is, theorems 1–3 and the considerations offered in support of them):

Theorem 1: A finite rational being cannot posit itself without ascribing to itself a free efficacy.   (III: 17; original in italics)

Theorem 2: The finite rational being cannot ascribe to itself a free efficacy in the world of sense without ascribing the same to others as well, and thus without assuming other finite rational beings besides itself.   (III: 30; original in italics)

Theorem 3: The finite rational being cannot assume other finite rational beings besides itself without positing itself as standing with these in a determinate relation, which one calls the relation of right.   (III: 41; original in italics)

The conclusion is evidently that every rational agent *qua* self-conscious cannot but posit itself as standing in the relation of right with others. But since to posit oneself as standing in the relation of right with others looks, at least on its face, to involve claiming rights oneself and acknowledging others' rights, it seems to these interpreters that Fichte means to argue that 'political rights are among the

---

[97] Fichte was a supporter of the revolution, for reasons outlined in *Contributions to the Correction of the Public's Judgment concerning the Revolution in France* (published 1793, reprinted 1795, VI: 39–288).

[98] Fichte's own family of origin appears to have been in this position, or something very close to it, depending on whether the provision that each be able to support himself from his property without resort to private charity subsumes the ability to support dependents, and whether that support, in the case of children, involves only nourishment or also adequate education. Cf. M. Kühn 2012.

[99] That such support is often undergirded by ideology is something Fichte himself points out in a later (1813) set of lectures on political right, where he suggests that the institution of slavery in the ancient world relied on the belief that a god had decreed it (IV: 507–8). It is, sadly, also something he exemplifies, most astonishingly in his justification for denying wives full legal personhood in the appendix on marriage and family law (III: 304–12).

[100] See e.g. A. Renaut 1986 and 1992; L. Ferry 1987–8; and G. Zöller 1998.

necessary conditions of self-consciousness.'[101] This claim would be difficult to reconcile with the claim that the choice of whether to become or remain the member of a commonwealth is an arbitrary one.[102] This apparent tension between the derivation of the third theorem and the characterization of the principle of right as a hypothetical imperative is thought by many to create a gap in the overall argument of the *Foundations*.[103]

Since it is important to my account of the place of rights in Fichte's ethical thought that the political sphere *not* be a source of independent categorical obligations (and so that the argument in *Foundations* §§3–4 not be intended to show that it is), I propose to address this set of worries in the two sections that follow. In §3.2.3.7, I examine more closely Fichte's account of what it is to *posit oneself as standing in a relation of right* with others; and in §3.2.3.8, I examine more closely Fichte's account of what it is to *have rights*.

3.2.3.7 THE SUMMONS AND THE PROBLEM OF RIGHT

The point of the *Foundations*, as I have said, is to propose a set of a priori constraints on any solution to the problem of right, that is, to the technical problem of coordinating the activity of rational agents engaged in planned action in a shared external world. In order to motivate his account of constraints on solutions, Fichte takes himself first to have to assure his readers that the problem is one they actually have, and that it is soluble in principle at least in some cases. The first main part of the *Foundations* (§§1–4) claims to give a transcendental deduction of the concept RIGHT, viz. an argument showing that the concept is a necessary one, in the sense of being possessed by any self-conscious being as such.

---

[101] F. Neuhouser 2000, p. xv. Cf. also P. Baumanns 1990, pp. 120, 124, 168.

[102] Neuhouser writes:

> Fichte often claims (e.g. SW III p. 9) that a theory of right can only establish what a community of free, rational individuals must look like if such a community were to exist; it cannot show *that* such a community ought to be. This claim is associated with his view that the decision to become a member of political society (not just a particular society, but political society in general) is wholly a matter of *Willkür*. But if living in a political community governed by the rules of right is required, as my interpretation claims, for the self-consciousness of individuality, and if such self-consciousness is an essential part of being a person, then, contrary to some of Fichte's assertions, it no longer seems to be a matter of arbitrary choice whether or not we enter such a political order.   (F. Neuhouser 1994, p. 179)

Darwall sees a similar tension: 'there are reasons for thinking that Fichte cannot hold to a voluntaristic interpretation if he is to maintain that the conditions for self-awareness are sufficient to validate the principle of right' (S. Darwall 2005). P. Franks (2005) and O. Ware (2010) also take there to be an at least *prima facie* problem here.

[103] Cf. L. Siep 1979, pp. 26–35; F. Neuhouser 1994, p. 171; F. Neuhouser 2000, p. xviii; P. Franks 2005, pp. 324–5; R. Williams 2006; O. Ware 2010. G. Herbert (1998) raises what looks like a related worry.

Since RIGHT is a technically practical concept (one whose instantiation is the solution to a practical problem), that task involves an articulation of the problem. The problem is: how can multiple rational agents co-exist as externally free? The second main part (§§5–7) claims to give a deduction of that concept's applicability, viz. an argument showing that and how the concept in question can be applied in the sort of experience of which self-conscious beings as such are the subjects. In the case of a technically practical concept like RIGHT, the aim is to show that the conditions of possibility of solutions to the problem could in principle obtain.

Fichte's ingenious move in the opening pages of the *Foundations* is to link the possibility of rational agency conscious of itself as such with a particular form of human interaction—the form of human interaction he calls a 'summons' or, alternatively, 'upbringing' (III: 39). As I have explained in §2.3.5 above, a summons is a demand that the summoned exercise her external causality in a way that does not interfere with the summoner's external causality in a sphere that the summons itself determines; and it is a demand conveyed in a way that likewise does not interfere with the external causality of the summoned.

The connection Fichte alleges between a summons and the possibility of self-conscious rational agency has been much discussed in the interpretive literature.[104] I have said in §2.3.5 that I take Fichte's basic claim to be that the disposition to form second-order evaluative attitudes, to engage in practical reflection, and so to impose normative demands of any kind upon oneself, is the product of this kind of social interaction. My concern in this section is not with the connection between the summons and self-conscious agency, but instead with the connection between the summons and the foundations of Fichte's theory of right. The discussion of summoning occurs first in the *Foundations* because it is through an analysis of the basic features of this form of social interaction that Fichte brings out many (though not all) of the determinations of problem of right.

Most fundamentally, for there to be a problem of right, there must be a multiplicity of rational agents, and so one primary aim of the summons argument is to establish that no self-conscious agent can plausibly assert its uniqueness, but must instead acknowledge that there are (or have been) individuals outside of itself—that 'if there are to be human beings at all, there must be more than one' (III: 39; original in italics). But although convincing the reader that practical

---

[104] A few examples (there are many more): P. Rohs 1991b, pp. 86ff.; F. Neuhouser, 2000; A. Honneth 2001; F. Neuhouser 2001; A. Renaut 2001; S. Darwall 2006, pp. 20ff., 252ff., *et passim*; A. Wood 2006.

solipsism is untenable is one primary aim of the summons argument, it is far from the only one. That is because although the existence of a problem of right requires a multiplicity of individuals, this is far from the only thing it requires.[105] Many of the other conditions, however, are themselves built into the summons situation; and so if Fichte succeeds in establishing that self-consciousness is possible only on the basis of a summons, he succeeds at the same time in establishing that these conditions—again, conditions for the existence of a *problem* of right—actually obtain if there is agency conscious of itself as such.

A first set of necessary conditions is causal, and it is laid out mainly in the deduction of the body and of reciprocal influence at III: 55–73. For two agents to stand in the summoned–summoner relation they must have wills that are immediately causally efficacious in some part of the external world (III: 58–9, 69). These parts of the world must be distinct, for were they not, the one could not distinguish her own efficacy from the efficacy of the other, and so could not conceive of herself as a distinct will. Each must have some sort of causal efficacy with respect to the will of the other, however, for there could be no interaction if their wills were wholly immune to one another's influence. Such efficacy cannot be immediate, for there could be no independence if their wills could work directly and immediately upon one another. Instead it must be mediate: the one must be able to act with her body upon the body (but not directly upon the will) of the other (III: 64–5, 69). Further, their interaction must be able to take two distinct forms: direct physical contact on the one hand, and signaling that acts upon the sense organs but does not involve direct physical contact on the other (III: 61–73). This is because they must be able not only to act upon one another in a way that violates the sphere that the summons will assign to each (must be vulnerable to one another's physical interference) but also to act upon one another in a way that does not violate it (must have some medium of influencing one another's wills apart from physical interference). It must, further, be the case that not every exercise of external causality on the part of the one impinges on the body of the other: there must be a physical space between and

---

[105] I believe I disagree with Neuhouser's reconstruction here, insofar as he seems to take Fichte's view to be that conceiving of oneself as an individual suffices for having the concept RIGHT (cf. F. Neuhouser 1994; F. Neuhouser 2001, p. 40). Part of the disagreement may rest on our disagreement about what Fichte means by 'individual' for these purposes. On my view, to be an individual is to be a locus of causal efficacy and rational deliberation numerically distinct from other such loci. No thicker conception of individuality is required in order to get any problem of coordination off the ground. But it seems to me that even Neuhouser's thicker conception of individuality does not suffice for the articulation of the problem of right. For articulating that problem requires appeal to considerations that cannot plausibly be built into the concept INDIVIDUAL on any interpretation, for example the consideration that the space individuals share is finite.

around them, within which their two bodies can causally interact in a mediated way (III: 68).

A second set of necessary conditions is epistemic. Fichte assumes without argument that the physical space separating agents is populated in part by other causally efficacious but non-rational beings, and that discovering one another within this environment is therefore a problem rational agents must be able to solve if they are to summon or be summoned. He claims in the deduction of application that nature has settled this question for us by giving us bodies of a certain sort, bodies that signal, naturally, that their owners are rational beings (III: 76–85).[106] But what he writes elsewhere (e.g. in §43 of the first appendix, one of the sections dedicated to the upbringing of children) makes much more sense:

It is a natural drive in human beings to suspect beings outside of themselves of rationality, where this is at all plausible, and to treat objects (for example, animals) as though they had it. The parents will treat their child in the same way, summoning it to free activity; and in this way rationality and freedom will gradually become manifest in it.   (III: 358)

The answer to the question of who is a rational being is settled through inter-action in which rationality and freedom are, or gradually become, manifest in behavior. (In fact this is stated, though not in such clear terms, already in the deduction (III: 37).)

A summons is a strategic interaction in the sense that what it is rational for each to do in it depends on her expectations about what the other will do, which she recognizes to depend in turn on the other's expectations about what she herself will do, and so on.[107] Fichte is here appealing to a general feature of such interactions: each participant can affect the expectations, and therefore the behavior, of the other participant, only by how she behaves herself. The sum-moned must do as she is asked if the summoner is to continue to regard her as a being who is at least potentially free and rational. But the summoner must do likewise—must obey the very constraints she is trying to impose—if she is to be recognized as issuing a summons. So recognition of one another as rational

---

[106] There are actually two accounts at III: 76–85, not clearly distinguished. On one, the form of the body is a kind of natural sign of its rational potential. Human bodies are distinguished from animal bodies in lacking an articulation that defines a determinate sphere of movement, but instead having an articulation that has 'infinite determinability.' On the other, we recognize other rational beings by the similarity of their bodies to ours.

[107] Typically, it is what Schelling called a 'mixed-motive' game, in which agents share an interest in coordination, but also have competing interests that cause them to favor different solutions. Cf. T. Schelling 1958, pp. 207ff. For another take on the relevance of Schelling's theory to Fichte's characterization of the summons, see N. Nomer 2010.

agents is necessarily connected to some behavioral expression, which must be present on both sides for recognition to take place.

Since it must take place in this kind of interaction, such recognition can only ever be mutual:

The relation of free beings to one another is therefore necessarily to be understood in the following way, and is posited as being so determined: the knowledge of the one individual by the other is conditioned on the other's treatment of it as free (that is, that the other limit his freedom through the concept of the freedom of the first). This mode of treatment is however conditioned on the action of the first toward the second, this action through the action and through the knowledge of the second, and so on to infinity. The relation of free beings to one another is thus the relation of interaction through intelligence and freedom. Neither can recognize the other if both do not reciprocally recognize one another. And neither can treat the other as a free being if both do not reciprocally treat one another that way. (III: 44)

In the absence of such behavior, they show up for one another as non-rational animals.

This epistemic point—that the one can know the other to be free and rational only because and to the extent that the other's actions demonstrate that it recognizes the freedom and rationality of the one—gives rise to constraints on rational conduct only for agents who want to appear to others to be rational beings. The summons need not be successful (III: 34, 44). Grasping the fact that I can affect others' behavior by affecting their expectations about my own does not constrain me to interact with them in that way. I have concepts other than 'rational being' under which I can (accurately) subsume those others (concepts like 'animal' and 'material object') and it is physically possible for me to act on others as if they fell only under such concepts (III: 86–7). It is irrational to do so only if I have ends inconsistent with others' treating me in exactly the same way, a result I can foresee as soon as I have any understanding of the situation. Fichte describes the irrationality involved in failure to respond appropriately to the summons as a 'theoretical' one (III: 47, 48, 50). But we must not be misled by this, since as we have seen in §2.2 all instrumental reasoning is theoretical reasoning on Fichte's view (cf. IV: 165–6).

Instrumental reasoning requires ends on which to operate, and we find these built into the summons situation as well. Both agents are assumed to have an interest in coordination on non-overlapping spheres of permissible activity, and thus already to have, or be capable of being inspired to have, their own bodily integrity, external causal efficacy, and ability to plan as ends. Likewise built in is a requirement of (again, instrumental) rationality to recognize the symmetry of the interests involved (III: 44–8). Agents refusing to recognize in others interests they know them to have can expect to come to no meeting of minds.

These specifications of the summons situation correspond, as they are meant to, to aspects of the problem of right. Right exists as a problem to be solved not only because there are many individual sites of deliberation and causal agency, but also because these must share a space of external action, because their exercises of their freedom can come into conflict, and because they have their own unimpeded causal efficacy as an end. It is in principle soluble only if they can agree to an arrangement that removes such conflict by a signaling mechanism that is not itself an instance of such conflict. Its solution is the outcome of a bargaining process in which individuals recognize one another as having standing to make claims on one another and mutually recognize those claims. (This is not to say that the bargaining power of each must be equal to that of all others, but only that each must derive some at least perceived benefit from the other's voluntary compliance with the agreement, if there is to be any.) Effectively signaling agreement requires actually adhering to the terms. Some form of cooperation is its expected outcome.

Fichte takes all of these conditions to be established as facts known to any self-conscious rational agent by the end of the deduction of applicability. Any being that has once been 'summoned' by or 'brought up' to be a rational being is able to understand the aspects of the strategic situation that I have just described, and to see that others are likewise able to understand them. The 'ongoing universal expectation' that all other rational beings will recognize me as a rational being (III: 45–6) and the correlative requirement of 'theoretical' consistency (III: 47, 48, 50, 86) that I cannot expect such recognition unless I recognize them in the same way (where such recognition is a behavioral, not a merely cognitive, fact) is just Fichte's articulation of what it means to posit oneself as standing in a relation of right with others.[108]

To posit oneself as standing in a relation of right with another is, then, to acknowledge that we two have, together, the problem of right, and that we have interests that typically dictate that we should go about solving this problem together, negotiating constraints on our respective activities to make them compatible. If we manage to solve this problem we will, collectively, take on new moral duties with respect to one another (duties whose fulfillment, because of the nature of the apparatus that makes them possible, will be a prudential imperative as well): duties of right (IV: 295–301; cf. III: 8–11).

---

[108] Here I agree with Nomer in his view that 'the "relation of right" is not a codified, patterned, or institutionalized relation; rather it takes the form of a negotiation to arrange the social space into non-conflicting spheres of activity' (N. Nomer 2010, p. 489).

On this interpretation, the outcome of the summons argument is consistent with Fichte's characterization of right as a technical science and the imperative of right as hypothetical. This does not seem to me to diminish either the originality or the significance of the argument. If it succeeds, it succeeds in connecting the possibility of self-conscious agency to a set of substantive normative claims that are, plausibly, foundational for political philosophy. That their normativity is only hypothetical in no way diminishes their political significance, since social organization is something virtually everyone has reason to want.

3.2.3.8 FICHTE'S POSITIVISM

It is surprisingly common for Fichte's readers to take the *Foundations* to be an account of what fundamental rights people *have*. It is only on the basis of this assumption that it seems plausible to regard Fichte's ambition there to be the derivation of political rights as necessary conditions of self-consciousness (a locution Fichte himself never employs); and it is surely this assumption that explains Neuhouser's understanding of original right as an account of actual rights (even though this conflicts with Fichte's own description of them as 'mere *fiction*' (III: 12)).[109] But the text leaves little room for error on this point: as we have seen, Fichte explicitly denies that what he is proposing is a theory of natural rights (III: 111–12, 148). If we bear in mind his account of the source of our interest in rights it is easy to see that 'natural rights' could not answer that interest. Only coercively enforced legal rights could do so.

We would expect someone holding such a view to recognize the existence of human beings who, because they are not cooperating members of existing commonwealths, are not rights-bearers. In fact Fichte describes six classes of such individuals in the *Foundations* and the *System of Ethics*. We have been introduced to two of them already: hermits (who refuse to have rights—IV: 238); and lawbreakers (who in the absence of some expiation contract forfeit their rights in breaking the law—III: 260, 271, 274–5, 278–80).

In discussing the requirement that any two individuals who are to stand in the relation of right with one another must be able to interact causally, Fichte describes a third class of rightless individuals: 'One misunderstands the concept of right entirely, when one speaks, for example, of the rights against the living of those long dead' (III: 56). Although Fichte does not say this, the causal interaction provision evidently has consequences for duties to future generations as well: although we have moral duties toward them, these cannot be construed as duties of right. So past and future individuals constitute a third class.

---

[109] Cf. F. Neuhouser 1994, p. 171; F. Neuhouser 2000, pp. xvi–xvii.

A fourth class is discussed in the section on cosmopolitan law: stateless people seeking to enter an established commonwealth from the outside. Migrants have only the sole right that (Fichte tells us) can properly be described as a 'natural' one: the right to *acquire* rights by entering into contracts with willing others (III: 383–4). This is best understood as an extra-political entitlement to demand a hearing, to enter into a process of negotiation (that may, legally, result in either their citizenship or their expulsion), which a migrant can claim just by demonstrating their ability to be a rights-bearer (which they do simply by making the first move in that process of negotiation—that is, by issuing a summons).

The fifth class is by far the most problematic for a reading on which the summons argument seeks to show that political rights are a condition of possibility of self-consciousness. Fichte uses the terms 'summons' and 'upbringing' interchangeably throughout the text, and this is because the paradigm case of summoning occurs in the context of child-rearing. Typical summoners are parents, and typical recipients of the summons are children. But, as we learn in the first appendix, 'the child, insofar as it is being brought up, is not at all free, and so not at all a possible subject of rights or duties' (III: 359). Children have no political rights at all, not even the right not to be killed by their parents (III: 361–2). Although the state may assign parents legal duties to sustain and raise their children, these are grounded in the arrangement parents maintain with other adults, not in any rights claims that might be made by or on behalf of the children themselves.

This class is especially significant because if the paradigm case of the summons is that of a parent summoning a (non-rights-bearing) child, not that of one adult making a demand on another adult (still less a demand of respect for some right that pre-exists the interaction), it seems very implausible to think that Fichte means, in arguing that self-consciousness depends on a summons, to argue that it depends in any way on political rights or the institutions that make them possible. The relation of dependence is instead the opposite: beings who have not (yet) been summoned are, in virtue of that fact, not (yet) capable of co-citizenship, not (yet) capable of having rights.

A sixth class consists of sets of individuals whose circumstances make the problem of right insoluble for them. Fichte assumes that all of the arrangements described in his theory of the social contract must be implementable by institutional mechanisms human beings can design for themselves (with no real or imagined threat of external enforcement to bind them), and describes in §16 constraints on governmental institutions adequate to that task. But he cautions that any actual solution to the problem of right will include determinations he has not described, imposed by the geographical and cultural situation of the people trying to solve it (III: 286ff.). We learn from his discussion of two sorts of case that he does not think it will always be soluble.

The first is the example, mentioned in §3.2.1.1, of a lifeboat that can hold only one of two shipwreck survivors. The example was a staple in texts on natural right in this period, but Fichte's approach to it is peculiar. He denies that the philosophy of right applies to such a case at all:

> The question of right is: how can multiple free beings coexist as such? This question presupposes that there is some possibility of coexistence. If this possibility is absent, then the question of the determination of this possibility disappears entirely, and with it the question of right.   (III: 253)

This conclusion might seem puzzling. This is after all a case in which a set of individuals must adjudicate their claims to a distributable resource. Why should the question not arise here? Fichte's answer displays his conceptualization of the problem of right as, fundamentally, a bargaining problem. The situation is one in which no meaningful cooperation is possible, since by stipulation there is no distribution that satisfies the most basic interests all parties to it have (in this case, survival), and so there is no possible agreement such that both parties stand to gain from it more than they stand to gain from unilateral action.

A different sort of case is discussed in §16. Fichte allows that the system of government he describes there cannot function if most citizens are sufficiently corrupt (III: 180–1). He does not explain exactly what he means, but the point seems to be that some minimal disposition to deal honestly and keep agreements in some proportion of members of a group is required if that group is to be able to solve the problem of right for itself.

We can conclude from these two discussions that Fichte takes the problem of right to be insoluble in principle in conditions of extreme scarcity or in the absence of some minimum of political culture. But it seems that even those for whom it is soluble in principle can fail to solve it in practice, simply because the technical problem that faces them is too complex for them to solve. The problem is solved only when everyone who would coexist with others as a free being among free beings in a stable and law-governed way is able to do so: when each can rationally plan, secure in the knowledge that others have on balance no prudential reason to interfere in those plans, when each is protected from physical violence and has a secure employment sufficient to fulfill her basic needs and those of her dependents.

It should be obvious, as soon as the solution is described in those terms, that we know of no historical instance of the problem of right having been (entirely) solved by any group of people. Far from denying this, Fichte explicitly characterizes right as a property had in degrees by different social organizations. The null degree is the complete absence of a constitution, of which even 'the worst is better than none' (XI: 125). 'Politics' is the discipline whose aim is to make 'progress from a not entirely right, but also not entirely un-right, constitution to one that is more right' (XI: 124), where what it is to be 'more right' is simply to better satisfy the fundamental interests set out in the 'original right' section of the *Foundations*.

Excepting the cases in which the problem is insoluble in principle, and holding fixed (artificially, granted) the *degree* to which it is solved (that is, holding fixed levels of violent and property crime and economic disenfranchisement), it seems clear enough that for most peoples at most times the problem of right is soluble in multiple roughly equally desirable ways.[110] In those cases, what determines which system is implemented is just the sum of the actual individual choices of the people involved, in the past and in the present (III: 152, 196). The *Foundations* is intended to articulate only a priori *constraints* on stable solutions to the problem of right. It does not purport to provide, itself, such a solution, because there can be no a priori solution.

> The principle of right says only that each should limit his use of his freedom with reference to the freedom of others; but it does not determine how far and to what objects the right of each extends. This must be declared explicitly, and in such a way that the declarations of all are consistent.   (III: 152; cf. III: 196)

This means that if we want to know what rights people have, the document to consult is not the *Foundations*, but the legislation of the state of which they are citizens. The law as it is (rather than the law as it ought to be by any normative standard) is what determines people's rights and others' corresponding obligations of right. This is why the obligations of right described in *System of Ethics* §18 are described only as obligations to become or remain a citizen of some actual state and to abide by its actual laws. There could be no richer description, since what rights individuals have depend on the positive law of the commonwealth to which they belong.

In each of the six cases of rightless individuals, as we should expect on such an account, although there are moral duties that concern them, none of those duties are duties of right, and all of them are importantly qualified by the fact that the individuals concerned are not rights-bearers. Parents are morally

---

[110] Fichte actually denies this (III: 107)—just as he denies that there can be more than one equally morally optimal action in any given situation (IV: 155, 195)—but this seems a failure of imagination not to be taken terribly seriously, since he appears to have commitments (e.g. to the free choice of careers by young people—IV: 272–3) that would entail the possibility of equally desirable solutions.

obliged to bring up their children, making them into rational beings and potential fellow citizens, while constraining their behavior in extralegal ways for their own and others' well-being until they reach that point (IV: 335–41). Hermits must, as we have seen, be avoided if they refuse to be integrated, since there is by hypothesis no rightful way of interacting with them (IV: 237–8). There can be no moral justification for allowing migrants to exist in political limbo: morally, they must be integrated, or, if this is genuinely impossible, deported (III: 383–5). Lawbreakers, insofar as they are in the act of breaking the law, and insofar as one is acting as a proxy for a state whose actual officers cannot effectively intervene, should be regarded as rightless (and this status explains the fact, noted in §3.2.3.2 above, that there is no moral prohibition on violating an attacker's property or bodily integrity in the act of defending his victim against him). Still, they should be protected from unnecessary harm on the grounds that they may yet be reintegrated. In each of these cases there is a moral obligation to try to integrate (or reintegrate) the individual in question into a commonwealth that would provide them with legal rights (where this is possible), and to protect and promote their rational agency in whatever other ways available until this can be done. But in none of these cases does Fichte describe any extralegal, moral, or 'natural' rights that individuals might claim in the absence of such integration.

3.2.3.9 PARTICULAR DUTIES

With this account of the place of rights in Fichte's ethics in mind, let us turn to an aspect of the view presented in the *System of Ethics* that I have not yet discussed in detail. I have described Fichte's moral theory as, structurally, a maximizing consequentialism. It might seem that the proponent of such a theory ought to approach the question of the adjudication of the conflicting claims of individuals in something like the way in which utilitarians are usually taken to approach it, distributing in whatever manner maximizes the total (alternatively, the average), the fact that it is distributed amongst persons adding no new considerations to the picture. The moral end as Fichte has described it does not itself dictate this approach, but many of Fichte's remarks suggest that he sees some appeal in it. This is especially evident in his discussions of tradeoffs involving the deliberator herself, in which cases he for the most part advocates treating one's own good as strictly on a par with the good of others.[111]

---

[111] Exceptions to this are several points where he seems to be arguing in favor of a morality of disproportionate self-sacrifice, claiming that one should forget one's own interests entirely in one's pursuit of the moral end (IV: 255, 259ff., 265, 269) and justifying the duty of self-preservation instrumentally (IV: 261, 269).

But, as we have seen, the end of coordination and the institutions that make it possible place limits on individuals' entitlement to make such decisions unilaterally. Fichte's discussion of 'universal' duties incorporates patient-centered constraints arising from the application, in the sphere of personal decision-making, of the most fundamental elements of the scheme of coordination that is laid out by the law. There are further obligations, not all legally encoded or coercively enforced, that also arise out of (natural or conventional) solutions to coordination problems. These are what Fichte calls 'particular' duties, which arise from individual roles in the social division of labor (IV: 258, 271–3, 325–65; III: 165, 175, 302). Like duties of right, particular duties are given an external justification rooted in the end of independence:

The end of furthering reason is the sole duty of all: this encompasses all others within itself; particular duties are duties only insofar as they relate to the achievement of that primary aim. I should carry out the particular duty of my estate and occupation not because I absolutely should, but because in my situation I further the end of reason in so doing. I should regard particular duty as a means to the accomplishment of the universal duty of all human beings, and not as an absolute end.   (IV: 325)

Particular duties do not trump universal ones (IV: 326), but they typically come first in the order of deliberation for individuals because, involving as they do solutions to coordination problems, they answer many questions left unanswered by universal duties.[112] Their function as mechanisms of coordination explains why Fichte argues that there is a general duty to submit oneself to some sort of division of social labor either by finding a place in an existing one, or by creating one where none exists (IV: 258, 271), and to make oneself physically and mentally fit for that chosen place (IV: 274).[113]

---

[112] This is true of all such duties, including duties to further the well-being of family members, as we have seen already in Fichte's consideration of duties of rescue in §3.2.1.1 above.

[113] In contrast with Hegel, Fichte argues that all such places must be taken on voluntarily. One does not have duties as woman or man, but only as spouse or parent (and although one has an obligation to become a spouse and parent where possible, the fulfillment of these obligations has moral worth only when freely undertaken). Similarly, one does not have duties as member of a social station fixed by birth, but only as pursuer of a voluntarily chosen calling. One must choose some vocation or other, and must choose it not according to inclination, but according to one's conviction that it best fits the measure of one's powers (IV: 272), given the options available and given that society agrees with one's judgment of those powers (IV: 273). But parents may not choose on their children's behalf; rather, everyone should receive a universal general education up to the age of majority, and should thereafter choose for himself (IV: 273). This position on education was radical at the time. Hegel takes the more traditional position—that *Stand* is typically determined by birth, and that education beyond what is required for carrying out one's occupation is unnecessary—even twenty years later, in the *Philosophy of Right*. It is, even now, the norm in the German-speaking world for vocational specialization in education to begin before the age of majority.

The state, the system of *Stände*, and other social conventions that Fichte does not discuss in detail, in fact answer the greater part of the questions we might have about what our duties to one another are (IV: 238–89, 259, 285–7, 301, 306–9). The moral end dictates obligations directly only where political and particular duties do not. It is a source of self-regarding duties and of some duties to others that are not duties of right or particular duties (e.g. duties to future generations); and it guides collective deliberation by citizens about which larger social goals to pursue among the many that are consistent with the maintenance of a rational social organization. But where it does figure directly in practical deliberation it does so in a way that tends to erase distinctions between persons. This is true from the perspective of both agent and patient: I should not care whether it is I or someone else who is the agent of moral progress, so long as it is made (IV: 232); I should regard myself as having no moral claim on resources beyond what I need in order to function as an effective agent of that end (IV: 255, 259–61, 269); and I should place my own well-being strictly on par with the well-being of others (IV: 269–71, 279–82, 289, 297–8, 302–6).

4

Formal Independence

With this understanding of the substance of Fichte's ethics and nature of the principle that informs it in hand, we can now turn to an examination of Fichte's account of the formal condition of moral worth. First, recall Fichte's summary statement of the moral principle in §13: 'The ethical drive demands *freedom*— for the sake of *freedom*'; alternatively, 'I should *act freely*, that I may *become free* [*Ich soll* frei handeln, *damit ich* frei werde]' (IV: 153). Fichte's explication of the senses of 'freedom' at issue in those statements was this: the second occurrence describes 'an objective state that should be brought about' (the state of 'complete independence of everything outside of us,' a state that is our 'absolute final end' as rational beings) and the first describes the actions to be taken to approach that state. These actions must have two properties in order to be 'free' in the relevant sense: they must be the right actions (meeting a 'material' condition); and they must have come about in the right way (meeting a 'formal' condition). The material condition ('what must happen' (IV: 153)) was the topic of Chapter 3. The formal condition ('*how* it must happen' (IV: 153)) is the topic of this chapter.

I have said (§1.3) that these two conditions are independent. An action can be formally correct without being, objectively, the action in the circumstances most conducive to the moral end (if, for example, the agent reasons responsibly from false premises, and bears no responsibility for those false beliefs). Conversely, an action can be materially correct without meeting the formal condition (if, for example, the agent rashly or against her better judgment performs an action that is objectively the correct one in the circumstances). This point that the two conditions are independent has seldom been appreciated in the literature on Fichte's ethics, although distinctions of this form are commonplace in the contemporary ethics literature, which abounds with ways of drawing the line between the 'objective' and 'subjective' rightness of action. Fichte also uses such language, calling the formal condition 'subjective' and the material condition 'objective.' Like many philosophers today, he takes praiseworthiness to attach to subjective rightness only. That is why he sometimes calls the 'formal' condition a condition on actions' 'morality' and the 'material' condition a condition on actions' 'legality' (e.g. at IV: 154 and 275), where 'legality' refers to substantive moral correctness, not (only) accordance with positive law.

4.1 Conscientiousness

Fichte devotes the first section of the third division of the *System of Ethics* (§14) to the general explication of the formal condition. He distinguishes two components of it and—in a coup of terminological unclarity—dubs these its 'formal' and 'material' aspects, respectively. (The material aspect of the formal condition is distinct from the material condition, as I will explain.)

The first (formal) component requires that the agent act not blindly and impulsively but thoughtfully and with consciousness of her duty (IV: 155–6), which in turn requires that she acquire a sufficiently firm conviction, before acting, about what morality demands (IV: 163). This component imposes a sort of due diligence constraint on the pursuit of the moral end, requiring that the agent be sufficiently subjectively confident in her judgment that morality demands this action of her now.

The second (material) component of the formal condition requires that the agent act on that achieved conviction, only on it, and because she has it (IV: 163). This component forbids not only immorally motivated action, but also normative deference to other agents or to tradition or authority.

It appears that failure along one of these two dimensions accompanies failure along the other in every case, on Fichte's view. The material component of the formal condition appears unsatisfiable in cases in which the formal component has not been satisfied; and Fichte has commitments which seem to preclude the possibility of violations of the material component that do not rest on violations of the formal one. I will return to this issue in more detail in what follows.

Fichte presents these two components as consequences that 'follow immediately' from the Kantian idea that morally worthy action must be action *from* duty, not merely action *in accordance with* duty (IV: 155–6). Both are captured in the commonly accepted idea that an action must be conscientious if it is to be morally worthy; and Fichte uses the language of conscience and conscientiousness freely in this section. 'The formal condition of the morality of our actions . . . consists in our decision to do what conscience demands because conscience demands it' (IV: 173). Or, stated as an imperative: 'Act always according to your best conviction of your duty; or: act according to your conscience' (IV: 156; original in italics). But although Fichte clearly intends to capture the Kantian idea of a good will (IV: 157), his discussion departs from Kant in focusing more attention on the first ('formal') component than on the second ('material') one.

Kant's focus in *Groundwork* I is on differentiating between the duty-motive and other motives (such as sympathy or prudence) that could lie behind the same behavior (such as assisting a person in need, or dealing fairly with a person one could easily exploit).[1] Although he acknowledges that it is possible to misjudge whether a given maxim is consistent with the moral law,[2] Kant does not raise or answer the question of what degree of certainty in a given moral judgment is required for reliance on it to count as action from duty. Nor does he raise or answer the question of how we know we have achieved that degree of certainty: how we know the process of practical deliberation has come to an end and provided us with a conviction about what to do, on which we can then conscientiously act. Fichte, by contrast, is chiefly concerned with these two questions—the second especially—in his discussion of the formal condition.

There seem to be two reasons for this difference in focus. The first is that Kant sees the application of the categorical imperative as epistemically relatively unproblematic, whereas Fichte, on whose view practical deliberation is as potentially error-prone as any other exercise of reflective judgment, takes himself to owe the reader both an account of what could give an agent sufficient confidence in its results to justify acting on them, and an account of how an agent can be sure he has in fact attained that level of confidence.

The second reason is that Kant sees agents as capable of failing to incorporate recognized moral obligations into their maxims, whereas Fichte claims that agents always act on the best reasons they are aware of having and therefore (since moral reasons are the best reasons there are) always act on their moral duty to the extent that they are aware of it. It is 'simply impossible and contradictory that someone might with distinct consciousness of what his duty is at the moment of action *consciously decide not to do his duty*' (IV: 191). Since, for Fichte, weakness of will manifests exclusively in epistemic irresponsibility, his account of what the formal condition requires emphasizes epistemic virtue. Both in his discussion of action successful according to the formal condition (in §15) and in his discussion of action unsuccessful according to that condition (in §16), the focus is on what it takes for the process of *deliberation* to go right or wrong.

---

[1] I. Kant 1900-, 4: 397-9; I. Kant 1996a, pp. 52-4.

[2] This acknowledgment comes in two passages in which Kant discusses the traditional doctrine that conscience cannot err. He remarks, in both passages, that the traditional doctrine is true if we understand it to assert only that an individual cannot err about whether he deliberated morally before performing a given action, and cannot err about his own subjective conviction regarding the rightness or wrongness of his act. What Kant denies, in both passages, is that the traditional doctrine is true if we understand it as asserting that an individual cannot be substantively wrong about any of his moral judgments (cf. I. Kant 1900-, 6: 401; I. Kant 1996a, pp. 529-30; I. Kant 1900-, 8: 268; I. Kant 1996b, p. 34). The passages are reproduced in full in footnotes 6 and 7 below.

4.1.1 Formal formal independence

Since the moral law prescribes progress toward an end (the second occurrence of 'freedom' in the formulation at IV: 153), any individual instance of practical deliberation will be a case of means–ends or part–whole reasoning subordinate to that end (as we saw already in §2.2). Recall:

> The moral law, in relation to empirical human beings, has a determinate *starting point*: the determinate limitation in which the individual (in which it initially finds itself) finds himself; it has a determinate (if never reachable) *goal*: absolute liberation from all limitation; and a completely determinate *way* along which it leads us: the order of nature. There is therefore for every determinate individual in any given situation only something determinate that is required by duty—and this, we can say, is what the moral law demands in its application to the temporal being. Call this determinate action or omission *x*. (IV: 166)

Fichte is careful in this section to emphasize that the moral principle specifies only the end, and that the faculty of reflective judgment does the rest of the work. The task of finding this *x* cannot be discharged by the practical faculty because the practical faculty 'is no faculty of cognition' (IV: 165). 'It cannot itself provide this *x*, but rather this *x* is to be sought through the—here freely reflecting—power of judgment' (IV: 166). This means that the process of engaging in and completing practical deliberation is just the same as any other instance of theoretical reasoning: our theoretical faculties run their course until they hit upon a satisfying answer to the question (in this case, the question of which action is the one that, in these circumstances, is most conducive to progress toward the end of absolute independence) (IV: 167).

What the formal condition requires is that this activity of reflective judgment proceed until it has reached 'a certain determinate conviction [*Überzeugung*] (= A)' (IV: 165), the content of A being that some determinate action is the action *x* that is required in this situation. Once this conviction has been attained, the material aspect of the formal condition requires that one act on, and only on, A.

The problem raised by the formal aspect of the formal condition is: how does one recognize that a given conclusion is the one demanded (i.e. that it amounts to the sought conviction, A) (IV: 166)? How does one acquire a sufficiently firm conviction that a proposed action lies within the series such as to be justified—formally or subjectively justified—in going forward with it?

Fichte takes this to be a special problem because of the account of the moral psychology of evil he will present in §16. On that account, human beings are prone to intellectual sloth, self-deception, and outright irresponsibility in theoretical reasoning, and these are the failings that lead them to fail to fulfill the formal condition. The question an agent concerned with fulfilling the formal condition must ask herself, then, is: is my current level of confidence in my judgment A sufficient to justify me in acting upon A? The worry such an agent has is that she may be deceiving herself, she may be biased, she may have overlooked evidence or simply failed to reflect adequately—may be guilty, in other words, of one of the failures described in §16 (which I will describe in §4.2 below).

This question is very easy to mistake for another question, one Fichte is *not* asking in this section. That other question is: is this *x* that I have hit upon after this process of deliberation the action that *as a matter of actual fact* lies on the path toward absolute independence? Fichte does not confuse these two questions in this portion of the text, as many of his readers have done. He assumes that any process of practical deliberation is fallible, and that at any point the *x* hit upon may in fact not be the action objectively required, that any conviction A may be in error. This is true even where the formal condition is fulfilled.

The textual evidence that Fichte took conscientious moral judgment to be fallible is decisive. We see some of that evidence in Fichte's discussion of the duties of individuals who conscientiously disagree (mentioned in §3.2.3.5).

If *the other* claims to have acted according to genuine conviction, and *I* act differently in the same situation, then *I* act just as unethically according to *his* conviction, as *he* does according to *mine*. Whose conviction should be the guide? Neither conviction, so long as they are contradictory; for each should absolutely act according to *his* conviction, and the formal condition of all morality consists in that.   (IV: 233)

Notice the explicit statement that what is at issue is (claimed) disagreement of *genuine* convictions (i.e. convictions meeting the formal condition). Given Fichte's (problematic, but unequivocal) view that in each situation there is exactly one materially correct action (IV: 155, 195), the scenario Fichte envisages in this passage is one in which at least one party is substantively mistaken, although both (by stipulation) fulfill the formal condition. Further, indirect, evidence that Fichte takes even impeccably exercised moral judgment to be fallible comes from consideration of the relevance of scientific progress to the moral project on his view of it. Fichte believes that there is progress in scientific knowledge, that this progress is ongoing (that is, that we will know more in the future than we do today, and that some of the things we believe today are false), and that such progress is a social achievement (that is, that an individual cannot on her own overcome her ignorance in all areas). But he also believes that theoretical knowledge is relevant to moral deliberation and that scientific progress subserves progress toward the moral end. These commitments together entail that we will inevitably draw some false conclusions in any instance of practical deliberation today, because we begin from some false premises and are ignorant of relevant true ones. Such false conclusions are not explained by failure to meet the formal condition, because if our beliefs are supported by the best science of our time, our having them cannot be a matter of epistemic sloth. But they will fall afoul of the material condition on moral correctness.

What Fichte writes in §15 must be read against the background assumption of deliberative fallibility. Indeed if we look carefully at the text we can see that the assumption of fallibility actually figures in the problem as he sets it up:

The formal law of morality declares: act solely in accordance with your conviction of your duty...

But when my conviction is in error, someone could say, then I have not done my duty, but instead done what is contrary to duty. To what extent can I be at ease [*ruhig*] in this [*sc.* in acting on my conviction]?   (IV: 163)

The fulfillment of the formal condition is a problem *because* I know I can err in my first-order moral judgments. Since I cannot rule out that I may be in error, the question is, how can I have sufficient confidence in my judgment A to be able to act conscientiously on that judgment? Must I not constantly second-guess myself? Notice that if the material condition were not independent of the formal one, this set of questions could never arise.

Many have thought that Fichte means to answer the worry he raises here by attempting to show that conscientious practical judgment is not fallible after all. But in fact it is clear that this entire discussion is premised on the possibility of error, and that it concerns only the *finality* of practical deliberation, under circumstances in which the agent can have no independent confirmation of the *veracity* of its result.

The fulfillment of the formal condition, Fichte tells us, requires certainty (*Gewissheit*). But what does he mean by 'certainty' here? We must, on the grounds just given, rule out that he means certainty in the factive sense that entails that one's judgment is true. Can he have in mind certainty in the purely subjective sense of indubitability? This is indeed the first possibility he floats:

But when my conviction is in error, someone could say, then I have not done my duty, but instead done what is contrary to duty. To what extent can I be at ease [*ruhig*] in this [*sc.* in acting on my conviction]? Evidently only insofar as I hold it to be not so much as possible that my conviction could be in error, nor possible that I should ever, in an unending existence, take it to be in error. I compare my action therefore not only against the concept of my current conviction, but I compare this conviction itself against the concept of my entire possible conviction, against the whole system of this, insofar as I can present it to myself in the present moment.   (IV: 163–4)

What is proposed is that I test the current conclusion against the whole set of my other judgments, actual and possible, that are relevant to its truth, as a way of assuring myself that I could never under any foreseeable circumstances deem this conclusion incorrect.

But Fichte immediately rejects this option, pointing out that the present appearance of coherence with these other judgments does not guarantee even the fact of their *coherence*; and that anyway even a coherent set of beliefs is not for that reason indubitable:

> But the whole system of my conviction itself can be given to me in no other way than through my present conviction about it. Just as I can err in the single case, I can also err in the judgment of my judgment, in the conviction about my whole conviction.
> Thus my entire morality, and with it my absolute independence and ease of conscience, remains dependent on accident. I must ... either take my chances [*auf gut Glück handeln*], which is contrary to conscience, or I may not act at all, but must spend my entire life undecided and in an eternal wavering to and fro between the pro and contra: if there is no absolute criterion of the correctness of my conviction about my duty.   (IV: 164)[3]

The danger Fichte sees here is not error, but rather an eternal state of indecision (cf. also XI: 137). How is one to extricate oneself from that state, *given* that one cannot rule out that one's judgment may be in error?

Fulfillment of the material demands of morality is 'dependent upon accident' in a straightforward sense, because these demands are substantive and because practical judgment can err in its determination of them. Satisfaction of the formal condition, by contrast, is supposed to be immune to luck, and so *not* dependent upon accident, because it attaches to moral merit (*Verdienst*). So there must be some way to know I have achieved the determinate conviction, A, demanded by the formal condition. There must be 'an absolute criterion of the correctness of my conviction about my duty' if the formal condition is to be fulfillable. The availability of such a criterion would rule out the possibility that I might, unbeknownst to myself, fail to act on the motive of duty because I have failed to secure a conviction on which to act. This is the problem Fichte sets out to solve in the following pages.

It is in the ensuing pages that he sketches the account of practical deliberation explained in §2.2 above: reflective judgment seeks the x that is the action (materially) required in the circumstances.

> The ethical drive expresses itself here, accordingly, as a drive toward a determinate cognition. Assuming that the power of judgment finds [this] x—something that appears

---

[3] I owe the correction of a translation error in this passage in M. Kosch 2014 to Mike Demo, whose thoughtful comments on that paper also prompted me to rethink what Fichte is saying in this part of the text.

to depend on good luck—[in this case] the drive to the cognition and the cognition [itself] coincide. The original I and the actual are in harmony, and there arises, as always in these cases (according to the proof above) a feeling.   (IV: 166–7)

What happens, subjectively, when our theoretical faculties have hit upon that *x*, is the occurrence of a feeling of 'cool approval' that is exactly similar to the one that accompanies the discovery of the answer to any theoretical question. 'In action we call what is approved in this way *right*; in cognition *true*,' but the feeling of settled conviction that replaces the feeling of doubt that precedes it is the same, because the same cognitive process underlies both (IV: 167).

So long as the power of judgment is still seeking, the free faculty of imagination wavers between opposed [conclusions], and because this seeking is the consequence of a drive and this [drive] has not been satisfied, there is present a feeling of doubt which, since the matter is of highest importance, is connected with worry. (I know that e.g. I *doubt*. How do I know this? Certainly not on the basis of the objective character of the judgment made. Doubt is something subjective. It can only be felt, just like its opposite, certainty.) As soon as the power of judgment finds what is demanded, that this is [in fact] what is demanded is made apparent through the feeling of harmony. The power of imagination is now bound and constrained [*gezwungen*], as in the case of every reality. I can do no other than to see the matter so. As in the case of every feeling, there is constraint. This gives *immediate certainty* in cognition, with which *peace and satisfaction* are connected.

(IV: 167–8; cf. IV: 170 and XI: 127)

This feeling of settled conviction in moral matters is called the voice of conscience. What Fichte tells us in this passage is that its presence answers the question of how one can be assured that the formal aspect of the formal condition is met (when it is) by answering the question of how one can be confident that one has indeed acquired a moral conviction (when one has).

This passage has been read, by Wood, Breazeale, Zöller, and others, as asserting that a feeling arising out of the harmony of the empirical and pure I occurs when, and only when, the judgment that *x* is the right thing to do is *objectively correct*.[4] But this is obviously inconsistent with the text, both on its own and in the context of the larger section, which after all has to do with how to meet the formal rather than the material condition on moral correctness. Fichte is quite explicit here that he is making a phenomenological observation about what it feels like to come to a judgment: 'whether I am doubtful or certain, I learn not through argument… but through an *immediate* feeling' (IV: 169). Readers of

---

[4] A. Wood 2000, p. 105; D. Breazeale 2012, p. 200; J. Schneewind and A. Wood 2012, p. 479. Wood has revised this view in A. Wood 2016.

Peirce will recognize Fichte's point.[5] The feeling occurs not when the judgment is *correct*, but when it has *been made*.

The voice of conscience, Fichte tells us, is both immediate and infallible (IV: 173). It is immediate because a feeling, and infallible because the feeling reflects the state of our own consciousness, occurring when, and only when, doubt is replaced by settled conviction. Fichte's view of the infallibility of conscience is thus like Kant's in that, for both, the epistemic function of conscience is entirely second-order.[6] That is why Fichte can take himself to be agreeing with Kant about conscience in this section.[7]

---

[5] C. Peirce 1877.

[6] Kant also claims that 'an erring conscience is an absurdity,' and in fact Fichte's whole way of framing the issue echoes some remarks of Kant's in his essay 'On the miscarriage of all philosophical trials in theodicy,' which appeared in the *Berlinische Monatsschrift* in 1791. Kant there writes:

> One cannot always stand by the *truth* of what one says to oneself or to another (for one can be mistaken); however, one can and must stand by the *truthfulness* of one's declaration or confession, because one has immediate consciousness of this. For in the first instance we compare what we say with the object in a logical judgment (through the understanding), whereas in the second instance...we compare what we say with the subject (before conscience).... We can call this truthfulness 'formal conscientiousness'; 'material conscientiousness' consists in the caution of not venturing anything on the danger that it might be wrong, whereas 'formal' conscientiousness consists in the consciousness of having applied this caution in a given case. —Moralists speak of an 'erring conscience.' But an erring conscience is an absurdity; and, if there were such a thing, then we could never be certain we have acted rightly, since even the judge in the last instance can still be in error. I can indeed err in the judgment *in which I believe* to be right, for this belongs to the understanding which alone judges objectively (rightly or wrongly); but in the judgment *whether I in fact believe* to be right (or merely pretend it) I absolutely cannot be mistaken, for this judgment—or rather this proposition—merely says that I judge the object in such-and-such a way.
> (I. Kant 1900–, 8: 267–8; I. Kant 1996b, p. 34)

In the *Metaphysics of Morals*, the view is the same:

> I shall here pass over the various divisions of conscience and note only that, as follows from what has been said, an *erring* conscience is an absurdity. For while I can indeed be mistaken at times in my objective judgment as to whether something is a duty or not, I cannot be mistaken in my subjective judgment as to whether I have submitted it to my practical reason (here in its role as judge) for such a judgment; for if I could be mistaken in that, I would have made no practical judgment at all, and in that case there would be neither truth nor error. (I. Kant 1900–, 6: 401; I. Kant 1996a, pp. 529–30)

Kant goes on to note that it follows from this that 'to act in accordance with conscience cannot itself be a duty; for if it were, there would have to be yet a second conscience in order for one to become aware of the act of the first. The duty here is only to cultivate one's conscience, to sharpen one's attentiveness to the voice of the inner judge and to use every means to obtain a hearing for it' (I. Kant 1900–, 6: 401; I. Kant 1996a, p. 530). But in *Religion within the Boundaries of Mere Reason* (in a passage Fichte cites) he seems to say the opposite—'*Conscience is a consciousness which is of itself a duty*'—and goes on to describe the duty of conscientiousness as something very like the duty Fichte describes in this part of the *System of Ethics* (I. Kant 1900–, 6: 185–6; I. Kant 1996b, pp. 202–3: the full quotation can be found in note 7).

[7] Fichte's interpreters, by contrast, take him to be disagreeing with Kant (and so take his claim in this section that he agrees with Kant to be a mistake). Breazeale contrasts Fichte's and Kant's

Fichte is careful to point out that the second-order judgment based upon this feeling is no guarantee of the substantive truth of an agent's first-order conviction. 'This criterion of correctness of our conviction is, as we have seen, an inner one. An outer, objective one does not exist...' (IV: 170).[8] He also cautions the reader that although it is correct to say that 'conscience is *the immediate consciousness of our determinate duty*' (IV: 173), we should take care not to take this statement out of context:

The formal condition of the morality of our actions, or their morality in the narrow sense, consists in [our] deciding to do what conscience demands simply because it demands it. But conscience is *the immediate consciousness of our determinate duty*. This is to be understood in no other way than the one in which it has been derived. For the

---

accounts of the role of conscience in deliberation, writing: 'Whereas for Kant, conscience is an inner tribunal that ascertains whether we have really determined our actions according to respect for the moral law, for Fichte it is precisely "an inner feeling within our conscience" that determines what is and is not our duty, a feeling that "never errs so long as we pay heed to its voice"' (D. Breazeale 2012, p. 200). Wood likewise contrasts these in J. Schneewind and A. Wood 2012 (pp. 480–1), though he revises this view in A. Wood 2016 (p. 164). On my interpretation, which Wood appears now to follow, Fichte is correct in his assessment of his agreement with Kant. The reader is invited to compare Fichte's position as here explained with the passage he cites from *Religion within the Boundaries of Mere Reason*:

> *Conscience is a consciousness which is of itself a duty.* But how can we think such a consciousness, when the consciousness of all our representations seems to be necessary only for logical purposes, hence only conditionally, whenever we want to clarify our representation; hence cannot be unconditional duty?
> It is a moral principle, requiring no proof, that we *ought to venture nothing where there is danger that it might be wrong (quod dubitas, ne feceris!* Pliny). So the *consciousness* that an action *which I want to undertake* is right, is unconditional duty. Now it is understanding, not conscience, which judges whether an action is in general right or wrong. And it is not absolutely necessary to know, of all possible actions, whether they are right or wrong. With respect to the action that *I* want to undertake, however, I must not only judge, and be of the opinion, that it is right; I must also be *certain* that it is. And this is a requirement of conscience to which is opposed *probabilism*, i.e. the principle that the mere opinion that an action may well be right is itself sufficient for undertaking it. Conscience could also be defined as *the moral faculty of judgment, passing judgment upon itself*, except that this definition would be much in need of prior clarification of the concepts contained in it. Conscience does not pass judgment upon actions as cases that stand under the law, for this is what reason does so far as it is subjectively practical (whence the *casus conscientiæ* and casuistry, as a kind of dialectic of conscience). Rather, here reason judges itself, whether it has actually undertaken, with all diligence, that examination of actions (whether they are right or wrong), and it calls upon the human being himself to witness *for* or *against* himself whether this has taken place or not.
> (I. Kant 1900–, 6: 185–6; I. Kant 1996b, pp. 202–3)

Fichte also agrees with Kant's judgment that 'if someone is aware that he has acted in accordance with his conscience, then as far as guilt or innocence is concerned nothing more can be required of him. It is incumbent upon him only to enlighten his *understanding* in the matter of what is or is not duty' (I. Kant 1900–, 6: 401; I. Kant 1996a, p. 530).

[8] Kant draws the same distinction at I. Kant 1900–, 6: 401; I. Kant 1996a, pp. 529–30.

consciousness of something determinate, as such, is never immediate, but is only found through an act of thought (materially, the consciousness of our duty is not immediate). But the consciousness *that* this determinate [thing] is duty is, when the determinate [thing] has been given, an immediate consciousness. The consciousness of duty is formally immediate. This formal consciousness is a bare feeling.

Conscience...does not provide the material; this is delivered only by the power of judgment, and conscience is no power of judgment; but it provides evidentness [*Evidenz*], and this sort of evidentness is found only in the case of consciousness of duty.   (IV: 173)

He reiterates the point in the second corollary:

So that the word *feeling* does not give rise to dangerous misunderstandings, let me be more precise: a theoretical proposition is not felt and cannot be felt; what is felt is rather the certainty and sure conviction connected with the thought of [that proposition when it has been] brought about according to theoretical laws.   (IV: 174–5; cf. GA 4–1: 86)

His claims about immediacy and feeling, in other words, are not to be taken to imply that one acquires the first-order conviction that x is the action to be performed in a given situation by 'immediately feeling' it. (This is a very good thing, for given the fact that what is involved is the upshot of a piece of theoretical reasoning, the view he here rejects would commit him to the 'immediacy' (in the same sense) of all knowledge.)

Although Fichte takes care to forestall any confusion between this inner, subjective condition on moral correctness and the outer, objective one—pointing out explicitly the distinctness of the formal and material conditions at the start of the discussion (IV: 156), emphasizing along the way that the formal criterion is subjective and inner, not 'an outer, objective' criterion (IV: 170), and returning to the contrast between formal and material conditions at the end of the discussion (IV: 172–3)—virtually everyone who has written about Fichte's ethics has mis-understood his doctrine of the infallibility of conscience, attributing to Fichte the view that this second-order feeling of settled conviction about a judgment in fact guarantees the substantive material correctness of the first order judgment it is about.

Hegel attributed this view to Fichte in several works;[9] and from Hegel this reading of the *System of Ethics* passed into the general philosophical imagination. It has long been standard in texts of the history of philosophy,[10] and is still nearly

---

[9] Cf. *Phänomenologie des Geistes* §§632–71 (G.W.F. Hegel 1986, vol. 3, pp. 464–94), and especially §635 (G.W.F. Hegel 1986, vol. 3, pp. 466–7); *Grundlinien der Philosophie des Rechts* §137 (G.W.F. Hegel 1986, vol. 7, pp. 254ff.).

[10] Cf. e.g. Coppleston, for whom Fichtean conscience is 'an absolute criterion of right and wrong' (F. Coppleston 1962, vol. 7, p. 65) and who praises Fichte for tracking the 'way in which the ordinary

universal even among scholars of Fichte.[11] That such an account is implausible has been charged by virtually everyone who has attributed it to Fichte, beginning with Hegel. That makes its persistence a puzzle, especially given that the texts themselves and the architectonic of the *System of Ethics* rule it out categorically. Why have readers been so confused about this issue? I can offer no complete explanation. Part of the problem is surely the fact, which I have already mentioned, that Fichte often uses apparently factive vocabulary ('certainty' and even 'truth') in this section, a permission he gives himself because he has described the section as being concerned only with what goes on from within the agent's subjective point of view. From my own perspective in the moment of deliberation, my fulfillment of the formal and material conditions cannot come apart: I cannot perform an action from duty if I do not believe that duty actually demands that action (that is, that the action

---

man is accustomed to speak about his moral convictions' (by saying, for example, 'I feel that this is the right thing to do') (F. Coppleston 1962, vol. 7, p. 66). Cf. also K. Fischer 1884, pp. 580ff.

[11] At least, this was true before the publication of M. Kosch 2014. Of course even then this reading was not strictly ubiquitous. Peter Rohs, for example, explicitly acknowledges the existence of a material standard of correctness of actions that is independent of the deliverance of conscience (P. Rohs 1991b, p. 109). But its continuing appeal was made salient to me in a 2012 APA presentation by Günter Zöller, who pointed to the 'criteriological' role of conscience as a feature of Fichte's ethical theory that should make it unattractive to contemporary Kantians. Conscience, according to Zöller's Fichte, is a source of immediate and infallible moral insight. 'Unlike in standard situations of applying a means–ends calculus as part of consequentialist reasoning Fichte's ethical deliberator does not actually consider the short-, medium- and long-range outcome of various courses of action vying for preferential selection and exclusive execution. Rather Fichte's ethical ego turns to his or her own conscience as a source of immediate, allegedly infallible insight, not weighing consequences but attending to an inner voice' (G. Zöller 2012, pp. 5–6). Allen Wood has supported Zöller's reading in correspondence, and defended parts of the criterial interpretation in a 2012 paper, arguing that on Fichte's account conscience is an infallible guide to substantive moral correctness, and contrasting Fichte's view of the role of conscience with Kant's (J. Schneewind and A. Wood 2012, pp. 479–81)—although in earlier work, Wood advanced an interpretation more in line with the one I advance here (cf. A. Wood 1990, pp. 176ff.), and in more recent work (A. Wood 2016) he seems to concede the points I make in M. Kosch 2014. Daniel Breazeale has also defended the criterial interpretation in a 2012 paper. Like Zöller, Breazeale calls conscience's role for Fichte 'criteriological' (D. Breazeale 2012, p. 202). Like Wood, he contrasts Fichte's view of conscience with that of Kant (D. Breazeale 2012, p. 200). Breazeale takes the exercise of reflecting judgment to be part of practical deliberation, but he sees its function not as ordinary calculative reasoning but instead as a process 'which produces in me a certain mental "harmony" with my feeling of independence, a harmony that is perceived as a *feeling* of "ought"' (D. Breazeale 2012, p. 200). He identifies that process of reflection with conscience itself (thereby giving conscience a first-order epistemic role), and attributes to Fichte the view that conscience is substantively infallible. 'What we have just described is nothing other than the operation of conscience, which, properly understood, is our unfailing moral guide in every concrete situation' (D. Breazeale 2012, p. 200). In earlier work, Breazeale describes Fichtean conscience as 'the positive criterion' of truth for moral beliefs, claiming that this criterion, though 'subjective,' is nevertheless the only one, and that it is, for Fichte, immune to error (D. Breazeale 1996, pp. 48–50). Gunnar Beck likewise remarks that, according to Fichte, 'by dint of our conscience . . . each man has direct, unmediated and complete awareness of what the moral law commands him . . . to do' (G. Beck 2008, p. 69).

fulfills the material condition). Only for an observer can an agent's fulfillment of formal and material conditions come apart. This is the possibility that interpreters have thought Fichte's account cannot accommodate; but there is no evidence in this section that Fichte means to rule it out.

Apart from Fichte's use of factive vocabulary, I see only one other possible explanation for this mistake. This is the set of remarks Fichte makes as he turns from discussion of the formal condition on moral worth to discussion of the material one at the beginning of §17. The main point being made there is that the account of the formal condition does not suffice for a scientific account of ethics. 'Either we must be able to determine *a priori* what conscience would approve in general, or we must admit that a doctrine of ethics, as a real and applicable science, is not possible' (IV: 208). But in passing Fichte remarks that, for everyday life, conscience suffices (IV: 208, 209). Whether there is a tension between this remark and the account of practical deliberation in §15 is a point that has divided interpreters.[12] I see none, but that is because I take it that many of the inferences involved in practical deliberation are made automatically and outside of conscious awareness, and that they are, inevitably, often based on premises that the agent has not consciously articulated. This was Fichte's view as well, as we can see at various points in the posthumously published appendix to the *System of Ethics* dedicated to strategies for moral self-improvement. There Fichte distinguishes between weighty actions that always prompt explicit deliberation and everyday actions performed more or less unthinkingly (XI: 130–1); he describes a process of habituation whereby complex actions that once required conscious deliberation about each step are rendered automatic by practice (XI: 133); and he describes 'unconscious premises of our judgments' as one of the primary sources of unclarity in our moral thinking (XI: 134).

If this is correct, the claim that for the most part the feeling of certainty in one's conviction is all that occurs, consciously, to the deliberating agent by no means entails that conscience has a first-order epistemic function.[13] Here again the

---

[12] Baumanns, for example, sees no contradiction here: 'To act conscientiously is not like acting instinctively. Conscientious action does not preclude a calculated choice of the right, a calculation of the required action' (P. Baumanns 1990, p. 146). But Wood has argued that this comment is proof that Fichte does not take practical deliberation to (ever) involve consequentialist calculation (in correspondence; cf. also A. Wood 2016, pp. 148, 177–80).

[13] Some 20th-century moral philosophers have inferred intuitionism in moral epistemology from the fact that moral judgment seems (in many cases) like being faced with 'the immediate consciousness of our determinate duty.' Sturgeon explains how the denial that moral inferences can take place outside of conscious awareness can motivate intuitionistic conclusions, and why this is a mistake, in N. Sturgeon 2002 (pp. 205ff.). Sturgeon's point is illuminating here, because the same (mistaken) conclusion seems to have been drawn by many of Fichte's readers.

parallel with theoretical (e.g. perceptual) judgment is clarifying. For example, when we are asked to judge whether two items are the same distance away but different sizes, or different distances away but the same size, in some cases we know the answer immediately and can state it with confidence, and in other cases we are unsure and aware that we are unsure. We (as perceivers) need be able to give no account of the perceptual cues and the inferences made from them that allow us to judge confidently in the first case. We may be aware only of the judgment and of our degree of confidence in it. But there are in fact such cues, and we in fact draw inferences on their basis, without being conscious of doing so; and moreover both the cues and the inferences can be examined and laid out systematically. I take Fichte to be pointing out that something similar is true in the practical case (relevantly similar: I do not mean to suggest that Fichte takes moral judgment to be in any other respect like perception).

Of course another thing Fichte may have in mind, when he writes that from the standpoint of ordinary deliberation conscience suffices, is that all one ever has to go on, in deciding what to do, is the outcome of the best practical reasoning one can muster, based on the facts as one believes them to be. The same could be said for any process or inquiry, however, and it hardly requires saying that there is no tension between this acknowledgment and the commitment to there being a fact of the matter about the substantive correctness of one's judgment that is independent of the judgment itself.

4.1.2 Material formal independence

Fichte claims in the third corollary in §15 that the voice of conscience may not be replaced by the judgment of an external authority as a guide to action. This is the material aspect of the formal condition: 'Whoever acts on authority, necessarily acts unconscientiously' (IV: 175; original in italics). He takes this material aspect to follow from the characterization he has given of the formal aspect, since the feeling of certainty that he has described comes only to one who has made a judgment himself:

[I]t is the exclusive condition of possibility of [the feeling of certainty] that the subject himself actually judged. Thus certainty and conviction of foreign judgments simply does not occur; and conscience can absolutely not allow itself to be led by authority.   (IV: 175)

But the claim in the final clause allows weaker and stronger interpretations; and only on the weaker interpretation does the material aspect follow uncontroversially from the formal aspect of the formal condition.

On the weaker interpretation, the final clause is just a restatement of the clause preceding it, and there is only one, relatively unproblematic claim in this passage: that no one else can, in the literal sense, make one's moral judgments for one in a way that produces the characteristic feeling of settled conviction. On the stronger interpretation, the final clause states a further conclusion: that deference to someone else's normative authority is never permissible, because one can never act conscientiously on judgments that arise from such deference. Whether the claim on the stronger interpretation follows from the claim on the weaker one is a matter of dispute.[14] Fichte often appears simply to assume that it does, or else not to notice that the weaker and stronger claims are distinct. At any rate he offers no argument linking the two.

But although the stronger claim is controversial, given other aspects of Fichte's view it would not be especially worrisome if it were the intended force of that final clause. For as he immediately explains, he does not mean it to rule out the possibility that individuals might learn, morally, from other individuals, and indeed that they might do so by accepting, in at least a provisional way, those others as moral authorities:

> One can however lead the research of human beings; one can offer them the premises of the judgment one hopes to produce, which can be taken on, provisionally, on authority. This is more or less the story of all human beings; they obtain through upbringing that on which the human race has reached consensus up until their epoch and which has henceforth become universal human belief, as the premises for their own judgments, which they for the most part take on without further examination . . . .
>
> But before he acts everyone is bound by conscience to *judge for himself* on the basis of those premises accepted in good faith, [and] himself to draw the final conclusions that immediately determine his action.   (IV: 176)

What is more, Fichte does not offer the usual Kantian reasons for denying that there can be moral expertise. Instead he argues that the ultimate authority of individual conscience is consistent with the demand for openness to moral persuasion by others (IV: 245–7), including moral experts, whose existence he admits (IV: 348–53).

Much of the second part of the third division is devoted to the practical problem of how to act in the face of moral disagreement with one's peers. In the recent literature, the debate about peer disagreement centers on how the agent should (unilaterally) adjust her credences in the face of it.[15] Fichte takes the mere fact of disagreement to be no reason to adjust one's credences. Instead, he takes it to be a reason to reflect further upon them and to discuss them with others, especially with others who disagree, with a view to reaching consensus on

---

[14] Cf. e.g. J. Raz 1979 and P. Soper 2002.
[15] Cf. D. Christensen 2007; A. Elga 2007; D. Enoch 2010; and R. Feldman and A. Warfield 2010.

the questions involved (IV: 229–53 *passim*). He takes the obligation of an agent whose mind is not changed by the substance of such discussions to be to stand her ground and to be guided by her own judgment. It is worth noting that this is hardly an extreme position; in fact it is taken to be the default position in the contemporary literature on moral deference.[16]

In the political context in which the discussion of normative deference often arises—the question of the nature of the political duty to obey a law with which one substantively disagrees—Fichte finds grounds other than a duty of deference (viz. the heuristic importance of disagreement and the high moral stakes) to avoid the anarchist consequences to which his thoughts about the material aspect of the formal condition might otherwise seem to lead. He does not intend any claim about the material aspect of the formal condition to grant blanket permission to conscientious objection to political authority (IV: 239–40). What he means to rule out is only the moral permissibility of acting against one's own firm, considered conviction and acting instead on the expressed conviction of some other agent, acting in a private capacity, or of trying to cause anyone else to do the same (IV: 233).

4.2 Moral Evil

The topic of §16 is how practical deliberation can go wrong or, as Fichte puts it in the section title, 'the cause of evil in the finite rational being.' The juxtaposition seems surprising until one reminds oneself that in calling improper deliberation the source of all 'evil' Fichte does not mean to claim that it is the source of all substantive moral failure, but only that it is the source of all *formal* moral failure. Of course Fichte does also think (unsurprisingly) that improper deliberation is the source of much substantive moral failure. But it is important to bear in mind that materially incorrect action due to blameless ignorance does not fall under the rubric 'evil' in the sense relevant to §16.

The discussion in §16 is split into three parts.[17] The first part (IV: 177–91) consists of the sketch of developmental psychology already described briefly in §2.3.2 above. The second part (IV: 191–8) is the core of the discussion of what

[16] That pure moral deference is problematic is taken as the default position both by those who defend that position (cf. e.g. S. McGrath 2009; and A. Hills 2009b; for an early and influential statement see R.P. Wolff 1970) and by those who seek to challenge it, defending pure moral deference in principle (cf. e.g. P. Soper 2002 and D. Koltonski 2010 and 2016).

[17] It is tempting to think that these three discussions were composed at different times and collected somewhat arbitrarily as Fichte was pulling together material for the lectures that became the *System of Ethics*. But this supposition is undermined by the fact that all three of these appear in the parallel discussion in the Mirbach notes of the 1796 lectures on moral philosophy (GA: 4–1: 100).

goes wrong in faulty deliberation. The third part (IV: 198–205) is an appendix dedicated to Fichte's interpretation of the Kantian doctrine of radical evil. The first part is, I take it, meant to provide a basis for the latter two, insofar as it develops the important idea that rationality, and standards of rationality, develop from an initial state in which the rational powers are entirely inactive, in a process that is both historical and psychological. The second part then describes what happens when the quality of an individual's judgment falls below a baseline already attained, set by her social milieu. The third links the tendency toward such lapses to a fundamental feature of human nature—*Trägheit* (laziness or inertia)—on the one hand and to two fundamental vices—cowardice and mendacity—on the other hand.

Let me begin by recapitulating Fichte's sketch of developmental psychology in the first part of §16. The initial state he describes is one in which the agent is conscious of the natural drive 'and acts according to its demands, with freedom (in the formal sense of this word) but without consciousness of this its freedom' (IV: 178). Should this individual reflect upon its situation it will free itself from instinct, but it will initially be able only to act on the natural drive in various ways. Such an individual acts on maxims (IV: 179). Since he is conscious only of the demands of the natural drive, and since the end of the natural drive is pleasure or enjoyment (*Genuß*), his highest maxim will be that of choosing 'what promises intensively and extensively the most pleasure' (IV: 180).

It is possible to remain one's entire life at this stage of minimal reflection, if nothing induces one to take a further step. 'In this sense, evil is inborn' (IV: 182). It is surpassed only when such an agent begins to ask himself, what *ought* to happen? Fichte points out that this asking cannot be the result of an intention the agent could have formed, on her own, ahead of time, because the transformation consists in acquiring a new concept—the categorical OUGHT—that was by hypothesis absent before.

Here is something incomprehensible; and it must be so, because we stand here at the boundary of comprehensibility in the doctrine of freedom [as] applied to the empirical subject. For so long as I do not yet stand at the higher point of reflection, it is not there for me at all; thus I can have no concept of what I ought, before I actually do it. It is nonetheless still the case that I absolutely ought to do it: that is, I ought to relative to another judger, who is familiar with this point, and relative to myself, when I [shall] have reached it. When [I reach that point] I will not excuse myself by appeal to my incapacity, but will instead rebuke myself for not having reached it long since.   (IV: 181–2)

What I ought to do (namely progress to a higher point of reflection) is something of which I have no concept before I spontaneously develop the concept, in which case I will have already done what I ought. On Fichte's view the necessary spur to this, as to the first stage of reflection, is social interaction. Each individual takes up the normative standards of his social milieu, and this is explained by the fact that, as we have seen, moral agency is the result of upbringing (IV: 184; GA 4–1: 87).

He next describes the possibility that an individual may become conscious of the drive to pure independence, but in a way that leads to an amoral striving for domination. Such an individual will be free in a different sense from the individual guided by the maxim of pleasure. The latter is free formally, but still fettered to nature and the end of enjoyment. He can satisfy the natural drive in more than one way; but it is still only the natural drive he must satisfy. The individual at this new, 'heroic' stage (IV: 190) becomes free materially as well: he has a choice between action on the end of pleasure and action on the end of independence (IV: 184; cf. XI: 135). In this case as well, the drive to absolute independence functions as a drive—that is, as an otherwise opaque source of motivation—and not as a law (IV: 185; cf. XI: 135). Typically such action occurs in outbursts against a background of behavior informed by the maxim of self-interest (IV: 186). This stage is in a certain sense an advance, insofar as the individual has independence as his conscious end, and is no longer in the grip of nature.

The remaining step is to bring this drive toward absolute independence to clear consciousness, transforming it from a blind and lawless drive 'to an absolutely commanding law' (IV: 191). This also is an act of reflection, and so spontaneity; it likewise relies in the typical case on social interaction. The person on the other side of this final transformation 'knows that he simply [*schlechthin*] ought'—that is, I take it, is aware of a categorical imperative—which requires that he make it his maxim 'always to do what duty demands *because duty demands it*' (IV: 191). So concludes the first part of §16.

In answering the question of how it is possible that an individual at such a stage might fail to fulfill the formal condition, Fichte begins by ruling out what might seem the most obvious answer:

It is simply impossible and contradictory that someone, in distinct consciousness of his duty in the moment of action, in full consciousness [*mit gutem Bewusstseyn*] *decides not to do his duty*; that he, rebelling against the law, refuses to obey it, and makes it his maxim not to do what is his duty, because it is his duty. Such a maxim would be devilish . . .   (IV: 191)

Evidently, Fichte means to refer here to Kant's denial, in *Religion within the Limits of Mere Reason*, that a human being can adopt the 'devilish' maxim of immorality for its own sake.[18] But he commits himself to far more than Kant does there, in this sentence and the ones that follow.

---

[18] I. Kant 1900–, 6: 35, 37; I. Kant 1996b, pp. 82, 84.

He argues that to be clearly conscious of one's duty means to demand some action of oneself, as intelligence; but to decide in full consciousness not to do one's duty would be to do the very opposite, and in the same moment, and this is impossible (IV: 191–2). The only possibility in the vicinity is that one's view of the requirement of duty is obscured (IV: 192). This seems to rule out a construal of the material aspect of the formal condition whereon violations of it can vary independently of violations of the formal aspect. If the consciousness of duty is clear and present, failure to act on the motive of duty is impossible. Fichte thus emphasizes here that this clear consciousness of duty is fragile: it remains only as long as one maintains it actively in reflection. If one lets it fall, the necessity of acting on it disappears (IV: 192).

Although it is possible for an agent to lose sight of his duty entirely, reverting to one of the earlier moral-developmental stages, the more common case is one in which the agent keeps sight of duty in general, but allows his consciousness of duty to become obscure (IV: 193–4). The mechanism of obscuring that Fichte describes is a process of abstraction. It is possible, he remarks, to abstract consciously and according to a rule; and there is nothing wrong with doing that. What happens when duty is obscured is a different, ruleless sort of abstraction, in which thought simply becomes less determinate. It is a natural propensity of human thought to fall into abstraction in this second sense, or never to become determinate to begin with. We are prone to think vague and general thoughts; we find precise and clearly defined thoughts more difficult to produce and maintain.

In the case of the thought of duty, there are three determinacies that may be lost to this sort of abstraction, and so three typical forms of moral error (IV: 194). One can, first, settle on the wrong action as the unique one required in the situation (perhaps because one has lost sight of the details that distinguish the action one would like to perform from the action one ought to perform in a given circumstance) (IV: 195). Or one can, second, make a determinate judgment as to the action, but an indeterminate judgment about the appropriate time to carry it out (a worry in the case of the many duties that are not firmly tied to the present moment—procrastination belongs here, as well as failure to appreciate the urgency of some task) (IV: 195). Finally, one can, third, lose sight of the determinacy of the form of the duty, taking the action to be recommended, or a good idea, but not a strict requirement (or more generally taking the deliverance of practical deliberation to be good counsel, to be followed when not too costly, but not an absolute demand) (IV: 195–6).

Fichte's description of the first sort of case is critical for understanding what he takes to be going on when clear consciousness of duty is lost; but it is also puzzling. He writes:

First, in each determinate situation a determinate action (among all those possible) is duty, and all of the others are contrary to duty. Only the concept of *this* action is accompanied by the above-described feeling of certainty and conviction. This determinacy of the action escapes us, while the form of the concept of duty remains. We grasp something else as duty, the sort of thing we might perhaps, for all we know, also do for the sake of duty, but which when we actually do it must, unbeknownst to us, in fact be demanded and determined by some inclination, since we have already lost the authentic guiding thread [*Leitfaden*] of conscience. We deceive ourselves in this case about what our duty itself is, and act, as one commonly says, from an erring conscience. But this error is and remains our fault [*unser Schuld*]. Had we held fast to the insight into duty that was already present (and this depends solely upon our freedom), we would not have erred. Here a very dangerous self-deception prevails, against which one need always be on guard.   (IV: 195)

What Fichte seems to be describing is a case in which I perform an action y, thinking it is morally required and that I am performing it from the motive of duty; but in fact some other action x was morally required in my situation, and I am, unbeknownst to myself, in fact performing y out of inclination. I am guilty of a sort of double wishful thinking: about what the right action is and what moves me to do the action I am doing. If we ask which is more fundamental, the judgment about the action or the shift in motivation, the answer appears to be: the shift in motivation. I have let go of the guiding thread of conscience and instead let inclination be my guide. This then explains the fact that I lose track of some morally relevant considerations, which in turn explains my lapse of judgment about which action to perform. I am blameworthy for the lapse of judgment, in this case, because the act of letting go of a prior grasp of duty was a free one.

How is the possibility of this scenario left open by the account in §15? We can start to answer that question by ruling out a reading on which, although x is the required action, this is something I could not know, and so my performance of y is (at least from my own current perspective) conscientious. Clearly x must be the *subjectively* rational action, in this case, first because we are after all still considering the formal condition, and second because, were it not, no self-deception at the level of motivation would be required to explain the fact that I have chosen y. Fichte is here drawing a distinction between the genuinely subjectively rational action (the action prescribed by the totality of the agent's relevant beliefs coupled with the moral end) and an action that appears subjectively rational (because prescribed by the beliefs actually accessed in this instance of practical reasoning, which constitute a proper subset of the totality and do not include all beliefs actually relevant in this action situation).[19]

---

[19] Cf. A. Sepielli 2014 for a similar distinction between two senses of 'subjective rationality.'

But is the idea then that we can fail to meet the formal condition *without knowing* that we have failed to meet it? This seems exactly what was supposed to be precluded in §15. One possibility is to understand Fichte as here assuming that the *motivation* to fulfill the formal condition—to act conscientiously—must be present in order for the verdict of conscience to be reliable, and that it is not present in this case. This would render the passage consistent with the account in §15. It would not explain why the case must involve self-deception, however: what prevents the agent registering the absence of the motive of conscientiousness? That the flaw must not be fully apparent to the agent seems the reason for the (otherwise puzzling) specification that the action performed be the sort of thing the agent might (in other circumstances) do from the motive of duty ('the sort of thing we might perhaps, for all we know, also do for the sake of duty'), since it is plausible to think that failures of conscientiousness can be more easily masked in cases with this feature.

Certainly Fichte wants to deny that failures of reflection are the result of any conscious policy: there is, he writes, no maxim of letting consciousness of duty become obscured (IV: 193). Instead, in all cases, the ultimate explanation of failure to maintain a precise and accurate representation of one's duty is an inborn laziness (*Trägheit*) with respect to the activity of reflection (IV: 199). This is the force that counters the motive of conscientiousness. It is the topic of the appendix, the third part of §16, where Fichte explains reflective sloth as the expression in us of a natural principle (IV: 199), a *power* (*Kraft*) of inertia (IV: 200). We all start out thoughtless, as children, and are prone to revert to thoughtlessness out of habit; indeed the very existence of habit is a manifestation of the inner force of inertia (IV: 200). '*Laziness*, that reproduces itself into infinity through long habituation, and soon becomes a complete incapacity for good, is the true, inborn radical evil, lying in human nature itself' (IV: 202). (Virtue, by contrast, cannot become a habit: 'Practice and vigilance, standing guard over oneself must be continual; no one is certain of his morality even for a moment without continual strenuous effort' (IV: 193; cf. IV: 199–204).)

From laziness spring the two other vices Fichte discusses in §16: cowardice (*Feigheit*) and mendacity (*Falschheit*). Cowardice is laziness about insisting on our freedom and independence in relation to others (IV: 202). It manifests in deference, one failure to meet the 'material' formal condition. Indeed, Fichte defines cowardice as unwillingness to insist on acting on one's own judgments already in §15 (IV: 175). Mendacity develops as a way of asserting one's will interpersonally when direct means cannot be employed, because of cowardice (IV: 203). These three—laziness, cowardice, and mendacity—are the three 'fundamental vices' of humanity (IV: 203).

In Fichte's discussion of laziness it is clear that what is at issue is primarily reflective sloth, and this puts the discussion firmly within the ambit of the formal condition as explained in §15. Cowardice and mendacity are not mere failures of reflection, however. These look like substantive failures (mendacity most obviously). Yet it seems to follow from the setup that the problems described in §16 must all have to do with failures of the reasoning process. Does this pose a problem for the thesis that formal and material conditions or moral worth are independent? I do not believe it does. What makes lying (the behavior at issue in the doctrine of duties) substantively wrong is its effects on the people deceived. What makes mendacity (the disposition at issue here) formally wrong is its effects on one's own deliberative practice. These are not unconnected; in fact a causal connection typically runs in both directions. But the fact that many substantive failures will invariably have their roots in formal failures is consistent with the existence of substantive moral failures that do not arise out of formal failures, as well as with the view that substantive and formal failures are fundamentally different in kind.

4.3 The Formal Condition and Formal Freedom

It is tempting to try to draw a line between blameworthy substantive failures and non-blameworthy ones by connecting the former, but not the latter, to formal failures. But it would be wrong to see this as part of Fichte's project in this section.[20] Certainly it is very difficult to see failures to meet the formal condition as blameworthy in any sense easily recognizable either today or in Fichte's own time. Formally insufficient decisions look instead, in virtue of their formal insufficiency, to be actions for which their agents are characteristically non-responsible.

This is because we typically take blameworthiness for an action to involve both knowledge of what it would be better to do and the ability to do that thing; but neither condition obtains in the case of the vicious agents of §16. That they are ignorant of what action is required at the time of action follows from Fichte's denial that anyone can clearly see their duty and yet fail to do it; and Fichte's repeated insistence that vicious agents are incapable of extracting themselves from vice without help is one of the most striking features of the discussion in §16. Although he concedes that it is possible for an agent to free herself spontaneously from thoughtlessness (IV: 193) and possible for individuals to raise themselves higher than the level of cultivation of character demanded by their

[20] My view on this has changed since M. Kosch 2013.

social milieu (IV: 204; cf. 184), he portrays such occurrences as rare, and emphasizes that vice is not a state from which one can typically extract oneself on one's own (IV: 201; cf. GA 4–1: 99). The vicious are capable of the greater effort that virtue would require (IV: 204), but they are typically unaware of their capacity for it and so incapable of spurring themselves to exercise it. The impetus to moral improvement 'must come from without' (IV: 204; cf. GA 4–1: 100).

I noted in §2.3.2 that Fichte's moral psychology in general is strikingly naturalistic, in a way that might seem at odds with his broadly Kantian assumptions, and especially with his insistence on the indeterministic spontaneity of human agency. I argued that the explanation for that is that he takes the will to be spontaneous and undetermined only insofar as, and because, the intellect is spontaneous and undetermined, and that there is for him nothing to the spontaneity of the will over and above the spontaneity of the intellect. His presentation of moral evil as explained by a natural principle of inertia is consistent with that picture, because what is involved is primarily an intellectual failure, and more precisely a failure of the intellect to assert itself over the 'nature' (in the form of the system of natural drives) of the finite rational being. That there can in fact be no conception of moral responsibility that would apply to vicious and virtuous agents alike is a consequence of this. Formal freedom varies together with excellence in reflection, which is itself moral excellence in the formal sense: the worse one's behavior, the less one is responsible for it; whereas the better it is, the more responsible for it one becomes.[21]

One final thing to note is Fichte's emphasis on the way in which one's virtue, one's responsibility, one's degree of intellectual activeness (all of which co-vary) all depend in turn on one's social and natural milieu. In §16 and §25 Fichte emphasizes the importance of examples of good moral conduct; in §18 he emphasizes the importance of dialogue among peers; in §16 and in §§27–30 he emphasizes the importance of education; and in §33 he emphasizes that the possibility of all of these depends on adequate nutrition, physical safety, and adequate leisure time, and therefore on the degree of control agents have over their natural environment. Fichte thought it was obvious that people deliberate poorly when they are exhausted from overwork or malnutrition, that they act without having come to a firm conviction about the right thing to do when circumstances force them to, and that people with more stressful or precarious

---

[21] That Fichte is still willing to remark at least in passing that their error is their 'own fault' (in a sense he does not specify) because the first loss of the thread of conscience is a 'free' act (IV: 295) is a puzzle, since what is involved in losing that thread is not an *act* of the intellect at all, but instead a failure of the intellect to act and so an *absence* of spontaneity.

lives make mistakes they might have avoided had their lives been less stressful or precarious. Education, leisure, health, safety, and many other material conditions contribute to deliberative integrity and thereby to the ability of agents to act conscientiously—to act *from* duty in something like the Kantian sense—on his view. That, and how, moral concern with the availability of the resources that make good deliberation possible (and so with material independence as described in Chapter 3) follows from concern with the ability of agents to act from duty is the topic to which I turn in Chapter 5.

5

Independence as Constitutive End

Independence in the formal sense—the fulfillment of the formal condition on moral worth—is perfection (one's own perfection, in the present instance) in the purely internal exercise of that disposition in virtue of which one is the appropriate addressee of moral imperatives to begin with: the disposition to set ends spontaneously on the basis of concepts of ends, through the activity of rational reflection. It is not difficult to see why Fichte might think this a constitutive end of rational agency, since what it involves is simply that one deliberate sincerely, completely, and responsibly, and act on the upshot of that deliberation—in other words, that one exercise that agency to the fullest extent.

But as I have emphasized, we misunderstand Fichte if we take this formal component to exhaust the constitutive end of rational agency as he understands it. The material component is the source of the substance of Fichte's doctrine of duties. Yet Fichte's claim that independence in this substantive sense is also a constitutive end of rational agency has been either dismissed as implausible or simply overlooked by generations of readers. My aim in Chapter 3 was to show that Fichte in fact held this view and that the project in the *System of Ethics* cannot be understood without it. But I said very little in that chapter in defense of the idea itself, and even less in response to the concerns of those who would dismiss it as implausible. That is the task of the present chapter.

I begin (§5.1) by showing why it is difficult for Kantians, especially those who accept something like the Kantian account of duties of right, to resist admitting the moral importance of substantive independence of nature in Fichte's sense. Then (§5.2) I present a reconstruction of Fichte's argument aimed at displaying its interest to a broader audience.[1] I begin with the basic Kantian assumption that

---

[1] My reconstruction will not appeal to everyone, since some commitments about the nature of value or obligation will rule out Fichte's approach from the outset. For example, if one believed the only thing of value to be individual happiness hedonistically conceived, it would follow that independence in Fichte's sense could have at most instrumental value; and thus that its value would be contingent and possibly limited. (Cf. e.g. G. Dworkin 1988 and J. Elster 2000 for further examples.) Of course someone holding such a view would also have to reject Fichte's claim that formal independence is a constitutive end of rational agency, and would disagree with Fichte on many other points as well.

the rational will constitutively aims at its own exercise, and describe and defend the additional premises Fichte needs if he is to argue from that assumption to the conclusion that there is a moral (and not merely a prudential) imperative to make technological and social progress with the aim of broadening the scope of possible rational plans of action. Finally (§5.3 and §5.4) I respond to some common and plausible objections to this conclusion not directed specifically at the premises spelled out in §5.2.

5.1 Material Independence and Kant's *Doctrine of Right*

It seems to me that anyone who accepts the basic Kantian starting point in the unconditional value of the exercise of the rational will must accept Fichte's conclusion that material independence with respect both to other agents and to natural forces is an obligatory end. Yet Kantians typically do not. More precisely, they (often) do accept in some form the claim that material independence with respect to other agents is an obligatory end; but they deny that material independence with respect to non-human natural forces is an obligatory end. What I will show in this section is that this distinction is untenable in its usual Kantian form, because the account of the value of interpersonal independence presupposed in Kant's *Doctrine of Right* itself relies on the value of independence *simpliciter*.

'Independence' here is to be understood in the narrow sense depicted in §3.1: freedom from interference in carrying out one's plans by forces powerful enough that they cannot be safely ignored or unpredictable enough that they cannot be effectively planned around. Whatever else is thought to be involved in the interpersonal independence at issue in Kant's *Doctrine of Right*, freedom from such interference on the part of other human beings will be part of it. (Differently put: 'external freedom,' however it is fully specified, will include independence in this narrow sense as part of its specification.[2]) This is the only sort of interference I have in mind throughout this section, and by 'independence' throughout I mean only freedom from such interference.

---

[2] As Uleman points out, it is difficult to give an account of what the external freedom at issue in the *Doctrine of Right* actually amounts to; but it is also required, for an adequate interpretation of the purpose of right, to have some specification, and especially important to have a specification that is not entirely circular (e.g. 'freedom from unrightful interference') (cf. J. Uleman 2004). Here I am assuming only the minimum that Kant's interpreters assume: that independence requires both freedom from susceptibility to assault and control over some (perhaps quite minimal) sphere of external action possibilities.

For Kant, as for Fichte, the problem of right is that of dividing the space of possible actions so as to allow multiple agents to co-exist in a way that preserves for each some sphere of independence in this sense; and the point of entering into a commonwealth is to secure the exercise of our own and others' external freedom. For Kant, as for Fichte, the principle of right is distinct from the moral principle and not a mere application of it;[3] but obligations of right become moral obligations for those who are members of a state; and there is a moral obligation to enter into an existing state or to institute one if none is present.

Since he takes it to be morally obligatory to enter into an arrangement whose defining characteristic is that it protects the external exercise of the freedom of agents from interference by other agents, Kant must take the external exercise of freedom to be a matter of moral importance. Otherwise, membership in a state might be prudent, but it would not (absent further assumptions) be morally obligatory. So both Kant and Fichte are committed to the view that the mutual independence of agents in their outer exercise of their rational agency is an object of moral concern. If it were not, there could be no moral problem with mutual interference, and so no moral requirement to enter into a set of relations whose sole purpose is to minimize such interference.

What separates the typical Kantian view from Fichte's is just a distinction between the moral status of interference stemming from other persons and of interference stemming from impersonal natural forces. Fichte is committed to the claim that freedom from *all* outside interference in the external exercise of rational agency is an object of moral concern; whereas Kant is usually read as having thought that *only* freedom from interference on the part of other agents is a matter of moral concern.[4]

Right concerns only the interactions of rational agents, and from this it follows that the science of right can occupy itself only with the sorts of interference agents can encounter from other agents. But it does not follow from this that the moral concern that underlies the moral duty to participate in a regime of right must itself be limited to concern with the sorts of interference agents can encounter from other agents. So someone defending the Kantian view will need an account

---

[3] The idea that the principle of right is not an application of the categorical imperative is controversial. In saying that it is not, I agree with T. Pogge 2002 and A. Wood 2002, and my reasons are essentially those that Wood enumerates.

[4] The consensus interpretation of Kant's *Doctrine of Right* is one on which its concern is with interpersonal independence exclusively. Cf. T. Pogge 2002; J. Uleman 2004; A. Ripstein 2009. Contemporary Kantians follow Kant in emphasizing the distinction between social limitations and natural ones. Rawls' distinction between natural and social primary goods, and his insistence that only the latter, but not the former, should be subject to the difference principle, is one example (J. Rawls 1999, 54, 87–9, 156, 447–8). Cf. T. Pogge 2007, 73–7 for discussion and critique of Rawls' rationale.

of what distinguishes independence of nature from independence of other agents, such that the latter but not the former is an object of moral concern.

The standard account appeals to the value of being one's own master, subject to no one else's will.[5] What is objectionable about interpersonal dependence is that it tends to bring one person's will under the sway of another's: it makes someone other than the agent his master. This Rousseauean justification is taken, by Kant's interpreters, as the basis for a distinction between social and natural limitations, because nature has no will to which anyone's might be subject.[6]

But while it is indeed true that nature has no will to which anyone's might be subject, and so can never be an agent's master in the sense in which another agent can be, this strategy for drawing a line between the moral value of independence of others and the moral value of independence of nature cannot, in the end, succeed. The problem with it comes into view as soon as one asks how it is that subjection to interference by another person in one's exercise of external freedom might be thought to undermine one's self-mastery.

Notice first that 'self-mastery' here cannot *mean* freedom from arbitrary interference in one's projects (and still less arbitrary interference on the part of other agents only), for the moral importance of that was just what was supposed to be explained. The self-mastery at issue must be something of acknowledged moral significance that does not already encompass freedom from arbitrary interference on the part of other agents. It must, plausibly, be something like the ability to make decisions that are genuinely one's own, to exercise one's rational agency in a way that allows one to be fully responsible for one's actions, to subject one's will to moral demands, or the like. (It does not matter, for my purposes, how exactly this is spelled out, since on every plausible (and non-question-begging) conception of (inner, moral) self-mastery, the objection I am about to raise will go through.)

Second, notice that there are relatively few actions that can directly and literally undermine moral self-mastery without simply destroying it, and even fewer that can bring one person's will directly and literally under the control of another's.[7] The most obvious examples are operations—like brainwashing, or the manipulations

---

[5] I. Kant 1900–, 6: 237–8; I. Kant 1996a, pp. 393–4. Cf. F. Neuhouser 1993; A. Ripstein 2009, chs. 2 and 3.

[6] Cf. J. Uleman 2004; A. Ripstein 2009. The thought is taken to be the one expressed by Rousseau in *Emile*: 'it is in man's nature to bear patiently with the nature of things, but not the ill-will of others' (*Emile* ¶262, bk. II; J.-J. Rousseau 1966, p. 110); 'The truly free man wants only what he can do and does as he pleases' (*Emile* ¶232, bk. II, J.-J. Rousseau 1966, p. 99).

[7] See S. Buss 2005 for a powerful case for this general point about the limitations of the psychological concept of autonomy alone as a source of moral constraints on manipulation and deception.

of nefarious neurosurgeons—that Kant could not possibly have had in mind. What is certain is that theft and robbery, breach of contract, most forms of assault, or the mere threat of more violent interference cannot bring one person's will directly and literally under the control of another's. Yet virtually all of the interference with external freedom contemplated in the *Doctrine of Right* is of this form.

If we then ask how it is that one agent could, by any amount of such interference, cause another agent to cease to be his own master *in the morally relevant sense* (as opposed to persuading him to acquiesce, of his own morally free will, to others' demands) we find it difficult to supply an answer on Kant's behalf. He elsewhere insists that everyone is capable, and knows himself capable, of resisting efforts to bend his will to another's, even where these efforts include the threat of immediate execution.[8]

But my aim here is not to argue that Kant's account of agency precludes an answer to the question. It is instead simply to point out that *some* answer is required. For if we did not care, to begin with, about our exercise of our external freedom—indeed about our ability to pursue relatively complex long-term plans in an external sphere of the sort protected by a regime of property—then other agents would not be able to undermine our self-mastery by interfering with our external freedom in the ways contemplated in the *Doctrine of Right*. And if that caring were morally optional, then participation in a regime of right would be morally optional as well.[9] Without an account of the moral value of external

---

[8] There is disagreement as to Kant's purpose in presenting the following thought experiment, but on no available account are we to conclude that the presence of the gallows undermines the threatened individual's self-mastery in the sense of his ability to determine his will in accordance with moral demands:

> Suppose someone asserts of his lustful inclination that, when the desired object and the opportunity are present, it is quite irresistible to him; ask him whether, if a gallows were erected in front of the house where he finds this opportunity and he would be hanged on it immediately after gratifying his lust, he would not then control his inclination. One need not conjecture very long what he would reply. But ask him whether, if his prince demanded, on pain of the same immediate execution, that he give false testimony against an honorable man whom the prince would like to destroy under a plausible pretext, he would consider it possible to overcome his love of life, however great it may be. He would perhaps not venture to assert whether he would do it or not, but he must admit without hesitation that it would be possible for him. (I. Kant 1900–, 5: 30; I. Kant 1996a, p. 163)

[9] One might object, here, that Kant bases many moral duties on universal human interests that are not themselves morally required. An example is the duty of beneficence, which rests on the de facto universal end of one's own happiness, which end is not itself morally enjoined. That is of course correct; and were we to see duties of right that way, the situation would be no worse than it already is with the account of some moral duties forbidding natural acts (i.e. acts, like murder and assault, whose possibility does not depend upon convention) whose maxims involve no contradiction in conception and which are, according to one of Kant's criteria, to be counted among imperfect

freedom, rights-violations would have no greater moral significance than insults: they might express others' lack of respect for one's person, but would have no significance beyond their role as vehicles for that expression.[10]

So what we would need, from a Kantian defending the general picture in the *Doctrine of Right* but rejecting Fichte's view, is an answer to the question just posed that does not concede Fichte's point about the value of independence *simpliciter*. Such an answer may be possible and it may support the claim that there is a deep moral difference between natural limitations and limitations imposed by other agents. What is certain is that this claim cannot be supported simply by the appeal to the value of self-mastery, because that appeal, in the form in which Kantians have articulated it, itself relies on the significance, from a moral point of view, of external limitations per se—limitations of the sort that can have their source in nature as well as other human beings.[11]

5.2 From Rational Agency to Material Independence

I now turn to the task of reconstructing Fichte's argument in a way that does not assume the moral significance of interpersonal independence in something like the sense at issue in Kant's philosophy of right.

---

duties for that reason. (See, for example, B. Herman 1993, ch. 6; C. Korsgaard 1996, ch. 3.) Kant never describes duties of right as imperfect; and it is anyway generally taken to be a problem for his moral theory that the duty to refrain from assault is less strict than the duty to refrain from deception. Far from providing a solution, this reply points to a broader problem in Kant's ethical theory, of which the problem I raise here then becomes an instance.

[10] Thanks to Rachana Kamtekar for pressing me to (try to) clarify the point here.

[11] Uleman and Ripstein both try to draw a principled line between limitations on freedom of action that are and are not the concern of right (in Kant's sense), and both appeal to the value of self-mastery. But even where interference by other agents is concerned, the line between rightful and unrightful intervention is difficult to draw (J. Uleman 2004; A. Ripstein 2009, p. 34). The problem is acknowledged as a problem by Uleman, but not by Ripstein. A deeper problem is that any such account presupposes that agents must have a moral interest in their external freedom, and Kant offers no story about why that should be the case. Pippin points this out (R. Pippin 1999). Pogge raises the worry that, once such an interest is established, it might force revisions to Kant's conception of a state of right:

> In particular, Kant must exclude the preferability of a legal order that, though it constrains persons' external freedom more than is necessary to establish mutually secured domains, enhances their external freedom on the whole by facilitating (for example, through technology) the removal of natural obstacles and threats or the creation of additional options. This difficulty does not come into view for Kant, because he does not clarify his notion of external freedom, and in particular, does not discuss what obstacles and threats are to count as reducing a person's external freedom. (T. Pogge 2002, p. 148n31)

5.2.1 *The argument in* Foundations *§11*

The justification Fichte offers for his assertion that every rational agent simply as such has as a constitutive end an environment secured against unpredictable, powerful forces of nature appeals to the same considerations that justify his claim that rational agents can co-exist as free only on the basis of a reliably enforced property agreement: the role of knowledge in rational planning, and the role of control in securing knowledge. That is why the first and most explicit version of the argument appears not in the *System of Ethics*, but instead already in the *Foundations of Natural Right*, in the passages from the discussion of original right in §11 that were cited in full in §3.2.2.3 above.

The argument we can draw from those passages is this:

(1)   An agent who aims to exercise her capacity rationally to set ends ought (*ceteris paribus*) to aim to obtain or maintain any conditions necessary for the exercise of that capacity.

(2)   Possession of knowledge concerning causal regularities and concerning the disposition of items in the environment is a condition necessary for the exercise of the capacity rationally to set ends.

(3)   An agent who aims to exercise her capacity rationally to set ends ought (*ceteris paribus*) to aim to obtain or maintain knowledge concerning causal regularities and concerning the disposition of items in the environment (1 and 2).

(4)   An environment secured against intervention by unpredictable, powerful forces uniquely facilitates the acquisition of knowledge concerning causal regularities and concerning the disposition of items in the environment.

(5)   An agent who aims at acquiring knowledge concerning causal regularities and concerning the disposition of items in the environment ought (*ceteris paribus*) to aim to obtain or secure any conditions uniquely facilitating its acquisition.

(6)   An agent who aims at acquiring knowledge concerning causal regularities and concerning the disposition of items in the environment ought (*ceteris paribus*) to aim to obtain or maintain an environment secured against intervention by unpredictable, powerful forces (4, 5).

(7)   An agent who aims to exercise her capacity rationally to set ends ought (*ceteris paribus*) to aim to obtain or maintain an environment secured against intervention by unpredictable, powerful forces (3, 6).

(8)   Every rational agent aims to exercise her capacity rationally to set ends.

(9)   Every rational agent ought (*ceteris paribus*) to aim to obtain or maintain an environment secured against intervention by unpredictable, powerful forces (7, 8).

This argument is valid. Since by 'to exercise her capacity rationally to set ends'
Fichte means only to exercise the internal, psychological capacity described in
Chapter 2 (to exercise freedom in the formulation of rational *plans* of action), and
since an environment secured against intervention by unpredictable, powerful
forces is not assumed to be itself a part of this capacity, it is non-question-begging.
Premises (1) and (5) are applications of the instrumental principle—(1) in its
more canonical (necessary conditions) form, (5) in a form that, while less commonly employed in the philosophical literature, figures more commonly in
everyday practical reasoning. (I will say what I mean by 'uniquely facilitates' in
that context in a moment.) The substantive premises that might be thought
controversial are, then, (2), (4), and (8).

As I have already noted, I have nothing to say in defense of (8) that goes
beyond the defenses already abundant in the contemporary Kantian literature.
But I will note one supposition behind it that might be thought relevant to the
argument. Fichte's theory is, like Kant's, a form of perfectionism; and like Kant
he takes it that the rational will aims, not at its own minimal exercise, but at its
own fullest exercise. Both assume, plausibly, that any capacity whose exercise
an agent takes to be valuable and that can be developed to different degrees is—
absent defeating conditions—a capacity that agent should want to develop to
the fullest degree, given constraints of time, energy, and resources, and given
the demands of other worthwhile ends (such as the end of developing other
valuable capacities, or the end of allowing other agents the latitude to develop
similarly valuable capacities).[12]

Premise (2) is just the claim, discussed in §2.3.1 above, that empirical knowledge is required for the exercise of the practical reflection that is part of rational

---

[12] The following objection was raised by Paul Katsafanas in comments on M. Kosch 2015a (as
presented at a workshop at Dartmouth College in the fall of 2013): It might seem plausible to think that
an agent with an interest in the exercise of her capacity rationally to set ends has an interest in obtaining
the conditions *minimally* necessary in order to exercise that capacity, but why think that such an agent
has an interest in obtaining the conditions conducive to the *maximal* or *most effective* exercise of that
capacity? I confessed at the time that I do not see the force of the objection. Take for example the
capacity to play the piano. It is plausible to think that if I value its development at all, I value its
development to the point of excellence—maximal excellence, given constraints (on resources for
instruction, and on time and energy that can be devoted to practicing, given that time, energy, and
material resources are finite, and that there are other capacities whose value calls for development). It is
difficult to see what could even motivate the thought that my valuing of it justifies *only* my development of it to the point at which I can play (say) a simple melody with one hand.

agency. Since no one can intentionally perform an action that she has no idea how to perform, or aim at an end she has no idea how to pursue, ignorance in a particular sphere precludes any rational end-setting within that sphere. Since all rational end-setting is the activity of finite agents operating in a world about which their a priori knowledge is limited, some empirical knowledge will be required for rational end-setting to take place.

As I noted in §2.3.1, we could substitute 'true beliefs' for 'knowledge' in the formulations above without loss of fidelity to Fichte's view; but we could not substitute 'beliefs' for 'knowledge.' The premise is not, in other words, the wholly uncontroversial point that intending to x entails having some beliefs pertinent to x-ing—at minimum, the belief that it is possible for one to x under the contemplated circumstances.[13] This means that the argument as formulated is open to objection on the grounds that mere belief, rather than knowledge or true belief, is the cognitive attitude that figures in the activity of rational end-setting, and that it is therefore only mere belief, rather than knowledge or true belief, that can properly be called a necessary condition of the exercise of rational agency.

As I pointed out in that section, this position is by no means obligatory: some philosophers have defended the view that an agent operating with false beliefs is rationally deficient simply in virtue of that fact. But others have held that practical rationality is a function only of the relations that hold between one's attitudes and that full rationality is consistent with wholly false empirical beliefs (perhaps with the proviso that they were not formed in rationally objectionable ways). Someone who held a view like this would reject (2); but the argument can be modified to accommodate this position, since those who hold it are unlikely to want to deny that rational end setters, *qua* rational, ought in general to aim at having true beliefs concerning means toward their ends. That is because (3) follows plausibly from

(10)   It is impossible to set any end sincerely while remaining entirely indifferent to the likelihood of achieving it.

(11)   Knowledge (or true belief) concerning the disposition of items in the environment and concerning causal regularities raises the likelihood of achieving one's ends.

---

[13] Familiar counterexamples (such as those proposed in M. Bratman 1987) to the view that intending to x entails believing that one will do x (cf. K. Setiya 2007), or that to intend to do x just is to believe that one will do x (cf. D. Velleman 1989), or is an attitude different from belief that still contributes to knowledge that one will do x (cf. G.E.M. Anscombe 1963), do not undermine the minimal supposition that intending to do x entails believing that it is at least possible for one to do x by the proposed means in the circumstances. In fact they do not undermine the stronger supposition, which would simplify Fichte's argument were he willing to use it, that to intend to x entails believing to some degree that one will x (cf. K. Setiya 2008; R. Holton 2009).

Knowledge is not here portrayed as a necessary condition of the exercise of rational agency, but instead as a facilitating condition of one of its presumed constitutive ends, namely success in the production of the result intended in the current instance. Although Fichte never explicitly articulates (10), his acceptance of it is evident and unsurprising. As we have seen, (11) figures explicitly in Fichte's reasoning about duties to support scientific research. Although there are counterexamples to it involving particular cases, as a general principle it is not controversial.

In §3.2.2.3, I discussed Fichte's reasons for thinking that an environment secured against unpredictable forces is required for an agent to have knowledge of the means at her disposal in any given instance of practical deliberation. Since the same sort of control over the environment plays a role in much scientific discovery (all experimentation relies on it), and since as we have seen Fichte is committed to the relevance of scientific knowledge to practical deliberation, there is good reason to attribute premise (4) to him.

Still, my articulation of premise (4) departs from Fichte's own argument in §11 of the *Foundations* on two counts. First, there he seems mainly (perhaps exclusively, although the text does not force this reading) concerned with knowledge of the disposition of items in the environment rather than with knowledge of general causal regularities. Second, he seems to be saying that security from the intervention of unpredictable and sufficiently powerful forces (in the case at issue there, the intervention of other rational agents) is a necessary condition, and not merely a facilitator, of such knowledge. That is, his claim seems both more narrow in scope, and more strong, than (4).

He explains, in those passages, that security from intervention on the part of other agents—indeed the sort of security that can be had only within a commonwealth with the power to enforce laws coercively—is required in part because human actions are entirely unpredictable (III: 115–16). In making this specification he allows that nature, whose action he takes to differ from the action of rational agents in being predictable in principle, might be dealt with in one of two different ways. We might secure our projects against certain types of interference (using mechanisms like dikes and firebreaks, mosquito nets and vaccines); or we might acquire the sort of exhaustive knowledge that would allow us to predict and therefore to plan around such interference *without* securing against it. That is, control (in the sense at issue) is not strictly a necessary condition of knowledge of means at our disposal, where only the forces of nature are concerned, on Fichte's view.

Of course, we do not have anything like the exhaustive knowledge that such prediction would require. But since we can adjust the scope of our projects to fit the predictive power that we in fact possess, we could in principle have all the knowledge of means at our disposal that our plans require—with the proviso that we keep our plans sufficiently simple, and sufficiently short-term, as to require no disposition of items that we cannot predict given what we currently know. The plans involved would have to be very simple indeed, and very short term. Such restriction would go against the tendency of the natural drive as well as every rational refinement of it; so it is not clear what could motivate it, on Fichte's picture, and it might therefore be fair to say that it is, psychologically speaking, impossible.

But even if the language of necessary conditions were appropriate in this case, it would still be clearly inappropriate in the case of the other sort of empirical knowledge that figures in the formation of rational plans of action: knowledge of causal regularities. Control may be strictly necessary for some discoveries that can be made only in specific experimental situations; but it is not in general necessary for knowledge of causal regularities, since these can sometimes simply be observed. Yet it is fair to say that control facilitates such knowledge and that science is accelerated by the application of existing knowledge in technology used in experimentation, and that we know of no replacement for this (hence, 'uniquely'). This is a point Fichte emphasized, as we have seen. Since it is also unproblematic to say that an environment secured against intervention by unpredictable, powerful forces (at least) facilitates knowledge concerning the disposition of items in the environment, I have used that language rather than the language of necessary conditions in premise (4).

A final question to answer is why an individual's concern for her knowledge (and so for her independence in the sense at issue) should go beyond a concern for the present moment—indeed should go beyond the mere hope that her current state of knowledge might suffice for the success of whatever intention she is currently in the process of forming. Given that there is nothing she can do, instantaneously, to remedy present ignorance, it does not seem that an interest in knowledge, and so in its necessary or facilitating conditions, could give rise to any imperatives at all for her, unless she has a concern for the fate of intentions beyond the present one.

To this question there are two answers. The first is that while a given agent's concern in a given instance may very well fail to extend beyond the mere hope that her beliefs suffice for success in that instance, this would itself involve a failure of rationality, on the assumption that her present deliberation is not rationally privileged by the mere fact that it is *her present* one. Fichte has, so far as I can see, nothing new to add to the familiar point that, in the absence of a qualitative difference between herself and another, or between her present and future selves, it would be irrational for her not to will the generalization of whatever conditions are required for the coherence of her present intention. But the point is plausible and some version of it is accepted by many moral philosophers.[14]

The second is that the plans of rational agents tend at every point toward a spontaneous increase in complexity and ambition, because the activity of rational end-setting is creative. To the extent that such an agent is self-aware, she will understand this, and understand that the current state of her knowledge, even if it does (luckily) suffice for the most minimal ends she is capable of forming at the moment, is unlikely to suffice for many ends that she (or others) will inevitably want to undertake at some point in the future. Once the connection between material independence and knowledge is acknowledged, then, it is a short step from the Kantian characterization of reason as a natural being's 'capacity to extend far beyond natural instinct the rules and aims of the use of all of its powers'[15] to Fichte's claim that there is a substantive moral imperative to expand the scope of possible rational plans of action. Kant, as I have said, takes it to be an empirical fact about rational end-setting that it tends to outstrip current knowledge, technology, and social organization and to force advances in those areas and so to expand its own reach. Fichte's view differs from Kant's in recognizing explicitly the feedback loop between the exercise of this creativity, the increasing demands upon empirical cognition arising from the new ends, the increasing demands upon technological control arising from those new cognitive demands, and the resulting broadening of the scope of this very creativity. If the exercise of rational agency is an end, and if that exercise is inherently creative, then an increase in knowledge will be an end as well; and if an increase in knowledge relies on an increase in independence in the sense at issue, then that also will be an end for rational agents simply as such.

Once we take into account this set of facts, together with the rational requirement to take into account the rational end-setting activity of future generations,

---

[14] T. Nagel 1970 and D. Parfit 1984 are the most important contemporary sources for arguments of this form. Kant's *Groundwork* was of course the most important source for Fichte himself; but Fichte's British consequentialist contemporaries were making the same argument. William Godwin, for example, in his *Enquiry Concerning Political Justice* (1793), in arguing against the permissibility of saving the life of one's own mother over that of a stranger capable of producing more good for humankind, in a situation in which only one can be saved (shortly after the passage reproduced in §3.2.1.1 above), asks 'What magic is there in the pronoun "my," to overturn the decisions of everlasting [in later editions: impartial] truth?' (W. Godwin 1793, vol. 1, p. 83). Even Fichte's claim that this familiar form of ethical argument derives from a requirement of consistency that is a principle of theoretical rather than practical reason, which seems a departure from Kant, is not as sharp a break as it might appear, since (as Engstrom has shown) Kant's employment of this principle has a theoretical analogue and is a general principle of both practical and theoretical reason. (Cf. S. Engstrom 2009, ch. 4.) Of course neither Fichte nor Kant nor Godwin draws the contemporary distinction between 'deontological' and 'consequentialist' conceptions of moral impartiality.

[15] I. Kant 1900–, 8: 18; I. Kant 2007, p. 109 (translation altered).

we can replace the argument drawn from *Foundations* §11 with one not articulated quite as succinctly anywhere in Fichte's writings, but one that seems to underlie his reasoning in texts from the *Lectures on the Scholar's Vocation* to the *System of Ethics*:

(12)   An agent who aims to exercise her capacity rationally to set ends ought to have as her aim the general exercise of the capacity rationally to set ends.

(8)   Every rational agent aims to exercise her capacity rationally to set ends.

(13)   Every agent ought to have as her aim the general exercise of the capacity rationally to set ends (12, 8).

(14)   An agent who has as her aim the general exercise of a capacity ought (*ceteris paribus*) to aim to obtain or maintain any condition necessary for the general exercise of that capacity.

(15)   The general possession of knowledge concerning causal regularities and concerning the disposition of items in the environment is a condition necessary for the general exercise of the capacity rationally to set ends.

(16)   Every agent ought (*ceteris paribus*) to aim to obtain or maintain the general possession of knowledge concerning causal regularities and concerning the disposition of items in the environment (13, 14, 15).

(17)   An environment secured against intervention by unpredictable, powerful forces acting on agents generally is a condition necessary for the general possession of knowledge concerning causal regularities and concerning the disposition of items in the environment.

(18)   Every agent ought (*ceteris paribus*) to aim to obtain or maintain an environment secured against intervention by unpredictable, powerful forces acting on agents generally (16, 17).

This formulation matches most closely the concise statement of the importance of material independence that we can see best in the *Lectures on the Scholar's Vocation*. (13) is the conclusion Fichte draws in the discussion of individuality in *System of Ethics* §18, discussed in §3.2.3.1 above. (14), (15), and (17) are reformulations of (1), (2), and (4). We can replace (4) with (17) because, when the exercise of rational agency is seen as an ever-expanding multigenerational project whose ends will inevitably, at some point in the future, rely on the most advanced scientific knowledge, independence of nature in the sense at issue is a necessary and not merely a uniquely facilitating condition of the continuing pursuit of that project. We could also, of course, replace (15) with analogues of (10) and (11).

5.2.2 Limiting conditions

There are, it is worth noting at this point, material ends that are rationally obligatory, on Fichte's picture, but that are not subsumable under the end of securing an environment free from interference, and that may even conflict with it. The most important of these, as Fichte emphasizes, is the end of social interaction. In fact we can construct an argument parallel to the argument above with an imperative of social interaction as its conclusion.

(1)   An agent who aims to exercise her capacity rationally to set ends ought (*ceteris paribus*) to aim to obtain or maintain any conditions necessary for the exercise of that capacity.

(19)   Social interaction is a condition necessary for the exercise of the capacity rationally to set ends.

(20)   An agent who aims to exercise her capacity rationally to set ends ought (*ceteris paribus*) to aim to obtain or maintain social interaction (1, 19).

(8)   Every rational agent aims to exercise her capacity rationally to set ends.

(21)   Every rational agent ought (*ceteris paribus*) to aim to obtain or maintain social interaction (20, 8).

The existence of such further conditions as social interaction is the reason for the *ceteris paribus* condition in the initial argument: obligatory ends beyond freedom from interference in one's plans arising from other agents and from forces of nature will condition the pursuit of these ends. (Conversely, the end of independence in the sense that involves control of the environment also in turn conditions these other ends. The end of social interaction, as we have seen, must be pursued within the constraints of a social structure that preserves, precisely, the material independence of rational agents from one another.)

This is an important point, since one underlying motivation for resistance to the idea that control over the environment is a constitutive end of rational agency, at least among contemporary readers and auditors, is the ease with which some particular formulations of that idea call to mind not only the specter of a post-industrial wasteland in which nature has been, indeed, mastered, but in a process that has left human life poorer rather than richer; but also the specter of a social world in which all other values (chiefly aesthetic values and the value of personal relationships) are sacrificed to the the values of efficiency and technological advance. I will address objections of this form in more detail in §5.4; here let me simply note that Fichte's emphasis on the existence and variety of such limiting conditions (which include the possibility of romantic and close personal relationships and certain forms of aesthetic experience, as well as the protection of the deliberative integrity of individual agents and the rightful distribution of freedoms) falls out of a commitment—plausibly the product of his interaction with Schiller and other critics of Kantian ethics in the early 1790s—to articulating an ethical theory that would reckon with the facts about what can actually make us better, given the sort of beings we actually are.[16]

5.2.3 Control as necessary end and control as end in itself

One concern that is often explicitly articulated about Fichte's view is that control is (perhaps as a conceptual truth, but in any case necessarily) a mere means, and so not even a candidate constitutive end.[17] My reconstruction of Fichte's argument might seem simply to concede this point; but I do not mean to do that, since it does not seem to me necessary to concede it.

It is important to distinguish the aim of showing that material independence is a rationally necessary end from that of showing that it is an end in itself. Fichte's aim is to establish that material independence with respect to nature is itself an obligatory end, its pursuit a categorical imperative (IV: 10, 54, 153, 155, 191). To do this he needs to establish that independence is a contentful and action-guiding end, and that its pursuit is not valuable merely as a means to the achievement of some particular, arbitrary ends (but not others), nor even merely as a means to some privileged but non-morally-obligatory end like happiness or well-being, but is itself rationally required. But he does not need to establish that it is, all on its own, an end in itself.

---

[16] The *Letters on the Aesthetic Education of the Human Being* contain only praise for what Schiller describes as Fichte's departure from Kant on this score. In a note to the fourth letter Schiller cites with approval the unity of personality of the morally ideal individual Fichte describes in the *Lectures on the Scholar's Vocation* (1794) (F. Schiller 1959, 8: 315); and in a note to the thirteenth he cites the *Foundations of the Wissenschaftslehre* (1794), crediting Fichte with the idea that one drive (Schiller calls it the 'rational' drive) does not simply subordinate the other (the 'sensuous' drive) in morally virtuous action, but rather modifies it, interacting with it on the model of reciprocal action (F. Schiller 1959, 8: 348). When the two of them had a falling out in the middle of 1795, soon after these letters were published, their breach was caused in part by Schiller's feeling that Fichte was borrowing too many of his ideas and methods without attribution (cf. especially the letter to Fichte of June 24, 1795, in which Schiller objects to the lack of distance between the first installments of Fichte's *On Spirit and Letter in Philosophy* and his own *Letters on the Aesthetic Education of the Human Being*). Schiller was not alone in thinking that Fichte had made this sort of advance over Kant. Cf. M. Kosch 2015b for more examples.

[17] Neuhouser, for example, argues that what it must mean for a subject to have independence is that the subject is able to accomplish its own purposes unhindered by natural impediments. But then those purposes, whatever they are, and not control over nature, are that subject's final end (F. Neuhouser 1990, p. 142). Elizabeth Anderson has also pressed an objection along these lines, in conversation.

In this respect the end of material independence does not differ remarkably from the end of refraining from acting on maxims unsuitable for universal legislation in a kingdom of ends. For Kant, only the good will is an end in itself. The categorical imperative is simply an articulation of what good willing consists in. Similarly, for Fichte, material independence is the substantive end that the rational will has insofar as it is rational. This is an articulation of what good willing consists in. But just as acting only on maxims suitable for universal legislation in a kingdom of ends is valuable only when it is the end of a rational agent acting conscientiously, so performing only those actions that lie in the series that leads at its limit to the independence of reason from everything outside of itself is valuable only when it is the end of a rational agent acting conscientiously. Kant and Fichte agree in giving the subjective condition on moral correctness an essential place in their accounts of moral worth. But just as it would be confused to think that one might object, against Kant, that on his account the categorical imperative is then not categorical after all, because adhering to it is only a means to the end of willing rationally, so it would be mistaken to object, against Fichte, that the end of independence is not a constitutive one after all, because it is only a means to the end of willing rationally.

5.3 Autonomy and Material Ethical Principles

Fichte's claim that self-sufficiency is our 'absolute final' end is nothing more than the claim that, beyond the perfection of the exercise of rational agency and the expansion of its scope, there is no further substantive end that a rational agent must, *qua* rational agent, have. He does not offer any arguments in support of the claim that there are no further obligatory ends, and may simply mean to fall back on Kant's arguments against the other material principles of ethics on offer, all of which (Kant argued) presuppose the heteronomy of the will. There would, however, be at least a *prima facie* problem with such an appeal, viz. that Kant had after all argued that *all* material principles presuppose heteronomy and that an autonomous ethical principle must therefore be purely formal. Fichte's principle, as I have presented it, is a material one, and so might seem to fall afoul of this argument. Far from being in a position to appeal to Kant here, then, Fichte seems to have an objection to answer.

A full answer to this line of objection would rely on an account of why autonomy, for Kant, might be thought to require formal principles, and what it is for a moral principle to be 'formal' in the relevant sense. A full answer is therefore beyond the scope of this book. But a brief look at Kant's arguments should suffice to reassure the reader that no very powerful objection can be

mounted from this direction. This is because Kant's arguments to the conclusion that all material principles must be principles of heteronomy rely dispro-
portionately on the *premise* that practical reason is the source of no substantive
ends. When directed against a view like Fichte's, they assume what they would
be asked to prove.

At *Critique of Practical Reason* 5: 22–8 Kant describes a 'material principle' as a
principle that both has as its content some end to be brought about, and has as its
determining ground some desire (typically, the desire that the end be brought
about) that has its source in sensibility.[18] These two criteria of materiality are
distinct, and some argument is required to show that all principles that are
material in the first sense must also be material in the second sense.[19]

In the case of the principle of happiness, the additional premise that would be
needed for such an argument comes from Kant's concept of the end of happiness,
on which it is a function of the satisfaction of sensible desires, which are simply
given. In the case of the ontological principle of perfection the additional premise
comes from the assumption that the concept of perfection is the concept of
something merely instrumental. Perfection is adequacy in bringing about ends—
in the human case, it is talent or skill.[20] A principle of perfection is empty in the
absence of given ends, Kant argues, because only these determine which talents or
skills are to be perfected. Such ends can be given only empirically, by the lower
faculty of desire, and so a theory based on the ontological principle of perfection
must be a theory of the heteronomy of the will in just the way and for just the
reason that a theory based on the principle of happiness must be.[21] (Since there is
no disagreement between Kant and Fichte about the theological principle of
perfection—whose status as a principle of heteronomy is uncontroversial
enough—nor about the 'external subjective' principles of *Metaphysics of Morals*
5: 40, I leave these aside.)

Kant's point in the case of the principle of happiness is relatively easy to see,
since it makes intuitive sense to think that a moral theory on which the agent
ought to take orders directly from the lower faculty of desire would be a theory of
heteronomy. His point in the case of the ontological principle of perfection is less
obvious. Again a full discussion of the relevant issues is beyond the scope of this
book, but it is important for understanding Kant's train of thought here that
the moral philosophers he was arguing against—notably Wolff, whom Kant

---

[18] I. Kant 1900–, 5: 22–8; I. Kant 1996a, pp. 155–62.
[19] For an argument for their distinctness, cf. D. Cummiskey 1996, ch. 3.
[20] I. Kant 1900–, 5: 41; I Kant 1996a, pp. 172–3.
[21] I. Kant 1900–, 5: 41; I. Kant 1996a, pp. 172–3.

mentions as an example—were perfectionists of a eudaimonistic stripe.[22] For them, perfection was excellence at fulfilling human desires in general; and so about them it is appropriate to say, as Kant does, that it is in the end always nature, in the form of sensible inclination, that is giving the law.[23] The distance between the subjective principle of happiness and the objective ontological principle of perfection that Kant has in mind is therefore not as great as it would appear, consisting largely in a disagreement about the availability for use in moral theory of an objective standard of happiness.

Fichte's differs from such theories in that on it the principle of morality is derived from an idea of self-sufficiency that is the product of practical reason itself (i.e. practical reason's idea of its own independence from everything that is not practical reason). Although the ethical drive relies (in part) on natural limitations for its content, it does not have the fulfillment of the natural drive *qua* drive as its end; nor does it have that drive itself *qua* drive as its determining ground. Fichte's theory is not a target of Kant's criticisms of theories embracing material ethical principles, then, because it is not among the forms of such theories that Kant considers.

'Autonomy' is not a term of which he made very much use, but Fichte does at one point explain why his account of ethics is 'autonomous' in Kant's sense. In this passage, he distinguishes three senses in which the term 'autonomy' can apply to his own view:

This legislation has been called, aptly, *autonomy* or self-legislation. It can be so described in three respects. First, assuming already the thought of [such a] law in general, and considering the I solely as free intelligence, the law becomes a law for it *to begin with* [*überhaupt*] only through the fact that it reflects upon it, and freely submits itself to it, i.e. that it self-actively makes it the inviolable maxim of all its willing; and moreover what this law demands in each *particular* case the intellect must first ... find through the power of judgment, and [it] must freely give itself the task of realizing the discovered concept. Thus all of moral existence is nothing other than an uninterrupted lawgiving of the rational being upon itself, and where this lawgiving breaks off, there immorality begins. Next, concerning the content of the law, nothing is demanded except absolute independence, absolute indeterminability by anything outside of the I. The material determination of the will in accordance with the law is therefore drawn solely from ourself; and all *heteronomy*, derivation of determining grounds from something outside of us, is precisely against the law. Finally, the whole concept of our necessary submission to a law arises solely through the absolutely free reflection of the I upon itself in its true essence, that is, in its self-sufficiency. As has been shown, the thought that has been derived [*sc.* the moral principle] does not force itself immediately [upon us], which would be wholly

---

[22] C. Wolff 1752; cf. I. Kant 1900-, 5: 40; I. Kant 1996a, p. 172.
[23] I. Kant 1900-, 4: 444; I. Kant 1996a, p. 92.

incomprehensible and would cancel the concept of an intelligence, nor [does it force itself upon us] by means of a feeling or the like, but is rather the condition, the necessary *manner* [*Weise*] of a free thinking. Thus it is the I itself that brings a lawlikeness to itself in this whole affair, and reason is thus in every regard its own law.

Here also, as it seems to me, we can clearly see how reason could be *practical*, and how this practical reason is not at all the so wonderful and incomprehensible thing that it has sometimes been regarded, not at all an as it were second reason, but the same [one] that all of us very well recognize as theoretical reason.   (IV: 56–7)

The first respect in which the moral principle can be described as a principle of autonomy, Fichte here writes, is that the authoritativeness of the law in general, and of what the law demands in each instance, is itself the product of the exercise of an agent's own practical reason. In the particular case, my conclusion that x is the thing to do is the result of my own exercise of reflecting judgment in the particular circumstances; in the more general case, my conviction that independence is my final end is the product of my own activity of practical reasoning. Moral demands do not come from outside of practical reason as inputs on which it must operate, but are instead the outputs of the activity of practical reasoning.

The second respect in which the moral principle can be described as a principle of autonomy concerns the principle's content: it is a principle of autonomy because what it demands is self-sufficiency, independence from anything not itself. This is the point of contention, and Fichte's remarks here seem directed toward Kant's discussions of material principles. In fact Fichte's efforts to distance his theory from any based on the end of happiness (either directly or instrumentally) may be motivated by a concern that his theory, though material in the first sense distinguished above, not be misconstrued as being material in the second sense as well.

The third respect in which the moral principle can be described as a principle of autonomy concerns the very idea that a rational being should proceed according to some law or principle to begin with. This is not something given (through feeling or in any other way), but comes as a recognition of its own essence, the essence of thinking. Fichte's assertion here of the identity of practical and theoretical reason is meant to underscore his claim that thinking, in any application, is essentially principled and essentially aims at its own independence, its freedom from determination by extraneous distorting influences.[24]

---

[24] This passage from the *System of Ethics* calls to mind the following passage from O'Neill's remarkable essay on *Groundwork* III:

A critical grounding of reason works by showing what it takes to orient thinking and acting by principles that do not fail even if used universally and reflexively. The key

Finally, although Fichte's principle is material in the first of the two senses articulated at *Critique of Practical Reason* 5: 22–6 because it prescribes an end, if we follow interpreters like Reath in thinking that 'a formal principle for Kant is a principle that is constitutive of some domain of cognition or rational activity . . . a principle that both constitutively guides that activity and serves as its internal regulative norm,'[25] then we can take Fichte's principle to be formal *while* prescribing an end.

But while this might be the ground that Fichte means to claim when he contrasts his system of ethics with 'material' systems (IV: 174), it does certainly appear that he took there to be some distance between his view and Kant's on this score, since he also explicitly contrasts his theory with 'purely formal' treatments of ethics (IV: 131, 147), under which category, as the context makes clear, he sorts Kant's. But regardless of whether there is in fact any disagreement with Kant here, it is at most in the wider sense of 'formal' articulated by Reath that it seems plausible to say that only formal principles can be principles of autonomy.[26] In the end it is simply not clear why an ethical principle based on the idea of the material self-sufficiency of practical reason with respect to everything that is not practical reason could not be a principle of autonomy.[27]

5.4 The Hegemony of Instrumental Reason?

As I have said, Fichte's idea that technological progress aimed at increased mastery of nature is a necessary end of rational agency has typically been met

idea behind the notion of a critique of pure reason is that we can find standards of reasoning by considering how we can and must discipline our thinking. However, this discipline is not to be thought of as externally imposed: rather it is *self-discipline* or *autonomy* in thinking. . . . Reason, the discipline of all disciplines, can only be and must be *self*-disciplined: the subordination of thinking or practice to other supposed authorities (state, church, experts, personal preferences) is not reason, but the abrogation of reason. Reason's discipline cannot be alien; it must be autonomous. . . . [Kant] argues not from reason to autonomy but from autonomy to reason. Only autonomous, self-disciplining beings can act on principles that we have grounds to call principles of reason.   (O. O'Neill 1989, pp. 56–7)

What O'Neill describes here sounds very much like what Fichte describes as the first and third respects in which his moral theory can be described as a theory of autonomy.

[25] A. Reath 2013, p. 180.

[26] Other senses of 'formal'—notably, the sense in which to be formal is to abstract from semantic content (cf. the discussion of the formality at issue in Kant's logic in J. MacFarlane 2000, ch. 4)— simply have no obvious connection to autonomy.

[27] Objections raised by Paul Katsafanas and Owen Ware motivated this section, and I benefited from discussion with Ware about the issues in it.

with either incomprehension or hostility. In this final section, I address what I take to be the chief sources of this hostility.

One such source appears to be a concern that this aspect of Fichte's thought is somehow objectionable from an environmental point of view. Whether this is so depends on the sort of environmental-ethical principle the objector has in mind. Fichte can, of course, embrace arguments for the value of the preservation of natural landscapes, of the diversity of species, of climate stability, and so on that are based on the value of those things to and for us (including, importantly, their aesthetic value, and their value to and for future generations). That he did not offer such arguments himself is a function of the absence, in eighteenth-century central Europe, of pressing threats stemming from environmental degradation. But in fact as soon as one poses clearly the question of whether global warming, pollution, deforestation, loss of species diversity, the destruction of natural beauty, and the like themselves expand human capabilities, or constitute ways in which humanity as a whole makes its projects less susceptible to derailment, it becomes evident that Fichte can offer stronger arguments for environmental conservation than other Kantians or indeed most consequentialists. That is because the best such arguments appeal to the value of preserving the capacities and opportunities of future generations.[28]

Deep ecologists and followers of the late Heidegger will disagree; but I have searched in vain for a plausible defense of such views.[29] Much of the conservative critique of technology, including Heidegger's, is directed not at technology per se, but only at new, unfamiliar technologies—technologies, in other words, that we do not yet know how to control.[30] But the fact that technology is a threat to our moral

---

[28] Wood also defends Fichte against the charge that his view would have negative environmental consequences, though not in the way I do here (A. Wood 1991, p. 18).

[29] Thanks to David Plunkett and to audiences at Dartmouth and the University of California at Riverside for much discussion of this issue. An anonymous referee has suggested that to respond to Heidegger on this point would require a more thoroughgoing examination of the anthropological assumptions on which Fichte's ethical theory rests than I undertake here, because, absent that, I have no grounds for dismissing Heideggerian objections motivated by Heidegger's own (different) anthropological assumptions. This objection misjudges the burden of proof. The anthropological assumptions on which Fichte relies are minimal: that we are embodied, multiple, rational, and that we have beliefs and desires and form intentions. This picture requires defense only against someone who would reject part of it. But Heidegger (as I read him) does not want to reject any of these assumptions, only to add additional ones. Those assumptions might suffice to overturn Fichte's conclusions, but the burden of proof in this case is on the defender of those additional assumptions.

[30] In a recent talk at Cornell, Harald Zils pointed out that conservative German writers like Heidegger and Jünger do not as a matter of fact portray *all* technology as bad. In his examination of the texts where a distinction between good and bad technology is drawn, and in the discussion that followed the paper, it emerged that the technologies portrayed as 'good' in these writers are uniformly old, outdated technologies and that their valorization has to do both with the idealization of the past and with the fact that these older technologies are *mastered*, under our control. We

aims when we cannot control it is not an objection to Fichte's view. It is an entailment of it. Commitment to the sacredness of nature or to the value (not to us or for us, but all on its own) of the preservation untouched of all or part of the natural world might inform resistance to an attitude toward technology like Fichte's; but it is not clear what acceptable ethical principle could have these commitments as a consequence.

Another source of hostility, from a slightly different direction, may be a concern of the sort articulated powerfully by Horkheimer and Adorno in *Dialectic of Enlightenment*, about the danger to human autonomy of the hegemony of instrumental reason. This is a two-pronged concern: on the one hand, the worry that an instrumental attitude toward nature is inextricably bound up with an instrumental attitude toward others, and on the other, the worry that an instrumental attitude toward nature is inextricably bound up with a repressive or sacrificial attitude toward the self. Of course Horkheimer and Adorno themselves do not mention Fichte in either Excursus, and the only explicit reference to Fichte in *Dialectic of Enlightenment*, in the first essay, touches on neither of these issues.[31] Still it may be worthwhile to say something about them here.

The first worry, articulated in the second Excursus, relies on a characterization of enlightenment practical philosophy according to which it is committed to formalism and rejects every substantive end as 'asserting the power of nature over mind.'[32] This characterization is of course at odds with Fichte's theory as I have presented it here. Fichte aspired to show that reason does have a

---

understand them, and the way they mediate our relation to the world. (Jeffrey Kirkwood made this last point, and it seems to me to have significance for critiques of technology well beyond the 20th-century German context.)

[31] It instead concerns a tension they see between practical and theoretical orientations in Fichte's thought. They describe Fichte's philosophy as 'the radical elaboration' of the 'classical demand to think thinking'—contrasting it with the modern aspiration to 'automate' thinking in service of the imperative to 'direct praxis'—but point out that this is an imperative 'Fichte himself also wanted to carry out.' (M. Horkheimer and T. Adorno 1988, p. 31; M. Horkheimer and T. Adorno 2002, p. 19; translation my own.) I find it interesting that they do not here accuse Fichte himself of 'reifying' thought into an 'automatic process that emulates a machine.' Instead the early *Wissenschaftslehre* is being held up as a model of philosophy in the classical spirit. As we have seen (cf. the 'limitative' aspect of the duty of intellectual self-cultivation in §3.2.2.2), the Fichte of 1798 does not accord to purely theoretical contemplation the status accorded to it by the ancients, a status Adorno evidently thinks it deserves. It has long been acknowledged that there is some tension between the primarily theoretical orientation of the first draft of the *Wissenschaftslehre* and the primarily practical orientation that emerged later in the 1790s. But that is not the tension Horkheimer and Adorno here diagnose. Their worry is with an alleged conflict between the *autonomy* of thought and the demand that it direct praxis. Fichte himself sees no conflict here, and in his defense I can only confess that I do not see any either.

[32] M. Horkheimer and T. Adorno 1988, p. 94; M. Horkheimer and T. Adorno 2002, p. 68.

substantive end of its own, and moreover one that forbids the assimilation of other rational beings to irrational nature (for reasons presented in §3.2.3). Were this line of criticism directed at Fichte it would presuppose—and so could not constitute evidence for—the failure of that aspiration. So in fact it seems to me no accident that the second Excursus is aimed specifically at Kant, and contains no reference to Fichte.

On the other hand, Fichte is indeed disposed to see the appropriate relation of reason to one's own psychological nature as one of control, and so inclined to admit, and even to embrace, the link between an instrumental attitude toward nature and a repressive or sacrificial attitude toward the self articulated mainly in *Dialectic of Enlightenment*'s first Excursus, for instance here:

In the moment in which the human being cuts himself off from the consciousness of himself as nature, all the aims for which he keeps himself alive, social progress, the heightening of material and intellectual forces, even consciousness itself, become void.[33]

Fichte simply rejects worries of this form, along with emphasis on the value of the individual and of subjectivity *qua* individual (in the sense of 'individual' Adorno has in mind, which surely encompasses disagreements of value judgments), as we have seen. Still even where Fichte talks about the 'annihilation of the individual and its fusion in the absolutely pure form of reason' (IV: 151) he does not have in mind the kind of 'annihilation' with which Horkheimer and Adorno are primarily concerned. So it is no accident that we find no reference to Fichte in the first Excursus either.

In fact there is no reason to think that Fichte could not take many of the moral and political worries articulated in *Dialectic of Enlightenment* to heart, attached as they are to a project, not of doing away with enlightenment or reversing the process of technological advance, but only of alerting us to its inevitable complications, especially in the context of late capitalism. (Whether from the perspective of the mid-twentieth century he could have been moved to share Horkheimer's and Adorno's pessimism about that project's prospects of success is a difficult question, and one I do not propose to answer.)

Still, it might be thought that there is a more general worry in this vicinity, a worry about the elevation of activity and the denigration of any passive, receptive attitude toward experience. Since personal relationships like friendship and familial and romantic love, as well as certain aesthetic experiences, non-contingently involve a loss of control, Fichte's view might seem unable to accommodate the

---

[33] M. Horkheimer and T. Adorno 1988, pp. 61–2; M. Horkheimer and T. Adorno 2002, pp. 42–3 (translation slightly altered).

value to human life of such experiences and relationships.[34] But there are two considerations that should, taken together, make this worry seem less pressing than it might at first appear.

First, recall the point made at the end of §5.2.2 about Fichte's appropriation of Schiller's critique of Kant. The independence that is the source of the material content of the obligatory ends of rational agents is the independence of finite, natural, social organisms like ourselves. If intimate relationships and aesthetic experience are necessary means toward independence for beings like us, then they are likewise obligatory (if subordinate) ends for us. I described in §3.2.2.5 how Fichte conceives of aesthetic experience as essential to the cultivation of individuals as moral beings, and so a source of moral duties. Here let me add that he takes the same to be true of intimate relationships, in particular the relationship of romantic love, which he discusses in §27. While he does not take the love, and lovability, on which romantic relationships depend to be themselves be the object of direct moral imperatives, he nevertheless takes it to be a duty not to remain unmarried through one's own fault or express intention (IV: 333). This is because, he thought, 'There are aspects of the human character, and indeed its most noble aspects, that can be cultivated only in marriage' (IV: 332), because love relationships make possible true friendship and motivate, naturally, humility and selflessness (IV: 332). 'The original tendency of the human being is egoistic; in marriage nature itself leads him to forget himself in another; and the marital union...is the sole natural path to the ennoblement of the human being' (IV: 332). This emphasis on the importance of romantic love, like that on the importance of aesthetic experience, is unsurprising given that Fichte developed his views in the Jena of the 1790s, at the center of the development of early German romanticism and in dialogue with its exponents.

That is the first consideration. The second is that the independence we are asking about, when we are asking whether, for instance, personal attachments might be detrimental to it, ought to be the independence of the whole of humanity, not that of a single individual. But while it is relatively easy to describe situations in which one's own individual independence might be undermined by some personal attachment, it is difficult to imagine circumstances in which collective human capacities would be expanded only if everyone were to avoid close personal relationships and the vulnerability inherent in them.

---

[34] John Martin Fischer has raised the objection that many ends central to human life—like involvement in love relationships—involve, precisely, absence or loss of control. Paul Katsafanas and Andrea Westlund have pressed the same point.

Of course it might still seem a matter of concern that, on a theory like Fichte's, the *feeling* of love, and the *pleasure* we take in the enjoyment of art, in adventure, surprise, and the like, are not unconditionally valuable in the way that the exercise of rational agency is unconditionally valuable. These values do have only a subordinate and instrumental place in his conception of the moral end. But the subordinate value of passive experience comes with the Kantian territory. It is also worth emphasizing that what is at stake in any objection along these lines is not the value of the *creative activity* of rational agents in building relationships, exploring the world, and producing cultural objects (and new ways of enjoying them). Those activities are not subordinate to the end of the exercise of rational agency and the expansion of scope for its exercise. They are constituents of it.

A final source of motivation for hostility toward the idea that technological progress aimed at increased mastery of nature is a necessary end of rational agency surely springs from resentment at the changes certain technological advances have wrought in certain long-established aspects of social life. Here again, though, it is difficult to locate a coherent worry that is not founded on assumptions that Fichte, correctly, emphatically rejects. Often the aspects of social organization that are destabilized in this way are reprehensible. A good example of this sort (though not one Fichte could have cited) is provided by technological advance in the control of fertility. While enhancing everyone's ability to form and carry out rational plans of life, modern reproductive technologies have at the same time eliminated mechanisms of control over women critical to the maintenance of the patriarchal order. Feminists and defenders of patriarchy alike have linked resistance to women's entitlement to employ these technologies to this very fact.[35]

---

[35] No feminist has put the point more forcefully than George Gilder, here:

> When the women demanded 'control over our own bodies,' they believed they were couching the issue in the least objectionable way. But ... they were in fact invoking one of the most extreme claims of the movement and striking at one of the most profound male vulnerabilities. For, in fact, few males have come to psychological terms with the existing birth-control technology; few recognize the extent to which it shifts the balance of sexual power further in favor of women. A man quite simply cannot now father a baby unless his wife is fully and deliberately agreeable.... Male procreativity is now dependent, to a degree unprecedented in history, on the active pleasure of women.   (G. Gilder 1986, pp. 106–7)

What Gilder is pointing out is that women could once be relatively easily coerced into pregnancy, and that modern reproductive technologies have made this traditional weapon of oppression less effective. 'This change in the sexual balance between men and women is still being absorbed by the society. People resist legal abortion on demand out of a sense of justifiable conservatism toward continued changes in the sexual constitution' (G. Gilder 1986, p. 107).

I take that to be a clear example in Fichte's favor; but it might be thought that examples could be cited that are more ambiguous. Many modern forms of exploitation, especially in the economic sphere, as well as many specifically modern dangers, plainly rely on specifically modern technologies. But here some care is in order. If the point is only that technology can outstrip the social organization required to put it to good use, and that technology misused can undermine rather than advance material independence, then it is not one Fichte needs to deny. He makes this point himself, using the example of weapons of war, in the *Vocation of Humankind* (II: 269). He takes that possibility, whose danger he clearly recognizes, to speak in favor of committing resources to education and to the research in human and social sciences that would light the way to improvements in social organization and in the moral dispositions of individuals. He does not take it to speak against the research in natural science that makes those improvements necessary. That seems the right response, and I have not been presented with an example of this sort that clearly speaks against Fichte's view.

6

Conclusion

In the chapter dedicated to the *System of Ethics* in his short introduction to Fichte's thought, Peter Rohs writes:

In intuitive substance, in universal insight, the *System of Ethics* belongs without doubt to the most important texts in the history of philosophy. The discursive element, the analytical cleanness in the details of the argumentation, is not of the same calibre. A work of this philosophical significance is thus something like a summons to its reader: to improve the discursive element where possible, but without loss to the intuitive substance.[1]

This book has been an effort to answer the summons Rohs describes: to identify and clarify Fichte's most important insights, and to present them systematically in a form accessible to a contemporary audience, without obscuring their intuitive appeal.

Fichte's central idea—that nature can place limits on our ability to govern ourselves and that knowledge can push back against those limits, and that anyone who values autonomy is thereby committed to the value of basic research and the development of autonomy-enhancing technologies—is not a prominent one in the mainstream of contemporary ethics. But it should be, for a number of reasons, the most salient of which (from an academic's perspective, at least) has to be the role it can play in grounding an account of duties to engage in and support education and fundamental research in the arts and sciences.

I hope in this book to have displayed the considerable philosophical interest of Fichte's ethical thought to an audience beyond scholars of German idealism, while doing justice to both the letter and the spirit of Fichte's texts. I hope also to have filled what is still an astonishing gap in existing historical scholarship, namely the absence of any book-length reconstruction of this central thesis of Fichte's normative ethics. No substantial treatment of Fichte's ethics to date has progressed beyond the portrayal of it as a strictly contentless ethics of conscience

[1] P. Rohs 1991b, p. 110.

popularized by Hegel two centuries ago.[2] Putting Fichte's account of conscience in its place, and showing that it cannot plausibly be read as precluding the possibility of the substantive normative ethics that in fact occupies nearly half of the book's pages, should clear the way for future research into Fichte's ethics that does justice to the wealth of insight Rohs describes.

[2] Cf. W. Jacobs 1967; P. Baumanns 1990; F. Neuhouser 1990; A. Wood 2016. The two exceptions I am aware of are P. Rohs 1991a and 1991b, both article-length works that do not reconstruct Fichte's central arguments.

Works Cited

Allgemeine Literatur-Zeitung, 1785–1849, Jena.

Anscombe, G.E.M., 1963, *Intention*, 2nd edition, Oxford: Blackwell.

Baumanns, Peter, 1990, *J.G. Fichte: Kritische Gesamtdarstellung seiner Philosophie*, Freiburg: K. Alber.

Baur, Michael, 2006, 'Fichte's Impossible Contract,' in Daniel Breazeale and Tom Rockmore, eds., *Rights, Bodies, and Recognition: New Essays on Fichte's Foundations of Natural Right*, Aldershot: Ashgate, pp. 11–25.

Beck, Gunnar, 2008, *Fichte and Kant on Freedom, Rights and Law*, Lanham: Lexington Books.

Bertoletti, S.F., 1990, *Impulso formazione e organismo: Per una storia del concetto di Bildungstrieb nella cultura tedesca*, Florence: Olschki.

Blumenbach, Johann Friedrich, 1789, *Über den Bildungstrieb und das Zeugungsgeschäfte*, 2nd edition, Göttingen: Dietrich.

Brand-Ballard, Jeffrey, 2004, 'Contractualism and Deontic Restrictions,' *Ethics* 114:2, pp. 269–300.

Bratman, M., 1987, *Intention, Plans, and Practical Reason*, Cambridge, MA: Harvard University Press.

Breazeale, Daniel, 1996, 'Certainty, Universal Validity, and Conviction,' in Daniel Breazeale and Tom Rockmore, eds., *New Perspectives on Fichte*, Atlantic Highlands: Humanities Press, pp. 35–59.

Breazeale, Daniel, 2012, 'In Defense of Fichte's Account of Ethical Deliberation,' *Archiv für Geschichte der Philosophie* 94, pp. 178–207.

Buss, Sarah, 2005, 'Valuing Autonomy and Respecting Persons: Manipulation, Seduction and the Basis of Moral Constraints,' *Ethics* 115:2, pp. 195–235.

Christensen, David, 2007, 'Epistemology and Disagreement: The Good News,' *Philosophical Review* 116:2, pp. 187–217.

Clarke, James A., 2009, 'Fichte and Hegel on Recognition,' *British Journal of the History of Philosophy* 17:2, pp. 365–85.

Cohen, G.A., 2011, *On the Currency of Egalitarian Justice, and Other Essays in Political Philosophy*, ed. Michael Otsuka, Princeton: Princeton University Press.

Coppleston, Frederick, 1962, *A History of Philosophy, Volume VII: From the Post-Kantian Idealists to Marx, Kierkegaard and Nietzsche*, New York: Doubleday.

Cummiskey, David, 1996, *Kantian Consequentialism*, New York: Oxford University Press.

Darwall, Stephen, 2005, 'Fichte and the Second-Person Standpoint,' *International Yearbook of German Idealism* 3, pp. 91–113.

Darwall, Stephen, 2006, *The Second-Person Standpoint*, Cambridge, MA: Harvard University Press.

Düsing, Edith, 1991, 'Das Problem der Individualität in Fichtes früher Ethik und Rechtslehre,' *Fichte-Studien* 3, pp. 29–50.

Dworkin, Gerald, 1988, 'Is More Choice Better than Less?' in G. Dworkin, *The Theory and Practice of Autonomy*, Cambridge: Cambridge University Press, pp. 61–81.

Elga, Adam, 2007, 'Reflection and Disagreement,' *Noûs*, 41:3, pp. 478–502.

Elster, Jon, 2000, *Ulysses Unbound*, Cambridge: Cambridge University Press.

Engstrom, Stephen, 2009, *The Form of Practical Knowledge*, Cambridge, MA: Harvard University Press.

Enoch, David, 2010, 'Not just a Truthometer: Taking Oneself Seriously (but Not Too Seriously) in Cases of Peer Disagreement,' *Mind* 119:476, pp. 953–97.

Erhard, Johann Benjamin, 1795, 'Apologie des Teufels,' *Philosophisches Journal einer Gesellschaft teutscher Gelehrten*, 1:2, pp. 1–140.

Feldman, Fred, 2006, 'Actual Utility, the Objection from Impracticality, and the Move to Expected Utility,' *Philosophical Studies* 129:1, pp. 49–79.

Feldman, Richard and Ted Warfield, 2010, *Disagreement*, Oxford: Oxford University Press.

Ferry, Luc, 1987–8, 'The Distinction Between Law and Ethics in the Early Philosophy of Fichte,' *Philosophical Forum* XIX: 2–3, pp. 182–96.

Feuerbach, Ludwig, 1848, *Pierre Bayle, ein Beitrag zur Geschichte der Philosophie und Menschheit*, 3rd edition, Leipzig: Wigand.

Fichte, Johann Gottlieb, 1962–2011, *Gesamtausgabe der Bayerischen Akademie der Wissenschaften*, ed. R. Lauth, H. Jacob, and H. Gliwitzky, Stuttgart-Bad Cannstatt: Friedrich Frommann Verlag.

Fichte, Johann Gottlieb, 1971, *Werke*, ed. I.H. Fichte, Berlin: de Gruyter.

Fischer, Kuno, 1884, *J.G. Fichte und seine Vorgänger*, 2nd edition, Munich: Bassermann.

Franks, Paul, 2005, *All or Nothing*, Cambridge, MA: Harvard University Press.

Friedens-Preliminarien, vol. 1, 1793, ed. 'The publisher of the secret tribunal,' Berlin: Voss.

Gibbard, Allen, 1978, 'Act-Utilitarian Agreements,' in Alvin I. Goldman and Jaegwon Kim, eds., *Values and Morals: Essays In Honor of William Frankena, Charles Stevenson, and Richard Brandt*, Dordrecht: D. Reidel, pp. 91–119.

Gibbard, Allen, 1990, *Utilitarianism and Coordination*, New York: Garland.

Gibbard, Allen, 2008, *Reconciling our Aims*, ed. Barry Stroud, New York: Oxford University Press.

Gilder, George, 1986, *Men and Marriage*, Gretna, LA: Pelican.

Godwin, William, 1793, *An Enquiry Concerning Political Justice and its Influence on General Virtue and Happiness*, 2 vols., London: J. and J. Robinson.

Hegel, G.W.F., 1986, *Werke*, 20 vols., Frankfurt am Main: Suhrkamp.

Henning, Tim, 2015, 'From Choice to Chance? Saving People, Fairness, and Lotteries,' *Philosophical Review* 124:2, pp. 169–206.

Henrich, Dieter, 1967, *Fichtes ursprüngliche Einsicht*, Frankfurt am Main: Klostermann.

Herbert, Gary B., 1998, 'Fichte's Deduction of Rights from Self-Consciousness,' *Interpretation* 25:2, pp. 201–22.

Herman, Barbara, 1993, *The Practice of Moral Judgment*, Cambridge, MA: Harvard University Press.

Herman, Barbara, 2007, *Moral Literacy*, Cambridge, MA: Harvard University Press.

Heydenreich, Karl Heinrich, 1794, *System des Naturrechts nach kritischen Prinzipien*, Leipzig: J.G. Feind.

Hills, Alison, 2009a, 'Happiness in the Groundwork,' in Jens Timmermann, ed., *Kant's Groundwork of the Metaphysics of Morals: A Critical Guide*, New York: Cambridge University Press, pp. 29–44.

Hills, Alison, 2009b, 'Moral Testimony and Moral Epistemology,' *Ethics* 120:1, pp. 94–127.

Holton, Richard, 2009, *Willing, Wanting, Waiting*, Oxford: Oxford University Press.

Honneth, Axel, 2001, 'Die transzendentale Notwendigkeit von Intersubjektivität (Zweiter Lehrsatz: §3),' in Jean-Christophe Merle, ed., *Johann Gottlieb Fichte: Grundlage des Naturrechts*, Berlin: Akademie Verlag, pp. 63–80.

Horkheimer, Max and Theodor Adorno, 1988, *Dialektik der Aufklärung. Philosophische Fragmente*, Frankfurt am Main: Fischer.

Horkheimer, Max and Theodor Adorno, 2002, *Dialectic of Enlightenment: Philosophical Fragments*, trans. Gunzelin Schmid Noerr, Stanford: Stanford University Press.

Howard-Snyder, Frances, 1997, 'The Rejection of Objective Consequentialism,' *Utilitas* 9:2, pp. 241–8.

Jackson, Frank, 1991, 'Decision-Theoretic Consequentialism and the Nearest and Dearest Objection,' *Ethics* 101:3, pp. 461–82.

Jacobs, Wilhelm G., 1967, *Trieb als sittliches Phänomen: Eine Untersuchung zur Grundlegung der Philosophie nach Kant und Fichte*, Bonn: H. Bouvier.

James, David, 2011, *Fichte's Social and Political Philosophy*, Cambridge: Cambridge University Press.

Kagan, Shelly, 2002, 'Kantianism for Consequentialists,' in Allen Wood, ed., *I. Kant, Groundwork for the Metaphysics of Morals*, New Haven: Yale University Press, pp. 111–56.

Kahnemann, Daniel, 2011, *Thinking, Fast and Slow*, New York: Farrar, Straus and Giroux.

Kant, Immanuel, 1900–, *Kants gesammelte Schriften*, ed. Königlich Preussische Akademie der Wissenschaften zu Berlin, Berlin: De Gruyter.

Kant, Immanuel, 1968, *Werke*, Akademie Textausgabe, ed. Königlich Preussische Akademie der Wissenschaften zu Berlin, Berlin: De Gruyter.

Kant, Immanuel, 1996a, *Practical Philosophy*, ed. M. Gregor and A. Wood, Cambridge: Cambridge University Press.

Kant, Immanuel, 1996b, *Religion and Rational Theology*, ed. A. Wood and G. di Giovanni, Cambridge: Cambridge University Press.

Kant, Immanuel, 1998, *Critique of Pure Reason*, ed. A. Wood and P. Guyer, Cambridge: Cambridge University Press.

Kant, Immanuel, 2000, *Critique of the Power of Judgment*, ed. P. Guyer and A. Wood, Cambridge: Cambridge University Press.

Kant, Immanuel, 2007, *Anthropology, History and Education*, ed. G. Zöller and R. Louden, Cambridge: Cambridge University Press.

Koltonski, Daniel, 2010, 'Political Obligation and Democratic Community.' Dissertation, Cornell University.

Koltonski, Daniel, 2016, 'A Good Friend Will Help You Move a Body: Friendship and the Problem of Moral Disagreement,' *Philosophical Review* 125:4, pp. 473–507.

Korsgaard, Christine, 1996, *Creating the Kingdom of Ends*, New York: Cambridge University Press.

Kosch, Michelle, 2006a, *Freedom and Reason in Kant, Schelling and Kierkegaard*, Oxford: Oxford University Press.

Kosch, Michelle, 2006b, 'Kierkegaard's Ethicist: Fichte's Role in Kierkegaard's Construction of the Ethical Standpoint,' *Archiv für Geschichte der Philosophie* 88, pp. 261–95.

Kosch, Michelle, 2013, 'Formal Freedom in Fichte's *System of Ethics*,' *International Yearbook of German Idealism* 9, pp. 150–68.

Kosch, Michelle, 2014, 'Practical Deliberation and the Voice of Conscience in Fichte's 1798 *System of Ethics*,' *Philosophers' Imprint* 14:30, pp. 1–16.

Kosch, Michelle, 2015a, 'Agency and Self-sufficiency in Fichte's Ethics,' *Philosophy and Phenomenological Research* 91:2, pp. 348–80 (first published online, March 2014, DOI: 10.1111/phpr.12085).

Kosch, Michelle, 2015b, 'Fichtean Kantianism in 19th Century Ethics,' *Journal of the History of Philosophy* 53:1, pp. 111–32.

Kosch, Michelle, 2017, 'Individuality and Rights in Fichte's Ethics,' *Philosophers' Imprint* 17:12, pp. 1–23.

Kühn, Manfred, 2012, *Johann Gottlieb Fichte: Ein Deutscher Philosoph*. Munich: Beck.

Larson, James, 1979, 'Vital Forces: Regulative Principles or Constitutive Agents? A Strategy in German Physiology, 1786–1802,' *Isis* 70:2, pp. 235–49.

Lenoir, Timothy, 1980, 'Kant, Blumenbach and Vital Materialism in German Biology,' *Isis* 71:1, pp. 77–108.

Lewis, David, 1969, *Convention: A Philosophical Study*, Cambridge, MA: Harvard University Press.

MacFarlane, John, 2000, 'What Does It Mean to Say that Logic is Formal?' Dissertation, University of Pittsburgh.

McGrath, Sarah, 2009, 'The Puzzle of Pure Moral Deference,' *Noûs Supplement: Philosophical Perspectives* 23:1, pp. 321–44.

Mill, John Stuart, 1985, *The Collected Works of John Stuart Mill*, vol. 10, *Essays on Ethics, Religion, and Society* (*Utilitarianism*), ed. J.M. Robson, Toronto: University of Toronto Press.

Nagel, Thomas, 1970, *The Possibility of Altruism*, Oxford: Clarendon Press.

Neuhouser, Frederick, 1990, *Fichte's Theory of Subjectivity*, Cambridge: Cambridge University Press.

Neuhouser, Frederick, 1993, 'Freedom, Dependence and the General Will,' *Philosophical Review* 102:3, pp. 363–95.

Neuhouser, Frederick, 1994, 'Fichte and the Relation between Right and Morality,' in Daniel Breazeale and Tom Rockmore, eds., *Fichte: Historical Contexts/Contemporary Controversies*, Atlantic Highlands: Humanities Press, pp. 158–80.

Neuhouser, Frederick, 2000, 'Introduction,' in Johann Gottlieb Fichte, *Foundations of Natural Right: According to the Principles of the Wissenschaftslehre*, ed. Frederick Neuhouser and trans. Michael Baur, Cambridge: Cambridge University Press.

Neuhouser, Frederick, 2001, 'The Efficacy of the Rational Being,' in Jean-Christophe Merle, ed., *Johann Gottlieb Fichte: Grundlage des Naturrechts*, Berlin: Akademie Verlag, pp. 39–49.

Nomer, Nedim, 2005, 'Fichte and the Idea of Liberal Socialism,' *Journal of Political Philosophy* 13, pp. 53–73.

Nomer, Nedim, 2010, 'Fichte and the Relationship between Self-Positing and Rights,' *Journal of the History of Philosophy* 48:4, pp. 469–90.

Nussbaum, Martha Craven, 1992, 'Human Functioning and Social Justice: In Defense of Aristotelian Essentialism,' *Political Theory* 20, pp. 202–46.

Nussbaum, Martha Craven, 2011, *Creating Capabilities: The Human Development Approach*, Cambridge, MA: Harvard University Press.

O'Neill, Onora, 1989, *Constructions of Reason*, Cambridge: Cambridge University Press.

Parfit, Derek, 1984, *Reasons and Persons*, Oxford: Oxford University Press.

Parfit, Derek, 2011, *On What Matters*, vols. 1 & 2, Oxford: Oxford University Press.

Peirce, Charles, 1877, 'The Fixation of Belief,' *Popular Science Monthly* 12, pp. 1–15.

Pippin, Robert, 1999, 'Dividing and Deriving in Kant's *Rechtslehre*,' in Ottfried Hoffe, ed., *Metaphysische Anfangsgründe der Rechtslehre*, Berlin: Akademie Verlag, pp. 63–86.

Pogge, Thomas, 2002, 'Is Kant's *Rechtslehre* a "Comprehensive Liberalism"?' in Mark Timmons, ed., *Kant's Metaphysics of Morals: Interpretive Essays*, Oxford: Oxford University Press, pp. 133–58.

Pogge, Thomas, 2007, *John Rawls*, New York: Oxford University Press.

Rawls, John, 1999, *A Theory of Justice*, 2nd edition, Cambridge, MA: Harvard University Press.

Raz, Joseph, 1979, *The Authority of Law*, Oxford: Clarendon Press.

Raz, Joseph, 1999, *Practical Reason and Norms*, 2nd edition, Oxford: Oxford University Press.

Reath, Andrews, 2013, 'Formal Approaches to Kant's Formula of Humanity,' in Sorin Baiasu and Mark Timmons, eds., *Kant on Practical Justification: Interpretive Essays*, Oxford: Oxford University Press.

Regan, Donald, 1980, *Utilitarianism and Co-operation*, Oxford: Clarendon Press.

Renaut, Alain, 1986, *Le Système du Droit: Philosophie et Droit dans la Pensée de Fichte*, Paris: Presses Universitaires de France.

Renaut, Alain, 1992, 'Fichte: Le Droit sans la Morale?' *Archives de Philosophie* 55:2, pp. 221–42.

Renaut, Alain, 2001, 'Deduktion des Rechts (Dritter Lehrsatz: §4),' in Jean-Christophe Merle, *Johann Gottlieb Fichte: Grundlage des Naturrechts*, Berlin: Akademie Verlag, pp. 81–95.

Richards, Robert, 2000, 'Kant and Blumenbach on the *Bildungstrieb*: A Historical Misunderstanding,' *Studies in History and Philosophy of Biological and Biomedical Sciences* 31:1, pp. 11–32.

Ripstein, Arthur, 2009, *Force and Freedom: Kant's Legal and Political Philosophy*, Cambridge, MA: Harvard University Press.

Rohs, Peter, 1991a, 'Der materiale Gehalt des Sittengesetzes nach Fichte's *Sittenlehre*,' *Fichte Studien* 3, pp. 170–83.

Rohs, Peter, 1991b, *Johann Gottlieb Fichte*, Munich: Beck.

Rousseau, Jean-Jacques, 1966, *Émile, ou de l'Éducation*, Paris: Garnier-Flammarion.

Sartorio, Carolina, 2009, 'Causation and Ethics,' in Helen Beebee, Christopher Hitchcock, and Peter Menzies, eds., *The Oxford Handbook of Causation*, Oxford: Oxford University Press.

Scheffler, Samuel, 1982, *The Rejection of Consequentialism*, Oxford: Oxford University Press.

Schelling, Thomas C., 1957, 'Bargaining, Communication and Limited War,' *Journal of Conflict Resolution* 1:1, pp. 19–36.

Schelling, Thomas C., 1958, 'The Strategy of Conflict: Prospectus for a Reorientation of Game Theory,' *Journal of Conflict Resolution* 2:3, pp. 203–64.

Schiller, Friedrich, 1959, *Gesammelte Werke*, ed. Alexander Abusch, Berlin: Aufbau-Verlag.

Schneewind, Jerome and Allen Wood, 2012, 'Moral Epistemology, 1788–1870,' in Allen Wood and Susan Hahn, eds., *The Cambridge History of Philosophy in the Nineteenth Century*, New York: Cambridge University Press, pp. 467–88.

Sen, Amartya, 1979, 'Utilitarianism and Welfarism,' *Journal of Philosophy* 76:9, pp. 463–89.

Sen, Amartya, 1985, 'Well-being, Agency and Freedom,' *Journal of Philosophy* 82:4, pp. 169–221.

Sen, Amartya, 1999, *Development as Freedom*, New York: Anchor Books.

Sen, Amartya, 2005, 'Human Rights and Capabilities,' *Journal of Human Development* 6, pp. 151–66.

Sen, Amartya, 2009, *The Idea of Justice*, Cambridge, MA: Harvard University Press.

Sepielli, Andrew, 2014, 'What to Do When You Don't Know What to Do When You Don't Know What to Do . . .' *Noûs* 48:3, pp. 521–44 (first published online, January 2013, DOI: 10.1111/nous.12010).

Setiya, Kieran, 2007, 'Cognitivism about Instrumental Reason,' *Ethics* 117:4, pp. 649–73.

Setiya, Kieran, 2008, 'Practical Knowledge,' *Ethics* 118:3, pp. 388–409.

Shell, Susan Meld, 1986, 'What Kant and Fichte Can Teach Us About Human Rights,' in Richard Kennington, ed., *The Philosophy of Immanuel Kant*, Washington DC: Catholic University Press, pp. 143–60.

Shell, Susan Meld, 1992, ' "A Determined Stand": Freedom and Security in Fichte's *Science of Right*,' *Polity* 25:1, pp. 95–121.

Siep, Ludwig, 1979, *Anerkennung als Prinzip der praktischen Philosophie: Untersuchung zu Hegels Jenaer Philosophie des Geistes*, Freiburg im Breisgau: Alber.

Sinott-Armstrong, Walter, 2015, 'Consequentialism,' *Stanford Encyclopedia of Philosophy* (Winter 2015 edition), ed. Edward N. Zalta, <http://plato.stanford.edu/archives/win2015/entries/consequentialism/>

Skyrms, Brian, 1996, *Evolution of the Social Contract*, Cambridge: Cambridge University Press.

Smith, Michael, 1994, *The Moral Problem*, Oxford: Blackwell.

Soper, Philip, 2002, *The Ethics of Deference*, Cambridge: Cambridge University Press.

Sturgeon, Nicholas, 2002, 'Ethical Intuitionism and Ethical Naturalism,' in Philip Stratton-Lake, ed., *Ethical Intuitionism: Re-evaluations*, Oxford: Oxford University Press.

Sugden, Robert, 2004, *The Economics of Rights, Co-operation, and Welfare*, 2nd edition, New York: Palgrave Macmillan.

Taurek, John M., 1977, 'Should the Numbers Count?' *Philosophy & Public Affairs* 6:4, pp. 293–316.

Uleman, Jennifer, 2004, 'External Freedom in Kant's *Rechtslehre*: Political, Metaphysical,' *Philosophy and Phenomenological Research* 68:3, pp. 578–601.

Uleman, Jennifer, 2010, *An Introduction to Kant's Moral Philosophy*, Cambridge: Cambridge University Press.

Vargas, Manuel, 2013, *Building Better Beings: A Theory of Moral Responsibility*, Oxford: Oxford University Press.

Velleman, J. David, 1989, *Practical Reflection*, Princeton: Princeton University Press.

Verweyen, Hansjürgen, 1975, *Recht und Sittlichkeit in J. G. Fichtes Gesellschaftslehre*, Freiburg: K. Alber.

Vogler, Candace, 2002, *Reasonably Vicious*, Cambridge, MA: Harvard University Press.

Ware, Owen, 2010, 'Fichte's Voluntarism,' *European Journal of Philosophy* 18:2, pp. 262–82.

Wiland, Eric, 2005, 'Monkeys, Typewriters, and Objective Consequentialism,' *Ratio* 18:3, pp. 352–60.

Williams, Bernard, 1973, 'A Critique of Utilitarianism,' in J.J.C. Smart and Bernard Williams, *Utilitarianism: For and Against*, Cambridge: Cambridge University Press.

Williams, Bernard, 1981, *Moral Luck*, Cambridge: Cambridge University Press.

Williams, Robert R., 2006, 'Recognition, Right and Social Contract,' in Daniel Breazeale and Tom Rockmore, eds., *Rights, Bodies, and Recognition: New Essays on Fichte's Foundations of Natural Right*, Aldershot: Ashgate, pp. 26–44.

Wolff, Christian, 1752, *Vernünfftige Gedancken von der Menschen Thun und Lassen, zu Beförderung ihrer Glückseligkeit*, new edition, Halle: Regnerischen Buchhandlung; 1976 reprint, Hildesheim: Olms.

Wolff, Robert Paul, 1970, *In Defense of Anarchism*, New York: Harper & Row.

Wood, Allen, 1990, *Hegel's Ethical Thought*, Cambridge: Cambridge University Press.

Wood, Allen, 1991, 'Fichte's Philosophical Revolution,' *Philosophical Topics* 19:2, pp. 1–28.

Wood, Allen, 2000, 'The "I" as Principle of Practical Philosophy,' in Sally Sedgwick, ed., *The Reception of Kant's Critical Philosophy*, Cambridge: Cambridge University Press.

Wood, Allen, 2001, 'Kant versus Eudaimonism,' in Predrag Cicovacki, ed., *Kant's Legacy: Essays in Honor of Lewis White Beck*, New York: University of Rochester Press, pp. 261–82.

Wood, Allen, 2002, 'The Final Form of Kant's Practical Philosophy,' in Mark Timmons, ed., *Kant's Metaphysics of Morals: Interpretative Essays*, Oxford: Oxford University Press.

Wood, Allen, 2006, 'Fichte's Intersubjective I,' *Inquiry* 49, pp. 62–79.

Wood, Allen, 2008, *Kantian Ethics*, New York: Cambridge University Press.

Wood, Allen, 2015, 'Von der Natur zur Freiheit (*System der Sittenlehre* §§9–13),' in Jean-Christophe Merle and Andreas Schmidt, eds., *Fichte: System der Sittenlehre*, Frankfurt: Klostermann, pp. 93–108.

Wood, Allen, 2016, *Fichte's Ethical Thought*, Oxford: Oxford University Press.

Zöller, Günter, 1998, 'Die Individualität des Ich in Fichtes zweiter Jenaer Wissenschafts-lehre (1796–99),' *Revue Internationale de Philosophie* 52:4, pp. 641–63.

Zöller, Günter, 2012, 'The Choice of the Philosopher,' comments on Michelle Kosch, 'Agency and Self-sufficiency in Fichte's Ethics,' symposium session, Pacific APA.

Index

Adorno, Theodor Wiesengrund 81, 173–4
aesthetic experience 73, 80–1, 165–6, 172–5
agent-centered constraints/restrictions 6,
    52n13, 57, 84n49, 89, 91
agent-centered prerogatives 6, 88
agent-neutral reasons/ends 6, 21–2, 58, 68, 81,
    88–9, 109, 113
agent-relative reasons/ends 20, 84n49, 88–9
agreement and disagreement, moral 21–2, 34,
    46, 58, 72, 108–12, 132–3, 142–3
art, see aesthetic experience, duties of fine
    artists
Ascetics as an Appendix to Ethics 28n30, 29, 71,
    98, 124, 134, 135, 140, 145
autonomy 1–6, 167–71, 173, 178

Bentham, Jeremy 44, 62n23
Blumenbach, Johann Friedrich 13–14, 25–7
    passim
Breazeale, Daniel 39n3, 135–7 passim, 139n11

calculative reasoning 17–18; see also practical
    deliberation, practical judgment
church 72–3, 110
Closed Commercial State 77, 103
conscience 95n65, 97, 128–49
    passim, 179–9
    freedom of 73, 94
consequentialism 6–7, 39n3, 44, 52, 60–7, 84,
    87–9, 91n58, 94–6, 112–13, 125, 140n12,
    163n14, 172
    maximizing 3, 37, 44, 52, 54–6, 63–4, 87,
        112–13, 125, 159
Contributions to the Correction of the Public's
    Judgment concerning the Revolution in
    France 98, 114n97
coordination 17–18, 51, 70, 75–6, 94–100,
    110–13, 117–20, 123, 126

Darwall, Stephen 31n35, 91n58, 115n102,
    116n104
deference, moral 129, 141–3, 148
disagreement, moral, see agreement and
    disagreement, moral
drives 9, 13–15, 23–9, 53, 150, 166n16
    Bildungstrieb 13–14, 25, 27n29
    mixed or ethical 28–9, 36, 43, 85, 87–8, 113,
        134–5, 169

natural 24–8, 33, 40–4, 85, 144–5, 162, 169
original 26–7
pure 26–8, 40–4, 144–5
social 96
duties 52–151 passim
    concerning aesthetic cultivation 46–7,
        80–1, 175
    concerning intellectual cultivation 52–3,
        70–5, 80–2, 83, 85–6
    concerning knowledge 24, 35, 45, 73–80,
        85–6, 158–64
    concerning moral cultivation 35, 70–3, 98–9,
        149–50, 175
    concerning physical protection/
        cultivation 30–1, 54–70
    concerning property 24, 54, 68–70, 75–8, 91,
        101–15 passim, 156–64 passim
    of beneficence 6–7, 69, 83–5, 156n9
    of fine artists, see duties concerning aesthetic
        cultivation
    of parents 34, 72–3, 118, 122, 124–6
    of religious leaders 34, 46–7, 72–3, 80
    of scholars and teachers 46–7, 78–80
    particular 46–7, 60, 70, 72–3, 79–80, 125–7
    perfect and imperfect 54, 83, 157n9
    positive and negative 52n13, 54, 59–60, 68,
        73, 81, 89–91, 107
    to set example of morality 34, 73, 82
    universal 53–4, 70–1, 125–7

effort, deliberative 4, 9, 29–30, 34, 110, 148–50
    passim
embodiment 3, 22, 30–1, 46, 53–4, 67–8, 70, 85,
    87, 93, 101, 105, 117–18
epistemic responsibility 66, 128–32, 143,
    147, 152
evil, moral 58, 67, 131–2, 143–51

Feuerbach, Ludwig 2, 78
formal condition of the morality of actions 6,
    9–10, 38, 66, 74, 109, 112, 128–51
formal ethical principles, see material and
    formal ethical principles
Foundations of Natural Right 24, 30–4 passim,
    47, 55n15, 58, 75–8, 87, 90–127 passim,
    158–64

Godwin, William 61–2, 65, 163n14

happiness 2, 5, 7, 20, 25, 27, 44, 60, 83–5, 166,
    168–70
Hegel, Georg Wilhelm Friedrich 2, 93n61,
    126n113, 138–9, 179
Horkheimer, Max 173–4

individuality 3, 31–4, 46, 53, 63–8, 78, 85–127
    passim, 166, 174
inertia (Trägheit) 29–30, 38, 110, 144, 148–50

Kant, Immanuel 1, 5–7, 13–16 passim, 18–22
    passim, 28–9, 35–6, 41, 47, 49n10, 51–2,
    54n14, 55–6, 72, 81–5 passim, 89, 96n68,
    98–9, 129–30, 136–7, 142, 144–5, 150–7
    passim, 159, 163, 167–76 passim
knowledge 2–4, 9, 22–4, 38, 51, 70, 110,
    132–3, 178
  duties concerning, see duties concerning
  knowledge

laziness (Trägheit), see inertia
Lectures on the Scholar's Vocation 5, 31, 47,
    51n12, 78, 84, 85n50, 96n71, 99, 104, 111,
    112, 164, 166n16
lifeboat cases 58–9, 63–4, 67, 123

Marx, Karl 2, 80
material and formal ethical principles 6, 40–2,
    167–71
material condition of the morality of
    actions 1–3, 6, 8–11, 17, 28, 36–129, 133,
    135, 140, 151, 166–7
maxims 20, 71, 130, 144, 167
Mill, John Stuart 21n21, 44, 62n23
Mirbach lecture notes 12, 14, 16, 21, 23n24, 30,
    35, 37, 49–50, 53, 58n18, 59–60, 73n35, 88,
    91, 109, 112, 138, 143n17, 145, 150
moral agreement/disagreement, see agreement
    and disagreement, moral
moral cultivation 25–9, 34–5, 71–3, 98–9,
    144–5, 149–50, 175; see also duties
    concerning moral cultivation
moral deference, see deference, moral
morally indifferent actions, no 72, 90n57,
    124n110, 132
moral responsibility 2–3, 12–16, 23, 29–30,
    34–6, 64–7 passim, 149–51, 155

Neuhouser, Frederick 12n1, 16n9, 30n34,
    31n35, 32, 39nn2–3, 92–3, 98n73, 99–101,
    111n93, 115nn101–3, 116n104, 117n105,
    121, 155n5, 166n17, 179n2
Nussbaum, Martha 84n49

Parfit, Derek 21nn20–1, 59n19, 88n55,
    96nn69–70, 107n91, 111n94, 163n14
patient-centered constraints 6, 91n58, 126;
    see also rights
practical deliberation 2, 4, 6, 9–10, 16–22,
    22–36 passim, 38, 45, 54, 57, 63, 66, 70–5,
    127, 131–41, 143–9, 169–71
practical judgment 6, 16–22, 38, 72, 110,
    129–49 passim, 169–71
property 24, 54, 68–70, 75–7, 101–15 passim,
    124–5, 156–64 passim; see also duties
    concerning property

reasoning, moral, see practical deliberation
reflection 1, 2, 8, 15–36 passim, 38, 41–3, 77, 82,
    116, 144–9 passim, 150, 159–60
Renaut, Alain 98–9, 114n100, 116n104
responsibility, see moral responsibility or
    epistemic responsibility
rights 6, 21, 24, 43, 50–1, 56, 58, 63–4, 68–70,
    74–8, 85–127 passim, 153–7; see also
    patient-centered constraints
Rohs, Peter 4n3, 24n26, 31n35, 39n1, 116n104,
    139n11, 178–9
Rousseau, Jean-Jacques 1, 98, 155

Scheffler, Samuel 88n54
Schelling, Friedrich Wilhelm Joseph von 26n27
Schelling, Thomas 95n63, 97n72, 118n107
scientific research 37, 78–80, 132–3, 161, 164
Schiller, Johann Christian Friedrich von 26n27,
    80, 166, 175
scholarship 46–7, 49, 74, 78–80; see also duties
    of scholars and teachers
self-consciousness 3, 16, 31–2, 54, 75, 114–17,
    121–2
self-determination 12–16, 25–7, 33, 41
self-respect 72
Sen, Amartya 7, 84
Smith, Michael 24n25
social contract 70, 75–7, 97, 100–10
spontaneity 8, 12–16, 27, 29, 33, 53, 57–8, 64–7,
    144–5, 150
summons 9, 31–4, 115–22

university, see scholarship, scientific research

Vocation of Humankind 8, 50, 77, 84, 177

Wood, Allen W. 19n15, 20, 22nn22–3, 31n35,
    36n41, 39n3, 49, 59–61, 63, 83n45,
    116n104, 135, 137n7, 139n11, 140n12,
    154n3, 172n28, 179n2

Printed and bound by CPI Group (UK) Ltd, Croydon, CR0 4YY